Dissonant Divas in Chicana Music

Dissonant Divas in Chicana Music

The Limits of *La Onda*

DEBORAH R. VARGAS

University of Minnesota Press
Minneapolis
London

Published by the University of Minnesota Press
111 Third Avenue South, Suite 290
Minneapolis, MN 55401-2520
http://www.upress.umn.edu

Library of Congress Cataloging-in-Publication Data

Vargas, Deborah R.
Dissonant divas in chicana music : the limits of la onda / Deborah R. Vargas.
Includes bibliographical references and index.
ISBN 978-0-8166-7316-2 (hc : alk. paper)
ISBN 978-0-8166-7317-9 (pb : alk. paper)
1. Music—Mexico—20th century—History and criticism. 2. Mexican Americans—Music. 3. Tejano music—History and criticism. 4. Gender identity in music. 5. Mexican American women. 6. Women musicians—United States. 7. Music—Social aspects. I. Title.
ML210.5.V37 2012
781.64089′6872073—dc23

2012002833

Contents

INTRODUCTION

Music, *Mejicanas*, and the Chicano Wave

On March 19, 2009, I attended a concert sponsored by the Esperanza Peace and Justice Center and Trinity University in San Antonio, Texas, the place where I was born and raised. The concert honored San Antonio singer Rita Vidaurri, whose career during the 1940s–50s extended from radio appearances on XEW radio in Mexico City to travels to Colombia singing her rancheras. Vidaurri and Lucha Reyes were also among the first *mexicanas* to wear *charro* pants while performing rancheras, thereby bucking the gendered norms of Mexican female performance and disrupting gendered national iconography.[1] The concert paid tribute to various local singers in San Antonio's music history, including Beatriz "La Paloma del Norte" Llamas, Blanquita "Blanca Rosas" Rodriguez, and Janet "La Perla Tapatia" Cortez. Having been sustained through the initiative of cofounding director Gloria Ramirez, the Esperanza Peace and Justice Center is an exemplary example of self-initiated public cultural projects that cultivate archives of and performance spaces for Chicana singers of past generations who have gone relatively unrecognized and unheard.[2]

The concert prompted me to reflect on the years I have conducted research on Chicana/Tejana singers and musicians and the profound significance of their music, which has gone relatively unengaged. Their absence in Chicano music history not only distorts musical and cultural knowledge but has shaped our understanding of Chicano music, borderlands social identities, and Chicana subjectivities. I was raised in a musical soundscape that fostered a bodily knowing of Tex-Mex music:

learning to dance everything in a counterclockwise circle, the smell of backyard barbeques that seemed to emanate from the sounds of an accordion, and the persistent way my polka-dancing feet move slow and low on the dance floor. I have carried this embodied knowledge to engage new spaces of knowing that revealed different stories and narratives of music than those held together by dominant tropes, historical narratives, and archives. For example, there was the time I spent at the home of Manuel Ayala, record collector in Corpus Christi, Texas. Ayala shared one of the rare 45 rpm recordings of "Las Nubes," the duet by Carmen y Laura recorded in the mid-1950s. Ayala explained how the version by Carmen y Laura has hardly ever been heard or circulated, and yet, two decades after Carmen y Laura's recording, Little Joe y La Familia recorded "Las Nubes" in 1972 for their album *Para La Gente*. It became an anthem for the United Farm Workers campaigns for workers' rights and economic justice. Still, I wondered to myself what different meanings Carmen y Laura's lyrics—"Ya todo se me acabó, no me puedo resistir. Si voy a seguir sufriendo mejor quisiera morir" (Now everything I have is finished, I can no longer endure. If I'm to continue suffering, it's best just to die)—might convey about Mexican Americans' experiences and subjectivities within a vastly changing post–World War II U.S. context. Then there was the time, after the first days of interviewing Rita Vidaurri, when she mentioned that my research would not be complete without looking into the career of deceased singer Eva Garza. After Vidaurri gave me contact information for Garza's sister Tina Moore, I showed up at her home the next day. Moore opened the door and, without even asking my name, said, "I've been waiting for you, for someone who'll listen to my sister's story, come in." Organized across Moore's kitchen table was an archive she had kept waiting, for someone to listen.

Although music has the power to shape the ways we imagine our social worlds and certain musical instruments have the power to narrate the experiences of communities, my research questions what it means to hear music through musical figures who so many have never had the opportunity to hear, not just musically, but experientially. I have often been reminded of the challenges of writing about Chicanas who have received such scant attention in public and institutional knowledge productions that, in part, give music so much of its power.

Dissonant Divas in Chicana Music assembles a dissonant cultural and sonic landscape of Chicana/Tejana singers and musicians since the early decades of the twentieth century to the present who—through performance, song, style, aesthetics, lived experience, voice, and instrumentation—are incompatible, inconsistent, unharmonious, and unsuitable within canonical Chicano/Tejano music narratives.[3] This book addresses the representational strategies of the female cultural producers who lived and performed throughout Texas, Mexico, Havana, and New York City, and across the Southwest, such as Rosita Fernández, Chelo Silva, Eva Ybarra, Ventura Alonzo, Eva Garza, Selena, Gloria Ríos, and Girl in a Coma. These singers and musicians have represented innovative instrumental and vocal stylings, evoked new passions and politics of the erotic, created new spatialities of belonging and modes of being Chicana/Tejana that offer us an alternative understanding of borderlands social identities. The musical figures in my analyses represent subject positions that are counter to, in excess of, and incompatible with what I refer to in this book as *la onda*'s heteronormative constructions of gender, citizenship, class resistance, home, femininity, and family.[4] In other words, the singers and musicians who populate this book do not easily fit the normative parameters of subjectivity in dominant academic and public cultural narratives of Chicano music and thus have been literally and discursively unheard, misheard, or overheard. Some singers, such as Eva Garza and Gloria Rios, are unfamiliar and relatively unknown. Others, such as Selena or Rosita Fernández, have registered loudly in music narratives and institutional histories. But I call attention to what has been muted within attempts to locate their musical production in dominant Chicano and American narratives. *Dissonant Divas* offers a new analytic of border cultural production that is usually rendered through hetero-masculinist logics of resistance and subordination. By centering cultural producers whose music, instrumentality, voice, embodiment, and performance produce a different epistemology, a way of knowing and of being in the borderlands, *Dissonant Divas* argues against simply reconciling nonnormative genders and sexualities within Chicano music by inserting their now sanctioned citizenship as women members. Instead, this book offers a feminist-of-color analysis of these figures' cultural contributions by advancing a notion of musical dissonance, a "dissonance" that I contend offers further complexity to analyses of gender and power within Chicana/o cultural productions.

Sounding *La Onda*: Music as a Sonic Imaginary of the Borderlands

I TAKE TO HEART that music is never void of power and always the site of gender, class, sexuality, and race politics. This book analyzes music with a focus on the politics of gender and sexuality. For minority communities in the United States, music has often been the mechanism for counterhistorical narratives, self-representation, and cultural empowerment. The most recognizable example of this is the contested site of jazz music and the ways jazz narratives have been a significant cultural mechanism for empowering self-representation for African Americans.[5] Simultaneously, productions of historical narratives, from the academic to the public sphere, have functioned as a device to integrate marginalized communities into the mainstream of American life. Early on in my attempts to excavate knowledge of Mexican American musicians and singers, it was apparent that there was a canonical formation of what is considered "Chicano" and often coined in the public sphere as "borderlands music." The term *la onda*—what generally translates as the "wave," "sound wave," or "force" but operates in this book precisely as the musical wave—is an umbrella term for Mexican American/Chicano/Tejano music. *La onda* also signifies the ways the broader public and Chicanas/os have claimed music as "our own," that is, the music that has emerged as a reflection and consequence of subordinate experiences living in the United States. I contend that Chicano music forms a sonic imaginary—understood as a musically sounded/sonic field where people come to understand, relate, and connect to notions of belonging, history, place, and cultural sensibilities—of Mexican-descent peoples and the often associated reference to a notion of borderlands. Moreover, through the analysis of the singers in this book, the borderlands sonic imaginary of *la onda* is theoretically approached according to Alicia Schmidt Camacho's theorizations of social imaginaries: that "cultural forms are not a reflection of the social . . . but rather the means by which subjects work through their connections to a larger totality and communicate a sense of relatedness to a particular time, place, and condition."[6]

La onda, in this book, operates to represent musics that have been prominent in academic and cultural institutional sites that have produced dominant discourses of sexuality, gender, class, race, geography, and language in the constructions of Chicano music. It should not be confused with "La onda Chicana" or "La onda Tejana" that is referred to briefly in chapter 5. This term has circulated in Chicano musicology as a particular moment or genre of Tejano orquesta music that Manuel Peña has defined as "the final stage of the evolution of orquesta Tejana style and its political aesthetic launched in the late 1960s by Little Joe and the Latinaires."[7]

For instance, it was common in my fieldwork to come across people referring to *la onda* as an umbrella term to designate music and musical innovations pertaining to a Mexican American/Chicano experience. Another example is the way *la onda* has circulated in music fan Web sites and public cultural projects such as the PBS documentary series *Latin Music USA,* which included segments such as "The Salsa Revolution" and "Divas and Superstars." In the documentary's third segment, "The Chicano Wave," *la onda* is intended to represent a range of Mexican American artists from Ritchie Valens, to Linda Ronstadt, to Santana and music from rock, to Tejano, to doo-wop. The subtitle to this segment also captures the ways in which my reference to *la onda* operates; the subtitle reads "Mexican-Americans have always been part of the USA, and their music tells a unique story."

I deploy *la onda* to describe the kinds of borderlands identities and cultural projects created by the knowledge productions of canonical Chicano music histories, including academic studies, public cultural institutions and exhibits, as well as documentary film. *La onda* represents a musical force of belonging, a sonic circuit of memory, and a wave of historical narratives that have come to designate the borderlands. Nonetheless, *la onda* has formed a borderlands imaginary that I argue has been constructed through rigid limits of heteronormative gender, sexuality, family, citizenship, home, and community. In fact, I argue that the musical construction of *la onda* has been dominated by cultural-nationalist tropes of "community" and "home." In Chicano studies, corrido, conjunto, rock, and orquesta music have been the focal point for narratives of survival, self-representation, cultural fusion, and belonging.[8] As a musical sound or cultural force, *la onda* has been sanctioned by scholars and public cultural projects throughout the twentieth century in a way that has produced constructions of the borderlands and Chicana/o subjects through a limited imaginary of belonging and social identities. *Dissonant Divas in Chicana Music* posits a feminist analysis of Chicana/Tejana singers who sound contradictions and complicities as well as push the heteronormative cultural-nationalist limits of *la onda*.

The singers and musicians discussed here create alternative sonic imaginaries of the borderlands. I read their cultural work to reimagine the borderlands as compatible with the ways Chicana feminist and cultural studies theorists such as Gloria Anzaldúa, Sonia Saldívar-Hull, Emma Pérez, and Rosa Linda Fregoso have theorized the borderlands as a historical-material location, as a trope for social identities in flux, and as a concept that calls attention to the cultural productions of heterogeneous Chicana/o subjectivies.[9] The borderlands imaginaries offered by the cultural work of these singers exemplifies this space as the psychic, cultural, political site of collision, violence, and promise that they have navigated; their musical representations demonstrate the negotiations of dual systems of power, knowledge, language, and culture that produce third ways of being or what Anzaldúa called the "facultad de nepantleras" (the faculty of those who reside in between). As such, the sonic imaginaries of the borderlands produced by these Chicana cultural laborers require a different way of understanding music by also engaging what is offstage and off page.

To listen for and to Chicana dissonant divas means engaging music not merely in its production or performance but also as socially constructed through the propriety central to discourses of instrumentation and furthermore as a social world that includes gossip about singers and their life choices, and song lyrics as possible testimonies of sexual desire and heartache that push the sonic limits of the borderlands. Thus, I consider the music of the singers and musicians encompassed by their life experiences, songs, performance, musicianship, and gender relations in relationship to *la onda*'s dominant constructions of gender and family, teleologies of cultural resistance, fixed notions of canonical musical archives, and prioritizations of race and class analysis. Thus, by listening beyond a teleology of cultural resistance that has prioritized race and class, *Dissonant Divas* centers music as a political project of gender and sexuality; it understands music as power in the borderlands.

My analysis turns our ears to how women wield instruments that epitomize the masculine, and to the gendered/sexual performances of emotion, vocality, and musicality, in order to analyze how Chicana singers and musicians push the limits of bounded geographies, break out of the accommodation/resistance binary, and create modes of belonging that challenge heteronormative notions of family and nation. I use the cultural knowledge produced by dissonant divas to understand the ways music has the power to reimagine histories, social identities, pleasure, and possibilities for resistance, as well as to rework complex notions of complicity, negotiation, spatiality, travel, and transnational cultural flows. *Dissonant Divas* engages Chicano music as a contested site of power and as a sonic force of possibilities and imagines the borderlands not as overdetermined by cultural-nationalist constructions of gender, geography, sexuality, language, class, and race.

There are certainly examples of alternative borderlands musical imaginaries that critically attend to gender, class, and race—for example, Anthony Macías's analysis of Chicana/o engagements with Latin jazz, mambo, and swing in Los Angles in *Mexican American Mojo: Popular Music, Dance, and Urban Culture in Los Angeles, 1935–1968,* and musical exhibitions such as the traveling exhibit *American Sabor* guest-curated by Michelle Habell-Pallán, Shannon Dudley, and Marisol Berríos-Miranda.[10] Yet, there remains a lack of sustained feminist analysis of Chicana musical figures, which thereby contributes to the replication of dominant tropes in academic research and exhibition practices that have sustained *la onda.* For example, the Tex-Mex sound is rendered almost exclusively through masculinist constructions of regionality. On the other hand, Chicano rock, highly dominated by West Coast historical narratives and a Los Angeles–based Eastside sound is not viewed as local or regional because of the construction of Los Angeles as a global city. Thus, while the singers in this book all are associated with Texas, having been born and/or raised there, *Dissonant Divas* attempts to work against the ways they may be overdetermined "regional" subjects through analysis of their travels, music, and experiential milieu; these are never disconnected from broader structural systems and cultural productions.

In the spirit of the Spanish-language question *¿qué onda?* (what's up? what's happening?), my reference to *la onda* very much signifies Chicano music as a musical scene or happening that conveys which politics, tensions, and tales get worked out and struggled over. As a contested site of musical power, my analysis of *la onda* requires us to understand "the scene"—composed of everything from gossip about singers, gender politics in recording, and memories channeled through lyrics and listening—as central to musical meaning. *La onda* has been a musical sonic imaginary for what has been happening in Mexican America. Thus, *Dissonant Divas in Chicana Music* represents a feminist-of-color interruption to the ways that what has been happening has most often been constructed through what I refer to as "*vato* vernacular," the sustained attention to Chicano voices, the coveted masculine homosocial spaces of conversation, and dominant historiography methods. The chapters that follow mobilize a feminist engagement with Chicano music through oral fragments of memories, self-cultivated archives, lyrical narratives, performance, and *chismes* (gossip) in order to argue that these, too, are part of what constitutes musical happenings. As such, the sonic imaginaries of the borderlands constructed by the singers in this book attempt to capture musical scenes that demand that we see gender, sexuality, and performance as central, if ignored, elements of *la onda*.

Diva Dissonance

THROUGHOUT THIS BOOK the terms "dissonance" and "dissonant" are used in combination with "diva" not as an identity label for the women but as a methodological and analytic device. Dissonance—as chaos, cacophony, disharmony, commotion, static—is deployed in this book to symbolize an interruption or disruption of the heteronormative and cultural-nationalist limits of *la onda* by Chicana/Tejana singers. Dissonance is representative of what Ajay Heble asserts as the "need to take stock of the social processes and institutional practices that frame (and are shaping) the production of knowledge both inside and outside the academy."[11] Furthermore, Heble argues that dissonance is that which sounds out of bounds in the music—such as angular melodies and improvisations—but also what we hear "when our critical practice might in some ways be said to be 'out of tune' with the musics and lives we seek to describe and interpret."[12] The "out-of-tuneness," as understood through the varied meanings of dissonance, commands our attention to music as power as well as to the power of music with regard to Chicana gender and sexuality. This is especially key when we consider nonnormative gender and sexuality as a sort of disturbance to the naturalized orders of knowledge production.[13]

Strategically, this book reclaims the term "diva" from its now gay camp sensibility or its derogatory reference to women of color who are said to be too much, too dramatic, too demanding.[14] It also must be noted that divas are not complete, closed Chicana subjectivities but represent highly contested, resistant, contradictory, and complicit subjectivities. Therefore, *diva* is referred to in this book to acknowledge the creative strategies too often misread or misrecognized that draw upon subordinate class strategies as well as racialized gender epistemologies for cultivating representations and cultural productions. The use of *diva* thus aims to draw attention away from descriptors of women-of-color musical figures as embodiments of excess that often dismiss struggles and negotiations with systems of power, and instead to critically examine their decisions and choices as often enabling them to reorient space, language, and femininity in the public sphere and for making music. Metaphorically speaking, the divas in my project register gender and sexuality that is too loud, too late, and too out of place for heteronormative legibility or audibility in *la onda,* ranging from the female bodies "unfit" for instrumental sound, to licentious singing performance, to life scripts of "inappropriate" wives and mothers.

This book is not centrally concerned with "recovering" Chicana music singers, nor is its intention to merely validate their cultural work as a feat of musical accomplishment equal to that of Chicano/Tejano men in music. Feminists of color have taught us that the goals of addition, integration, and visibility of women and queers long elided from canonical histories is shortsighted and does nothing to advance analysis of gender and sexuality as classifying systems of power. Although I find it critical to dedicate entire chapters to selected singers—because my hope is that this will not be the last project dedicated to these artists—my intention is to avoid containing the singers I write about within the limits of visibility and integration.

Exceptional Divas, or "She's No Lydia Mendoza"

In April 2006, I presented a paper on Selena at "Para la Gente: Symposium on Texas-Mexican Music, Culture, and Society" sponsored by the University of Texas at Austin. After the panel ended with the audience's somewhat predictable discussion of how great Selena was because she was so beautiful and had commercial success, I chatted with an audience member. He wanted to follow up on his comment that the reason more Mexican American women aren't written about is that they haven't accomplished much. In response, I rattled off several names of singers and musicians, including Eva Garza and duets such as Las Hermanas Cantú. His response indicated that he was not very impressed by Garza: "I mean, she's no Lydia Mendoza or anything."

I've come to recognize this response in many conversations. Responses to my work are either uncritically positive—"these women belong in the history too"—or they remind me that the women I study "come nowhere near Lydia Mendoza." Lydia Mendoza and Selena represent the musical bookends of Mexican American women singers during the twentieth century. Both have become not only the Chicana icons of borderlands music but, for the most part, the Chicanas who have garnered the most sustained attention by scholars and curators of public cultural exhibits. And yet, one can recognize the ways in which the distinction between Mendoza as "musician" and Selena as "singer" still represents the kind of musical discourse that marks Mendoza as what I refer to as an "exceptional exemption" in music. In other words, she is one of the few women greats considered exceptional enough in musical talent and skill to be an exemption to the heteromasculinist rule of canonical music histories. The idea that Chicana singers must be as exceptional in recording or career longevity as Lydia Mendoza to be worthy of historicization and analysis disrespects the rich potential for analyzing issues pertaining to everything from alternative archives in music and cultural production, to working-class and other modes of femininity, to homosociality, to nonheteronormative sexualities.

It goes without saying that Lydia Mendoza is worthy of all current and future attention to her cultural work. Two key texts by Yolanda Broyles-González and Chris Strachwitch and James Nicolopulos have contributed key docmentation and analysis of her music and her struggles to succeed in a male-dominated field.[15] No other female singer—and few male singers—of her generation recorded as many songs as Mendoza. Mendoza was an exceptional musical figure, yet my reference to "exceptional exemption" is precisely to point out that such levels of talent and accomplishment should not be the categorical justification that drives the analytic attention to Chicana singers. My invocation of "exceptional exemption" draws attention to a politics of historiography in Chicano music that too often has operated in an inclusion/exclusion and master/mediocre dynamic. Lifting artists such as Lydia Mendoza to the level of exceptional status not only forecloses on the experiences of other performers but also works to reproduce a normative ideology of gender, sexuality, and race among Chicana cultural producers. By these normative standards, an artist such as Selena—who neither was a musician nor wrote her own lyrics—can be considered an exceptional musical figure if she is figured in discourses of "la reina Tejana" (Tejano queen) as good daughter and citizen.

Chicanas who performed, recorded, and sang throughout the twentieth century often certainly don't measure up to the accomplishment and longevity of Mendoza, whose representation was as a singer of the poor, as a musician, and as a soft-spoken, humble woman. Mendoza's representation as "la cancionera de los pobres" (the singer of the poor)—popular among working-class and migrant workers in the borderlands—fits the necessary class subject position of cultural resistance symbolized in canonical texts.[16] Often reproduced narratives of Mendoza's dedication to traveling and singing to poor migrant laborers and her recording success in ranchera and corrido music have contributed to the representation of her as the prototypical Chicana singer easily consonant with music as a mode of cultural resistance. When Mendoza is held up in music narratives as *the* Chicana, it does not allow for the consideration of other Chicana singers who may align their cultural work with middle-class femininity, nonnormative family constructions, and queer sexualities and expressions of desire. The dissonant divas in this book thus honor Mendoza's musical legacy, not by measuring up to it but rather by illuminating different manifestations of power heretofore propelled by dominant narratives of Chicano music.

Sounding Divas

The Chicana singers and musicians in this book represent Chicana music that propels alternative sonic imaginaries of the borderlands that, in the words of Mary Pat Brady, "insist that one can embrace multiple contradictions and refuse the impossible effort to synthesize them fully."[17] The book charts through Chicana musical dissonance as an interruption to overdetermined geographic and gendered parameters of Tex-Mex as well as regional assumptions of Tejana singers as somehow disconnected from the national, international, and transnational. Thus, the reference to *mejicanas* in the title of this Introduction demonstrates new social identities, different configurations of gender, and alternative notions of place prompted by these Chicana singers. The term *mejicanas* sympolizes the connections and contestations between the terms *mejicana,* "Mexican American," "Chicana," and "Tejana" that are/were negotiated by these singers and musicians. *Mejicana* serves to remind us that Chicanas represent subjectivities produced in negotiation of multiple nation-making projects, from legally sanctioned U.S. citizenship to notions of belonging within Chicano/Tejano cultural-national formations. Thus, *mejicana* symbolizes the metaphoric and theoretical notion of Chicana feminist articulations of the borderlands as an imaginary that embraces the odd, the liminal, and the in between.[18]

The first three chapters of the book draw attention to the multiple nation-making projects reflected in contested identity formations of Texas-Mexican, *mexicano,* and Mexican American.[19] The three chapters represent the ways Chicanas have disrupted the gender, class, and sexuality boundaries arguably held in place by Tex-Mex conjunto and corrido music. They engage canonical studies of Tex-Mex conjunto and corrido music by critically reflecting on the historical subject formation of the Texas-Mexican or the Tejano; in other words, they offer a feminist assessment of Tex-Mex conjunto and corrido music that engages Texan and Tejano cultural nationalism and the multiple nation-making projects that shape constructions of race and gender for Tejanas and are echoed in musical production and narrative strategies of Tex-Mex music.

Chapter 1, "Remember the Alamo, Remember Rosita Fernández," begins the book with a musical figure who does not easily reconcile with the past and who will not allow us to forget the Alamo. This chapter presents the six-decade career—spanning radio, recording, movies, and live performance—of Rosita Fernández. Nicknamed "la rosa de San Antonio" (San Antonio's rose), Fernández's representation—too simply deemed "commercial"—is consistently staged within an Anglo-Texan colonial imaginary. Fernández's musical dissonance is marked by chaos and commotion; she is a musical figure whose representation is shaped as much by resistance as by complicity. As such, she represents an unsettled and at times contradictory Tejana subjectivity that allows us a more critical and complex entry into any considerations of Tejano/Tex-Mex music and cultural production. Fernández is unique because, unlike other singers of her generation, there is a legible and institutionalized archive of her musical contributions. Yet, she is metaphorically too abundant to contain within resistant calls to "forget the Alamo" that therefore have left her marginal to Chicano music.

The following two chapters focus on Chicana singers in relation to Tex-Mex corrido and conjunto music, musical genres that have served as examples of cultural resistance mechanisms to the legacy of racist violence and subordination of *mexicanos,* marked by years such as 1836, 1845, and 1848. Chapter 2, "Borders, Bullets, *Besos:* The Ballad of Chelo Silva," analyzes Chelo Silva's nonconformity to gender norms through her interpretations of boleros during the 1950s and 1960s. I argue that Silva's performance legacy—discursively constituted through desire, sexual excess, and emotional trauma characteristic of boleros—is dissonant within a canonical formation of Chicano music where Tex-Mex corrido music and the figure of Américo Paredes, Silva's former husband, have held so much power. The analysis in this chapter critically considers Silva's boleros as a "border ballad" and offers different configurations of power and resistance in heretofore unexplored elements of Tex-Mex corrido musical legacy. Chapter 3, "Tex-Mex Conjunto Accordion Masculinity: The Queer Discord of Eva Ybarra and Ventura Alonzo," brings the female body to bear on the Tex-Mex conjunto accordion, as the musical sounding of *Tejas,* particularly through the accordion, has given conjunto music its distinctive sound. I begin with an overview of music, performance, and labor in the early career of accordionist Ventura Alonzo that forms a queer analytic I refer to as *curiosidad* (the odd, the curious, the funny); I then move to a focus on Tejana accordionist Eva Ybarra to examine how the female body has been deemed incompatible with the accordion, a musical sound that has been considered "the heartbeat of a people."

Chapters 4 and 5 challenge the construction of Tejana subjectivities as overdetermined by gender, geographic, and nationalist parameters of regionality or locality. These two chapters reflect—extending Licia

Fiol-Matta's articulation of "divascape"—those musical soundscapes not bounded by nationalist genres but rather shaped by the desires, excursions, and possibilities of where divas' music takes us.[20] Eva Garza and Selena reimagine the borderlands through their formation of divascapes, travel, and the cultivation of north-to-south and south-to-south flows of music. These Chicana singers enable a sonic imaginary of the borderlands according to new musical mappings of both Tejana subjectivity and Chicano music. Chapter 4, "Sonido de las Américas: Crossing South–South Borders with Eva Garza," analyzes the transnational musical trajectory of Eva Garza from the late 1930s to the early 1960s that extends from San Antonio to New York, Mexico City, and Havana. Her literal and musical movements across gender and geographic borders reflect not only her music but also a life story that articulates nonheteronormative temporalities of family and citizenship among and between multiple scales of musical nation building. Chapter 5, "Giving Us That Brown Soul: Selena's Departures and Arrivals," theorizes a notion of "brown soul" by following the sound of Selena's music along a north-to-south trajectory. Through critical race and gender analysis of Selena's contemporary "musical crossover," I reveal the African diasporic sound we cannot hear when we comprehend Selena within a heteronormative construction of "la reina Tejana" (queen of Tejano music), a musical representation that is reduced to geographically, gendered, and racially reductive notions of crossover. Moreover, I assert that Selena's cumbia sounds, as well as her funk- and disco-influenced style, produce a Chicano musical configuration of "brown soul" that is queer, thereby reimagining the borderlands through often elided and marginalized social and cultural constructions of blackness and queerness.

The Epilogue, "The Borderlands Rock Reverb of Gloria Ríos and Girl in a Coma," explores the reverberations of Chicana rock music, from Gloria Ríos's 1950s rock-and-roll *grito* to the shouts in Girl in a Coma's punk music.

When I began this project many years ago, I quickly learned that I was going to have to assemble an archive by consistently questioning the notion of an archive and committing myself to understanding the power of musical sound and the powerful histories often not narrativized through the audibly or empirically decipherable. This has taken me to places—metaphoric and geographic—that I did not expect. Listening to and for the singers in *Dissonant Divas in Chicana Music* has required me to be open to listening for details I didn't want to hear, sitting with silences and innuendo, and hearing the same memories over and over; it also required unexpected travels to voting booths, to bingo games, to pick up groceries, and to an island I never expected to visit. Consequently, the women whose lives and works I examine required that I be as open in my analytic travels as they were in their musical travels. These Chicana singers have channeled their voices, bodies, and musical instruments and they have imagined desires, economic comfort, love, revenge, future, public recognition, pasts, home, travels, family, and claims of identities for themselves. Listening to and through the dissonance of these singers encourages our engagement with their music, their lives, critical assessments of music histories, and of all the complicated and contested alternative imaginaries of the borderlands their cultural work forges.

ONE

Remember the Alamo, Remember Rosita Fernández

Rosita y San Antonio son inseparables
Rosita and San Antonio are inseparable
—cover of Rosita Fernández's record *San Antonio*

SOUND MARKS PLACE. Music channels memory. Memories establish a presence. Place engenders social identities. Social identities are given presence through music. Sonic imaginaries possess histories. Histories—as canonical narratives, silences, ephemera, oral tellings, scandalous *chisme* (gossip), in the shape of dissonant figures—are contested struggles over remembering. To remember is a high-stakes project. It does not always result in healing, in uncovering or discovering an empowering subject or narrative, in resolving the past, or making the present more secure. To remember is a high-stakes project because it requires a commitment to engage contradiction, vulnerability, and complicity through complex struggles over power. To remember Rosita requires us to remember the Alamo.[1]

Rosita remembered the power of musical sound from an early age, recalling in an interview how impressed she was by the way a singing voice seemed to have the ability to hold attention and suspend time. She recalled that when she was a little girl, her father had one major rule in their home: that her mother's singing would not compete with anything else in the household. Anytime the children were near, Rosita's father would call them to attention to pause from what they were doing because "your mama is singing." Rosita's father believed that to make disruptive sounds or not give full attention would dishonor their mother's voice; Rosita and her siblings would have to interrupt what they were doing until their mother was finished.[2] In her recollections, Rosita noted not so much what her mother sang but the power that singing had for imagining other places and emotions. Her memories evoked not only her mother's voice and songs but also relationships with siblings, a cultivation of her own sense of cultural identity, and everyday social relations as she was growing up. Rosita's own singing voice and musical performances would come to represent a powerful sonic instrument, not only with regard to entertaining audiences but also for the ways her representation and singing experiences would form an alternative channel for constructions of Chicana/o and Tejana/o subjectivities and cultural identity formations.

I begin *Dissonant Divas* with Rosita Fernández because, of the women represented in this book, she is the one with the longest musical trajectory, the largest institutional archive, and diverse experience across musical media. Thus, Rosita sets the tone of dissonance in this book, a feminist critique of who and why musical figures are remembered, legible, and heard in what I refer to as *la onda* of the sonic imaginary of the borderlands as represented by Chicano canonical music. Moreover, remembering Rosita requires a commitment to grapple with contested histories of Anglo–Mexican relations, internal class conflicts, and contradictions within cultural-nationalist configurations of resistance to subordination. Howard Lamar provides an appropriate depiction of Texas that captures the complicated essence of Rosita Fernández and the spirit of dissonance as feminist critique: "Texas is not so much a place, but a commotion."[3] The commotion that is and has been Texas is symbolized by turmoil, disorder, and chaos corresponding to the unique social, political, and cultural shifts experienced by racialized populations. Such Texas commotion, I argue, conveys the residual sounds of multiple wars, nation-building projects, and identity formations fraught with contradiction and contestations.[4] Rosita Fernández represents such dissonant commotion through chaotic class mobility, language static, and a *mexicana* cultural identity that is not in order with cultural-nationalist narratives of Tejano or Chicano musical subjects. Rosita sounds a dissonance within a hegemonic imaginary of Tejano and Chicano borderlands music that has made little effort—with the exception of commercial or middle-class discourse—to reckon with her musical career.

Rosita Fernández has been everywhere in San Antonio's musical history as well as in songs that have signified the city itself. If one follows the key historical shifts in music media, one will see a career that spanned early Spanish-language phonograph recordings, English- and Spanish-language radio broadcasts, jukeboxes, film, and television. What one recognizes in looking through her institutional archive is that she is a ubiquitous San Antonio singing presence—at a local event, in the newspaper pictured next to an important person visiting the city, or at the downtown Riverwalk performing at the Fiesta Noche de Río. For people in San Antonio, Rosita has been the city's public face. As a public personality, she was larger than life—or at least taller than the five-foot, two-inch singer I interacted with—always singing and always dressed to perfection in her *china poblana* dresses. It seemed that anything related to San Antonio had Rosita attached to it. During her sixty-plus-year career as a performer, entertainer, and singer, she has been recognized by local and regional institutions: she was inducted into the San Antonio Musicians Hall of Fame, the San Antonio Women's Hall of Fame, and the Tejano Music Hall of Fame. As her career evolved in the 1970s, she was increasingly asked to be the city's unofficial cultural ambassador.[5] In the spirit of Rosita's recollection of her as a child hearing her mother sing, I am curious as to why Chicano music has not paid more critical attention to Rosita and what listening to her offers the sonic imaginary of the borderlands.

Surprisingly, Rosita has not received a great deal of attention or fame outside of San Antonio despite a six-decade career that marks her as one of the most active Mexican American women public performers of the twentieth century. I contend that her dissonance within *la onda* is a result of her being imagined through two conjoined sonic projects of nationalist music and folklore, namely, the battle cry "Remember the Alamo!" and the Chicano musical sound wave I refer to as *la onda,* whose canonical project has been a historical and cultural response to such racist and imperialist discourses about Mexicans channeled through such acts of remembering the Alamo. Rosita is as indivisible from the historically fraught call to "remember the Alamo" as she is illegible within Chicano canonical discourses of *la onda* that have prioritized heteromasculinist working-class *mexicano* subjects and experiences. Her cultural work is outside of the class, gender, and linguistic norms that uphold an authentic borderlands imaginary. Moreover, her desire for both economic security and professional recognition within a masculinist music industry is rendered as a cacophonous Mexican representation with a Tejano musical public culture where the call to "remember the Alamo" necessarily entails cultural resistance through the act of forgetting rather than alternative possibilities of remembering. Rosita Fernández exemplifies a figure of Chicana musical dissonance—analyzed through song, language, biographical narrative, and racialized gender representation—whose subjectivity does not register easily with either Texan independence or Chicano/Tejano cultural nationalism; to reckon with Fernández's musical figuration means to engage contradiction, ambiguity, and disorder within a dominant borderlands musical imaginary that has been sustained by notions of commercial music as inauthentic, English language as acculturated, and economic success as accommodationist.

I maintain that Rosita's indelible presence in San Antonio's public culture insists that we, in fact, remember the Alamo by remembering Rosita. The figurative call to "remember Rosita" is not intended to fit Rosita Fernández's *mexicana* representation within the Anglo Texan racist discourse; nor does remembering Rosita prompt forgetting the Alamo and its legacy of racist folklore. Rather, the kind of remembering I call for activates a reclaiming of *mexicano* subject formation within Texan cultural nationalism that bursts the limits of victim/oppressor or hero/villain binaries that have sustained both Texan and Tejano cultural nationalisms through a call to "remember the Alamo." Rosita Fernández's cultural work insists on a remembering that provokes differing, often competing constructions of Tejano history and identity formations through a *mexicana*'s experiences with negotiating English-language, commercial white audiences, and her racialized gender and sexuality as a singer within a masculinized Chicano/Tejano music world.

The first section of this chapter reviews historical narratives of the efforts to establish the Republic of Texas—as interlinked with folklore and popular Texas songs—that continually echo within San Antonio's public culture. Such mythic tales reproduce representations of *mexicanos* as either complicit with or resistant to Texan independence from Mexico. The chapter proceeds to analyze Rosita's personal experiences as well as her public representation as closely aligned with the Alamo. Her inseparability from Texan cultural nationalism, her singing in English, and her comfortable class status produced a Chicana singing figure disharmonious with racialized gender and class representations of the canonical Chicano/Tejano sonic imaginary of the borderlands. A feminist analysis of Rosita Fernández emphasizes that her efforts to establish a singing career produced an ambiguous, contested, and complicated racialized subjectivity of Tejanas and Tejanos that does not register in the discursive project to "forget the Alamo." The last section interrogates two sites of public memory—a bridge and a costume—that symbolize the chaos, commotion, or what I refer to as Chicana diva dissonance within the borderlands sonic imaginary.

Rosita stands at the crossroads of how San Antonio has been sounded as "the cradle of Texan independence" with *mexicano* representation being figured as either faithful victimization to or deceitful support of Anglo Texan hegemony.[6] My call to remember Rosita is a call to attention, a call to remember her musical career that moves beyond her representation as a commercial singer or San Antonio's entertainment novelty. Remembering Rosita symbolizes an alternative to forgetting the Alamo or to remembering those whose cultural work fits easily within the symbolism of cultural resistance that has muted the complicated realities by which race, gender, and sexuality shaped the careers and choices of women singers in early decades of the twentieth century. Remember: the Alamo—Rosita—San Antonio. Rosita Fernández has been difficult to hear because she is a mere mention in Chicano music histories despite the loud presence of her institutional archive. Following the sounds of her career requires us to open our ears to less stable sonic imaginaries of the borderlands and of Tejano representations and subjectivities.

San Antonio: So Far from Mexico, So Close to Texas

Porfirio Díaz, president of Mexico from 1876 to 1911, declared in 1900: "¡Pobre México! Tan lejos de dios y tan cerca de los Estados Unidos" (Poor Mexico! So far from God, and so close to the United States).[7] Although there are numerous interpretations of Díaz's original lamentation, it has been rechanneled many times over to describe the tension-filled yet codependent historic relationship existing between Mexico and the United States long before Díaz uttered those words. San Antonio has had a similarly troubled relationship between and within Mexican and Texan national imaginaries. Distinct from parts of what is now the U.S. Southwest, Texas was the site of bloody battles for independence from Spain (1811–14) that resulted in torture, mass executions, rape, abandonment of towns, beheading, and placing of heads and dismembered bodies on pikes in town squares, and then the 1836 Texas revolt, the 1842 Mexican attempts to reconquer Texas, the 1846–48 U.S.–Mexican War, and skirmishes resulting from the increasing racial violence against Tejanos after the 1840s.[8] In what is now known as the state of Texas, borders crossed peoples, nationalities shifted, and Mexicans became displaced and disempowered in ways unique to the larger region. Raúl Coronado argues that the acts of Anglo violence against Mexicans that included lynchings and the turmoil resulting from the number of wars and battles can be described as a "culture of war."[9] The residual racist discourses still echo in calls to remember the Alamo, to remember San Antonio, and to comprehend Tejana/o subjectivities as eternally too far from Mexico yet inescapable from monuments that reproduce *mexicano* racialization within a Texan national imaginary.

Founded around 1716, San Antonio de Valero Mission (originally San Antonio de Padua) would come to be known less as a place for Christianizing the region's Native peoples and more as a fortress, the site of numerous conflicts prior to its historic 1836 siege by Mexican military forces.[10] In fact, the Alamo was occupied by Mexican forces almost continuously from 1803 to 1835, when it was surrendered to Texan forces.[11] To paraphrase Howard Lamar, Texas is not so much a place, but a commotion.

The Texas imaginary is also comprised of multiple national flags that have laid claim to this territory. From 1519 to 1865, most of the geographic landscape of Texas was claimed by Spain, France, Mexico, the Republic of Texas, the United States of America, and the Confederate States of America.[12] From 1685 to 1690, France desired to expand its base in French Louisiana when René-Robert Cavelier, Sieur de La Salle founded a colony named Ft. St. Louis near the Texas Gulf Coast. From 1519 to 1685 and 1690 to 1821, Spanish conquest laid claim to present-day Mexico and Texas. Texas was in fact one of the interior provinces of New Spain from 1690 to 1821. The Mexican War of Independence lasted from 1810 to 1821 and by 1820 only two thousand Hispanic citizens remained in Texas as Spain finally relinquished control of the former New Spain. Texas became a province of the newly formed nation of Mexico and the geographic region was referred to as Coahuila y Tejas. After its annexation in 1845, from 1861 to 1865 Texas also distinguished itself as a Confederate state during the American Civil War.[13]

The most pivotal shift that directly pertains to the commotion that comes to represent Texas occurred when General Antonio López de Santa Anna overturned the Mexican Federalist Constitution of 1824. Santa Anna's move toward Centralist government collided with the Mexican government's previous permission for immigration from the United States into Texas. By 1834, approximately thirty thousand Anglos shared the region with only eight thousand Mexicans. "The residents of the San Antonio River valley from Bexar to La Bahía and southward to Refugio felt the brunt of war as early as October 1835 and withstood its ravages for almost a year as their lands were occupied and re-occupied by the contending armies."[14] During 1835–36, the power over this contested region of Texas changed sides four times.[15]

Initially, Bejareños (mostly residents of Mexican descent from the Béxar region) stood in opposition to Santa Anna's Mexican Centralist movement. In fact, from this opposition emerged one of the most legendary figures associated with the Texas Revolution, Juan Seguín, who traveled to Coahuila in a failed attempt to assist Federalist Coahuila-Tejas Governor Agustín Viesca to maintain his authority. Like Seguín, many Mexican Texans fought to preserve the 1824 Mexican Constitution. No matter the support Mexican Texans provided to the Federalist cause, tensions between Anglos—forcibly claiming rights to property, including cattle, food, and land—and Mexican Texans escalated because some Mexican Texans also fought alongside General Santa Anna. Tensions escalated when the Texas cause shifted from a stance of maintaining a Federalist government within the Mexican nation toward complete independence. Most Tejanos immediately equated this shift toward national sovereignty with permanent minority status within an Anglicized Texas nation:

> Few of them joined or re-enrolled in military service until after the conclusion of the battle of the Alamo. War weariness, dissatisfaction with the goal of Texas independence, and their earlier losses of private property combined to reduce the *Bejareños* support for the cause of resisting the Centralists.[16]

What is clear in reviewing these historical events, and what is often lost in critiques of Anglo Texans' call for an independent republic (which often results in an us-versus-them radicalized dynamic), is that "persons of Mexican descent in Texas did not speak with one voice, act with one purpose, or suffer to an equal degree."[17] For example, the 1836 revolt pitted Tejano family members against one another; it was not uncommon for siblings and parents to be on different sides, as when a brother who fought with Santa Anna's Mexican forces at the Alamo later received permission to bury his brother who had died defending the Alamo.[18] Approximately one hundred Tejanos showed support for Texas independence, while others cooperated with Santa Anna's army. Gathered at the San Fernando church in the center of town, Seguín addressed the crowd to honor those who had perished in defense of the Alamo, stating: "The venerable remains of our worthy companions as witnesses, I invite you to declare to the entire world, 'Texas shall be free and independent, or we shall perish in glorious combat.'"[19] Regardless of what side Tejanos stood on, most would not be saved from the racist violence by Anglo Texans, especially when it came to land rights. Mexican Texans attempted to become good citizens and integrate themselves into political office, but their status declined rapidly.[20]

To view the Battle of the Alamo in terms of sides is inaccurate at best. At worst, doing so elides the complexity necessary to understand *mexicano* subjectivities in Texas. This tumultuous history of internal and external conflict over historically fraught instances of nation building have shaped heterogeneous Tejano social identities. Tejanos observed the siege of the Alamo, the battle, and its aftermath from a diversity of perspectives. "Some Tejanos witnessed these events from within the Alamo, some left the garrison as couriers and scouts, some watched from the distance, and others left San Antonio during the hostilities, returning only after the battle was over."[21] In fact, during the decades following Texas independence, many petitions and depositions were filed in land-claim cases for Tejano heirs of defenders of the Alamo.[22]

The siege and the final assault of the Alamo in 1836 constitute the most celebrated, even mythological, military engagement in Texas history.[23] Not only was the Republic of Texas established through the outcome of this war, but this battle also presaged the eventual annexation of Texas into the United States. The U.S.–Mexican War would result in the 1848 Treaty of Guadalupe Hidalgo, through which the United States annexed more than half of Mexico's territory.[24]

Although the popular assumption is that the Alamo was the site where Texas established its independence from Mexico, the decisive battle occurred some weeks later at San Jacinto near present-day Houston.[25] The Battle of San Jacinto marked the conclusion of the Texas Revolution, after which Texas declared its independence from Mexico.[26] Nonetheless, the Battle of the Alamo is arguably equally significant because the defeat of Texans by Mexican forces would become the most momentous event of the Texas nationalist imaginary and the one often cited in discourses of Tejano cultural resistance captured by the phrase "Forget the Alamo." Yet, what is indisputable is that Tejano subjectivities in the nineteenth century were products of an ambiguous relationship to both Texan supporters of independence from Mexico and also Mexican forces led by Santa Anna and the move for a centralist government. Simply stated, Tejanos were caught between two undesirable outcomes because they preferred a reconfiguration of their political authority over Texas in light of the Mexican government's move toward a centralist government; yet this also did not equate to a pro-Texan republic stance.

Tejanos preferred to remain under Mexico but did not find their visions supported by Mexico's shift to establish a centralist government. As David Weber states, "In a larger sense, members of the Béxar *ayuntamiento* of 1832–33 found themselves caught between succumbing to pressures from Anglo-Americans, who formed the numerical majority in Texas, or remaining loyal to Mexican procedures and traditions. It was a dilemma that Mexicans in Texas would come to understand all too well after Texas won independence in 1836."[27] As such, what is often lost in contemporary discourses of Tejanos having defeated Anglo Texans at the Alamo and then having been defeated by Anglo Texans at the Battle of San Jacinto is that Tejanos were not merely subordinate to Anglo Texan desires for independence from Mexico because some Tejanos fought on the side of Texas forces, not fully aligned with Mexico's centralist goals. Simultaneously, Tejanos who fought on the side of Anglo Texans cannot be represented as having been fully in support of Texas's independence from Mexico. This complexity is lost in contemporary cultural productions that result from either racist discourses of Anglo hegemony over *mexicanos* in Texas or the representation of Tejanos as completely defeated victims who lost Texas to Anglo Texan forces desiring to separate themselves from Mexico. Thus, it is more productive to describe the contemporary legacies of Tejano identity formations as residual configurations of such structural complexity.

Remember the Alamo!

San Antonio de Béxar remains an enduring discursive topography of racial conflict and violence in what is now recognized as the city of San Antonio, an inescapable past made present every time one hears reference to the battle cry "Remember the Alamo!"[28] The Alamo as icon, institution, and cultural symbol has also been part of what it means to be *mexicano* in Texas and, by extension, what is echoed in the term "Tejano." For example, in 1980 the Texas Talent Musicians Association deemed San Antonio the "Tejano Music Capital of the World." Although there is much debate in musicology about origins, genres, and musical styles that emerged and transformed throughout the twentieth century to define what Guadalupe San Miguel calls "Tejano sound, a style unique to Texas and different from traditional Mexican music," the term "Tejano" and its sonic claim to the city of San Antonio exemplify the ways it has marked multiple, contested, and varied projects of cultural production that are linked to discourses of Texan racial hegemony, as the national proverb "Remember the Alamo!" has been central to the construction of social identities and cultural projects in the "making of Texas."[29] For example, even in the latter part of the twentieth century it was common to come across bands with names such as Ruben Ramos and the Texas Revolution or taglines for radio stations such as Tejano 107.5, where listeners who call in to the station follow identifying themselves by name with the tagline "and I'm Tejano and proud." Tejano music serves as a way to claim a Tejano identity through prideful enactments of Tejano cultural stagings that, according to Maylei Blackwell's assertion about Chicano cultural nationalism, is "forged through the recuperation or discovery of a historical legacy suppressed by colonization. More than an act of reclamation, it [is] the production of a Chicano identity."[30] The circulation of the term "Tejano," whether as an enactment of self-identity, an effort to distinguish a musical genre, or a historical construction of a population, hails the ever-present calls to remember.

The battle cry "Remember the Alamo!" insists on the construction of heroes and villains as delineated by racialized gender binaries: Texans/Mexicans, brave valiant heroes/ruthless uncivilized cowards, pure white femininity/savage racialized femininity, and freedom/tyranny, to name just a few. From required Texas history class in public schools to the multiple Alamo-themed Hollywood cinematic productions, it is nearly impossible to escape the grand narrative of the "ruthless dictator" Santa Anna whose forces defeated the likes of Davy Crockett, James Travis, and Jim Bowie, "American" heroes who fought to their death in defense of the Alamo fortress for Texas's independence:[31]

> The battle of the Alamo was not in vain, for Santa Anna's army is tattered and needs weeks to recuperate from its victory. Less than six weeks later, Sam Houston's army defeats Santa Anna's forces at San Jacinto, screaming, "Remember the Alamo! The Alamo! The Alamo! The Alamo!"[32]

Geographic locality, the literal mapping of the Texas–Mexico border, and the link between national boundaries and battles over geographic frontiers are central to the nation-building project of Texas. Texan nationalism thus permeates institutional knowledge—from textbooks to museums, from the Battle of San Jacinto to Texan folk and popular songs. One need only step foot into the Texas State History Museum rotunda to comprehend the grandeur that is the Texas nationalist imaginary:

> "Texas is the finest portion of the globe that has ever blessed my vision." (Sam Houston, 1833)
>
> "I will never forsake Texas and her cause. I am her son." (José Antonio Navarro, 1842)
>
> "Texas is rich in unredeemed dreams." (Larry McMurtry, 1968)[33]

These statements exemplify Ernest Renan's theorization of a nation built on rich legacies of memories and a heroic heritage of great men and glory: "The nation, like the individual, is the culmination of a long past of endeavors, sacrifice and devotion."[34]

The call to "remember the Alamo" has worked to align Anglo masculinity with heroism and valor while simultaneously representing *mexicano* masculinity with deceit and racial subordination. While some

Chicano cultural production, especially film and corrido music, has produced counternarratives that expose the realities of violent racial oppression, labor exploitation, and forced turnover of *mexicano* property rights, such narratives and representations, as Rosa Linda Fregoso has suggested, have drawn less critical attention to gender and sexuality as interlinked with race and class.[35] Alternative and counterhistories are suppressed rememberings that eventually break through, as if bursting through a stitch that has desperately held a nationalist narrative seam together; thus, in addition to analyzing productions of alternative or counternarratives and representational icons, it is also critical to explore the tension, the pulling and tugging at seams that either hold or break open. I find it especially critical to explore productions, representations, and singing icons like Rosita Fernández who present contradictions, complicities, and ambivalences in relation to Anglo Texas racial hegemony.

Analyzing figures such as Rosita Fernández becomes particularly significant when we think about the politics of race, gender, sexuality, and class in constructing forms of cultural resistance to racism, especially when she cultivated such an intelligible personal archive that is institutionalized, but has remained an indecipherable absence in historical documentation and scholarly analyses of Chicano cultural production and social identities.[36] In San Antonio, there is no greater cultural symbol of the ways in which racial ambivalence stands in opposition to racism and defies a sexist Chicano/Tejano music industry than Rosita Fernández.

Rosita's subjectivity has not functioned as a mechanism for simply forgetting the Alamo, nor have her songs and performances seamlessly succumbed to racist and sexist ideologies of *mexicanas*. Although her ubiquity in San Antonio's public culture during the last decades of the twentieth century was too often cast as novelty or commercial culture, her iconicity has called for a feminist engagement since the emerging decades of her career. Rosita's career and life choices operate much like a dual operating screen, overshadowing the elements of history that are too violent for Chicanos/Tejanos to acknowledge while projecting onto other aspects of history alternative subjectivities that disrupt a tidily produced, unproblematically chiastic Texas nationalist imaginary. Fernández's career is at odds with a mainstream rendering of a dichotomous "remember the Alamo"—that is, as a cultural imperative that allows only for an uncomplicated Anglo-Texan accommodation and overdetermined masculinist project of Chicano cultural resistance. For example, colleagues and friends often express to me, with no small measure of certainty, that *mexicanos* in Texas who attend San Antonio's Fiesta Week activities held annually in April to commemorate the Battle of San Jacinto are actively celebrating the defeat of "our *gente*"[37] because they just don't know any better or because they choose to not assert a critical stance against such racist symbolism. This type of comment implicates a figure like Rosita Fernández and also exemplifies the need to move through dissonance—represented by contradiction, complicity, and ambivalence—that cannot be neatly ordered into race, class, and gender constructions of "our *gente*."

So much of the metaphoric commotion that constitutes Texas history emanates from the cultural-nationalist folklore and unofficial state songs that reify hegemonic racist narratives of freedom and independence. Iterations of "Texas, Our Texas," "Beautiful, Beautiful Texas," "Deep in the Heart of Texas," and "The Eyes of Texas" exemplify why contemporary marketing slogans such as "Texas. It's like a Whole Other Country" (a slogan of the State of Texas Tourist Bureau) resonate with the public. Such Texan folk and popular songs rely on a subordinate racialized subject defeated by a hegemonic Anglo Texan subject in an oft-repeated, unproblematized script. The state song, "Texas, Our Texas," and the folk favorite of typical Texas history classes, "Beautiful, Beautiful Texas," offer two salient examples:

Texas, Our Texas
(William J. Marsh and Gladys Yoakum Wright)

Texas, our Texas! All hail the mighty State!
Texas, our Texas! So wonderful, so great!
Boldest and grandest, withstanding ev'ry test;
O Empire wide and glorious, you stand supremely blessed.

Refrain

God bless you Texas! And keep you brave and strong,
That you may grow in power and worth, Throughout the ages long.

Texas, O Texas! Your freeborn single star,
Sends out its radiance to nations near and far.
Emblem of freedom! It sets our hearts aglow,
With thoughts of San Jacinto and glorious Alamo.

Refrain

Texas, dear Texas! From tyrant grip now free,
Shines forth in splendor your star of destiny!
Mother of heroes! We come your children true,
Proclaiming our allegiance, our faith, our love for you.

Refrain

Beautiful, Beautiful Texas
(W. Lee O'Daniel)

Oh beautiful, beautiful Texas
The most beautiful state that I know
We're proud of our forefathers
Who fought at the Alamo.

You may live on the plains or the mountains
Or down where the sea breezes blow,
But, you'll still be in beautiful Texas
The most beautiful state that I know.

Perhaps no other songs have circulated so widely and enduringly to produce sonic imaginaries of Texas and reproduce Texan cultural nationalism as "The Yellow Rose of Texas" and "San Antonio Rose." More significantly, both of these songs exemplify the central figure of the racialized woman, here named Rose, in the project of nation building: both employ the rose as a trope for Texan independence. The name Rose romanticizes the imperialist underpinnings of racialized and racist discourses of *mexicana* gender and sexuality, or what Shelly Streeby refers to as "the centrality of entanglements of class, race, gender, sexuality and empire in nineteenth-century U.S. culture."[38] These two songs in particular have reverberated across generations, appearing everywhere from history textbooks to popular films and television shows. There are numerous versions that include different terminology based on historical context and regional dialect. Nonetheless, the examples below capture the general essence of the song.

The Yellow Rose of Texas
(J. K.)

There's a yellow rose in Texas, I'm going there to see.
I know she's waiting for me, nobody only me.
She cried so when I left her, it like to broke her heart.
And if we ever meet again, we never more shall part.

Chorus

She's the sweetest little rosebud, that Texas ever knew.
Her eyes are bright as diamonds, they sparkle like the dew.
You may talk about your Clementine, and sing of Rosy Lee,
But the yellow rose of Texas, is the only one for me.

Chorus

Oh, I'm going back to find her, my heart is full of woe.
We'll sing the songs together, that we sang so long ago.
I'll pick the banjo gaily, and sing the songs of yore.
The Yellow Rose of Texas, shall be mine forever more.

The following is an explicitly racist version of "The Yellow Rose of Texas":

There's a yellow rose in Texas,
That I am a going to see,
No other darky knows her,
No darky only me
She cried so when I left her
It like to broke my heart,
And if I ever find her,
We nevermore will part.

Chorus

She's the sweetest rose of color
This darky ever knew,
Her eyes are bright as diamonds,
They sparkle like the dew;
You may talk about your Dearest May,
And sing of Rosa Lee,
But the yellow rose of Texas
Beats the belles of Tennessee.

While there are numerous and competing folktales, historical analyses, and fiction texts devoted to the subject, Emily D. West (the supposed subject of the song), and the origins of the song, there is nonetheless a common folklore about who and why the song was written.[39] As Trudier Harris argues, "the Battle of San Jacinto, the song—these are the people, the time, the place, the incident, and the creation surrounding it that have merged history, legend, biography, and musical composition. No matter who would desire otherwise, the links are now inseparable in viewing the story of the song and its presumed subject, Emily D. West."[40]

According to Texan folklore legend, "The Yellow Rose of Texas" was written in honor of twenty-one-year-old Emily D. West, a "mulatta" slave—described in folktales as "mulatta" or "light-skinned"— indentured to James Morgan, who was said to have sent word to General Sam Houston that General Santa Anna was on the move toward his troops before the Battle of San Jacinto. According to the official Web site of the Alamo, the "yellow" of the song's title stems from the use of yellow to designate slaves of African descent with lighter-toned skin.[41] According to Texan legend, West is said to have distracted Santa Anna by utilizing her sexual prowess to assure General Sam Houston enough time to organize and carry out his attack. The Battle of San Jacinto was supposedly won because Emily West was able to use her sexual power to overcome Sam Houston.

"The Yellow Rose of Texas" fulfills the stereotypes of African American women as hypersexual.[42] Moreover, the prominent place of the song in reproducing Texan nationalism exemplifies characteristically reductive representations of *mexicana* and African American women in cultural nationalist narratives. According to the folklore, West was thanked for her participation in helping to defeat Santa Anna by being granted her freedom from slavery. The spirit of the song is intended to honor the fight for Texas sovereignty or, in the popular saying, "Ms. Emily was free and so was Texas."[43] Trudier Harris asserts that Emily D. West's body has been exploited in at least three different ways by historians, folklorists, and the general public's reproduction of this icon: first, the "body" of the song has been used to shape Texas and American history; second, West's corporeality is used to imagine unity in order to displace animosity and distrust; and third, the body of Emily D. West has been represented as someone whose primary concern was the welfare of Texas instead of her own.[44]

Although racist Texan folklore songs pertaining to African Americans and *mexicanos* in Texas are composed through racist discourses corresponding to unique historical circumstances, the figure of the rose is one similar trope deployed in folk songs that center *mexicana* racialized sexuality. The symbolism and songs that feature the rose might be understood as a legacy of "The Yellow Rose of Texas." The most common popular song that exemplifies this is "San Antonio Rose." Again, the rose as metaphor for *mexicanas* is fixed to San Antonio's cultural imaginary. Originally, the song was recorded by Bob Wills and the Texas Playboys in 1936[45] as an instrumental version with Wills's fiddle accompanied only by a steel guitar. The song's lyrics were written by Wills and sung by one of the Playboys, Tommy Duncan, in the hit version called the "New San Antonio Rose" released in 1940.[46] One of Wills's top four best-selling songs, "New San Antonio Rose" became his signature tune and set the stage for what was to become a new genre of music referred to as Texas Swing. Versions of how Wills came up with "San Antonio Rose" reveal his significant musical influences through interactions with African Americans and *mexicanos*.

According to Frank Jennings, one tale recounts how Wills learned the instrumental tune from Mexican ranch hands in the area of Texas where he grew up.[47] Al Strickland claims that Wills's nuclear family was very poor.[48] Wills himself was forced to join his family in the cotton fields when he was only five: "It was during these days in the cotton fields that Bob picked up some of his old fiddle tunes. He would listen to black cotton pickers working beside him, humming blues tunes. He never forgot them."[49] Although Jennings does not mention *mexicanos* explicitly in his account of Wills's family labor history, historians provide insightful documentation regarding cotton labor to suggest that Wills likely also worked alongside Mexican cotton pickers.[50] Charles Townsend claims that Wills composed an early version of "San Antonio Rose" called "Spanish Two Step" while in New Mexico, where he played in a band composed of several Mexican fiddlers.[51] Whatever the origins of "San Antonio Rose," the Mexican musical influence is clear by merely listening to mariachi influences in the 1940 recorded version. The song demonstrates the central symbolism of the rose for San Antonio. "San

Antonio Rose" has circulated in various forms since Wills popularized the tune. It was recorded by Patsy Cline and Asleep at the Wheel, and countless bars and dance halls across Texas are named after it. The wide circulation of the song thus replays a racial discourse that continues to propel a Texas nationalist imaginary of freedom and bravery:

New San Antonio Rose
(Bob Wills)

Deep within my heart lies a melody
A song of Old San Antone
Where in dreams I live with a memory
Beneath the stars all alone.

It was there I found beside the Alamo
Enchantment strange as the blue, up above
A moonlit pass that only she would know
Still hears my broken song of love.

Moon in all your splendor know only my heart
Call back my Rose, Rose of San Antone
Lips so sweet and tender like petals falling apart
Speak once again of my love my own.

Broken song, empty words I know
Still live in my heart all alone
For that moonlit pass by the Alamo
And rose, my rose of San Antone.

In Western symbology the rose is arguably one of the most coveted flowers. Perhaps no other species of plant has been beset with such a wide range of associations with human emotions, from white for sympathy to red for passion. Whether the rose provides a name for one's daughter or is placed at the altar of the Virgen de Guadalupe on her feast day, December 12, it symbolizes femininity in honor of nation and family. Texan nationalist folklore and popular culture offer an explicit connection between the rose—whether as flower or female—and the hegemonic narrative tales of Texas's fight for independence. Variations of the name Rose, including its Spanish variants Rosa and Rosita, represent a racialized and gendered trope that reifies hegemonic constructions of freedom, independence, bravery, autonomy, and superiority through and upon the racially sexualized bodies of women of color.[52]

The name Rosita—and, by extension, "San Antonio Rose" and "la Rosa de San Antonio"—is imbued with racially gendered connotations of *mexicanidad*. The name Rosita often represents a caricature of Mexican culture and identity, as is evident in innumerable movies with the token "Latin" character named Rosita or Juanita or María. A more quotidian example is the Rosarita® food label.[53] The brand label, perhaps best known for Rosarita Refried Beans, features a visual image of a girl we are to assume is Rosarita, complete with olive skin, a red rose pinned in her hair, and a *charro* hat. "Rosarita" signifies authentic *mexicanidad*. Much like her male counterpart, Juan, Rosarita does not need to speak or provide any experiential context of her life. Certainly, the mere naming of a character Rosa or Juan provides the audience or viewer with enough information to conveniently consume one-dimensional racist stereotypes.

Ironically, Rosita Fernández would step directly into this caricature of the *mexicana* as the imaginary of "the rose" of San Antonio. Both Rosita and husband Raúl recalled a time when there were relatively no *mexicana*/Spanish-language singers on radio, especially on programs geared toward an English-speaking audience of Anglo Texans. In one of our interviews, Rosita and her husband Raúl recalled an experience after having won a radio talent contest, when the radio station's staff began to negotiate the name and content of her program that she had won as a prize. Raúl recalled:

> Then there was an audition for a Gebhardt Chili Powder program and she was elected to sing. They told her she would have to change her name from whatever it was to Rosita.

Rosita observed:

> I told them "That's my name." They said, "Wonderful."[54]

The show already had a "Rosita" personality because Gebhardt Chili, among other San Antonio food producers, was at the forefront of marketing commercial Mexican food across the country.[55] The prefabricated image of a stereotypical "Rosita" already central to this marketing campaign conveniently became overlaid onto a real-life singer of "south of the border" music.[56] Rosita Fernández then became "Rosita" the performer.

Unfortunately, this early occurrence was a precursor to the racialized, gendered discursive baggage Rosita was to negotiate throughout her future career.

Throughout her six-decade career in music recording, stage performance, and public appearances in Spanish- and English-language media, Rosita Fernández was uniquely intertwined with San Antonio's public cultural landscape. She has represented both a cultural counterpublic to the Anglo Texan nation and the "Mexican señorita" that reinforces a racist representation of *mexicana* womanhood. She is the "rose of Texas," discursively stabilizing the coexistence of two opposing cultural and racial systems articulated by competing masculinities, the resistant Tejano subject and the Texan frontier subject. However, this Rosita of Texas can never merely represent the "rose" of the Texas nation because she cannot simply be reduced to a powerless racialized female figure who upholds hegemonic Texan masculinity.

Remember Rosita

Rosita Fernández was born in Monterrey, Mexico, in 1918 to Petra San Miguel and Cesar Fernández. Around 1924, she and her family migrated through Laredo into Texas. The family eventually settled in San Antonio when Rosita was nine. For Rosita, the era during which she and her family crossed the U.S.–Texas border into Laredo was not characterized by an explicit demarcation between the United States and Mexico, as Rosita recalls:

> La frontera no existía. Era muy fácil. Mi papá y mamá con tanta familia, pues cuando nos inmigraron nos pasamos por acá por Laredo, Tejas. Lo que cobraban entonces eran cinco dólares por cada persona y tres y medio o cuatro por los chiquillos. Era mucho más fácil.[57]
>
> The border didn't exist. It was very easy. My father and mother, with so much family, well, when we immigrated, we came through Laredo, Texas. What they charged then was five dollars per person and $3.50 or four for the little ones. It was so much easier.

For Rosita, San Antonio has always been "home," a place where Mexico remained through her strong commitment to Mexican cultural traditions

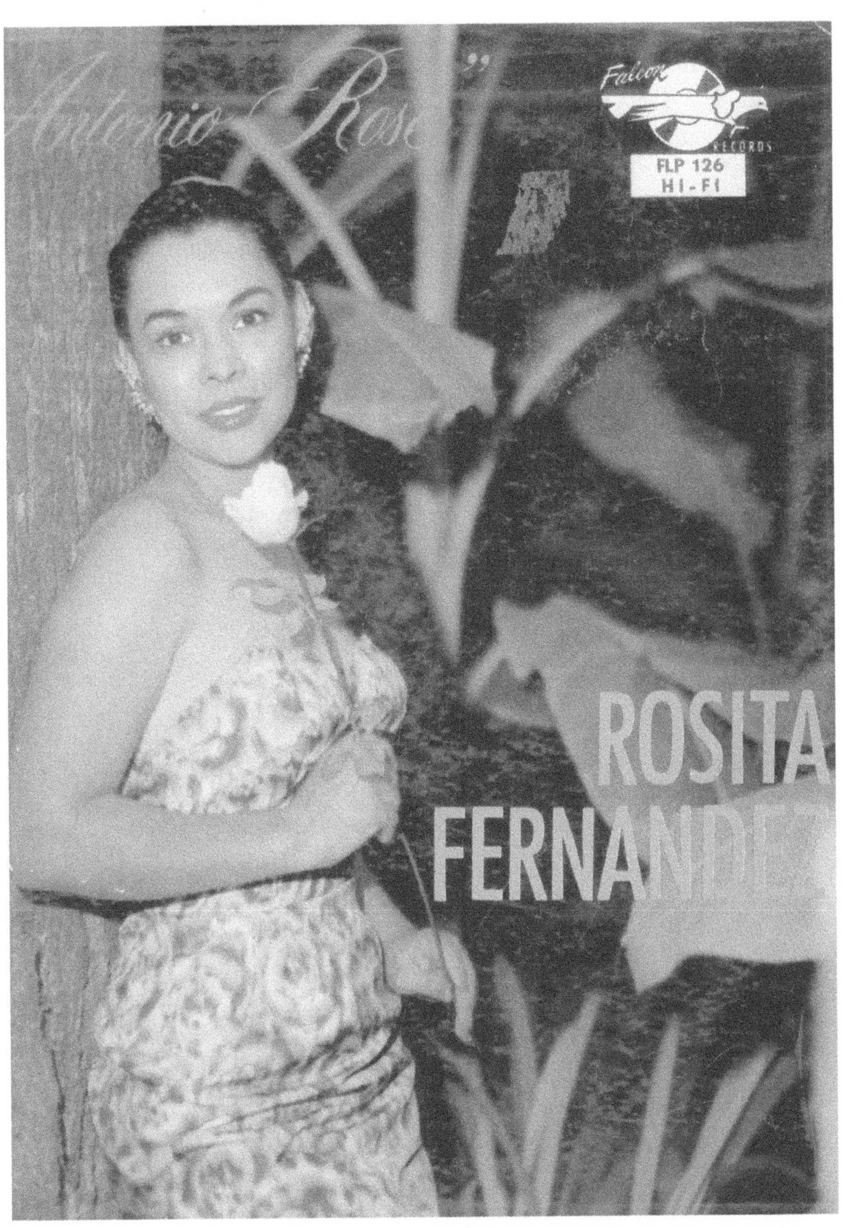

Rosita Fernández holds a yellow rose on the cover of her LP *San Antonio Rose.*

of live singing and dance. Rosita had been performing since the late 1920s as the lead singer of the Trío San Miguel, which included her mother's brothers Santiago, Sotero, and Fernando. The Trío, featuring Rosita, traveled—much like other *mexicano* singers during that time—in *carpas* (tent shows) following migrant paths throughout South and Central Texas. Rosita also sang during the earliest days of radio being broadcast throughout San Antonio. Initially, she earned two dollars a week performing on thirty-minute shows and singing Frito-Lay corn chip jingles seven days a week, and eventually she became a favorite singer on various regional radio shows in San Antonio between the 1930s and 1950s.[58]

Rosita's earliest stage for singing was live performance. At the time *mexicana* singers like Rosita could find work in traveling shows such as

San Antonio radio in the early 1930s. Rosita Fernández is the woman on the left in the background at right. Rosita Fernández Papers, MS 18, University of Texas at San Antonio Libraries Special Collections.

La Carpa Cubana or Stout Jackson's El Teatro Carpa.[59] She and the Trío San Miguel worked almost exclusively for Jackson's *carpa*. Some *carpas* traveled while others were more like short-run live open theaters.[60] In early decades of the twentieth century, *carpas* represented an alternative to segregated dance halls and public theaters that specifically disallowed non-Anglo audiences and performers. A typical tent show would feature Spanish-language movies and sometimes would charge the audience a bit more to include a variety show. Rosita and her uncles traveled throughout South Texas, often in Robstown, Falfurrias, Alice, San Antonio, and San Marcos. Jackson's shows filled a special niche in South Texas entertainment. Jackson observed that although in the 1930s the ratio of Tejano/*mexicano* to Anglo population was six to four, no entertainment was being marketed to Spanish-speaking *mexicano* residents.[61] Jackson seized the opportunity to make money by screening Spanish-language movies he would bring over from Mexico to screen in big circus tents that became makeshift theaters. Eventually, Jackson would feature some of the finest Mexican entertainers of the time, such as Cantinflas, Dolores del Río, Tin Tan, Jorge Negrete, and Pedro Almendáriz.[62]

The 1920s–30s marked a transformative period for music and sound technology. Not only did patterns of listening change with radio broadcasting but, as with the history of cinema, differences particular to race, class, and gender were consistently at the center of discourses of representation for communities of color and immigrants changing the landscape of U.S. culture.[63] Radio's content both shaped and reflected class and race discourse through songs, featured singers, and programs. Radio indeed shaped memories, notions of place, social relations, and a sense of who the listener was and his or her place in San Antonio or, more broadly, South Texas.[64] Because of the limited language structure of radio in the early decades of the twentieth century, it was not uncommon for Spanish-language singers like Rosita to sing to English-language speaking publics. Voice and content—whether performances or music—created a powerful combination for the formation of racialized representations as well as racialized gender constructions of *mexicanas* because women singers appeared to a lesser extent on radio. Rosita Fernández was one of very few *mexicana* representations audibly channeled over radio.

Rosita began her career on WOAI radio when Spanish-language radio emerged through a brokerage system set up by Anglo radio station owners throughout the Southwest during the 1920s to the 1930s. On-air contests offered Rosita her initial opportunities to perform on radio; for instance, she and her sister, Berta, won a contest sponsored by the radio program *La hora Anáhuac* in the early 1930s. *La hora Anáhuac*—precursor to San Antonio Spanish-language radio station KEDA—featured some of the earliest *mexicana/o* singers and musicians of the time.[65]

> First there was a Spanish program out of an Anglo station, *La hora Anáhuac*. They would buy one or two hours from the main station, like KTSA now. They would rent the two hours, the one or two hours, and we would perform.[66]

Beginning in 1932, Rosita performed on several music programs on WOAI radio (at that time a local affiliate of Texas Quality Network), where she also was contracted by local companies to sing commercial radio jingles.[67] Rosita's voice encouraged San Antonio's *mexicano* public to purchase Lone Star Beer, Pearl Beer, Falstaff Beer, and White Wing Flour Tortillas.[68] WOAI radio programs were among the first commercial radio broadcasts in the country: "The biggest Mexican music sponsors on English-language radio on WOAI was Frito Lay and Gebhart Chili Powder," recalled husband Raúl Almaguer.[69]

It is critical to note the significance of San Antonio as a key site of the first Spanish-language radio broadcasts. According to Félix Gutiérrez and Jorge Schement, one of the first successful Spanish-language radio brokered programs was in 1928 by Manuel Dávila on KONO in San Antonio.[70] By the 1930s, WOAI was broadcasting musical performances, soap operas, and agricultural news. Thus, radio imagined a sense of place and of bodies in that place through songs, vocals, commercial products, sounds, and stories that were unique from imaginaries in live performance. Rosita was among the earliest Spanish-language singers to appear on radio and among the first voices to shape *mexicana* representations in this period. Moreover, she was one of the few women singing in Spanish to a primarily English-speaking or Anglo audience. In fact, she took evening English-language classes as a teenager at a local high school because she realized that any opportunity she had for a career in music hinged on her knowing the English language.[71] Eventually, in 1946, KCOR, which began with just four hours of Spanish-language programming, became the first Chicano-owned full-time Spanish-language radio station in the United States. Although there is no official accounting of how many recordings were purchased by *mexicanos* in the Southwest during the 1920s and 1930s, they were "sufficiently acculturated to the electronic age to be receptive to the commercialization of their traditional music."[72] Moreover, we can ascertain that there was significant enough of a Spanish-speaking market for east coast recording companies to establish recording studios in places such as Dallas, San Antonio, and Los Angeles to record regional singers.[73]

Rosita quickly learned to negotiate language and song while singing to both English- and Spanish-speaking publics. Raúl, she says, would translate familiar English-language tunes—including "The Tennessee Waltz," "Slow Poke," and "I Came to Your Wedding"—into Spanish so that "American" radio audiences could find the music more appealing and so that she herself could maintain better vocal command.[74] English-language translation was a common characteristic of Rosita's music. In this way, her representation of "Mexican" music was made accessible and racially nonthreatening to Anglo audiences.[75]

Rosita described the experience of singing to two different publics this way:

> Cantaba un poco en inglés para complacer a todos, a tanto el americano como el mexicano, y el mexicano también fue muy acostumbrado a la música americana pero más en español porque allí era, a mí me gustaba muchísimo, claro. Pero lo mismo en el americano y así canté en los dos idiomas.[76]
>
> I sang a bit in English in order to please everybody, the American just as much as the *mexicano*, and the *mexicano* also was very accustomed to American music but preferred more the music in Spanish because that's what, that is what I enjoyed very much. But equally in American, and this is how I came to sing in both languages.

In fact, musical exchanges among Spanish and English songs were more common than one might assume. Many of today's standards of Texas and American folk and country music originated with Mexican musical compositions for non-Spanish-speaking writers and singers. For example, the famous waltz "Sobre las Olas" became a standard among fiddle players.[77]

Thus, Rosita's moving between English and Spanish performances on radio broadcasts cannot be understood by a one-dimensional rendering of assimilationist practices. Instead, her experiences require that we consider her as more complex than a subordinate "Mexican" fixed within a context of Anglo superiority. Savvy in pursuing economic success for herself, Rosita demonstrates a complex and contradictory dissonant diva who reflects *mexicano*–Anglo Texas relations in South Texas that cannot be reduced to Spanish-language, non-wage-earning, and domestic sphere parameters of *mexicana* gender that conform to the dominant representation during the 1930s and 1940s.[78]

Rosita Fernández was among the key women who contributed to the electronic reverberation of music. She made her first single with the Trío San Miguel in 1931.[79] Her recording career included solo performances and various duets, most often with Laura Hernández, half of the

Rosita Fernández performs at the Teatro Alameda in San Antonio, early 1950s. Rosita Fernández Papers, MS 18, University of Texas at San Antonio Libraries Special Collections.

legendary Tejano sister duet Carmen y Laura. Rosita, both as a soloist and along with her sister Berta under the name Las Dinámicas Estrellitas, recorded for such labels as Decca, RCA Victor, Bluebird, and Brunswick, along with smaller regional Tejano labels such as Discos Ideal and Falcon. In the 1950s, Rosita was often accompanied by legendary Tejano orquestas, including the Beto Villa orquesta and the Eduardo Martínez orquesta. In terms of what she preferred, she remembers always preferring to be onstage singing live. Despite increased opportunities at recording and her preference for live performance, Rosita was partial to radio because it meant more consistent work and pay.

The mid-1940s marked a significant shift from audio technology to audiovisual technology with the first broadcasts of English-language television. In October 1949, Rosita became the "public face" of the city of San Antonio when she was chosen to perform on the city's first live television broadcast, an event held at the White Plaza Hotel and sponsored

Rosita Fernández on WOAI radio broadcast in San Antonio, mid-1940s. Rosita Fernández Papers, MS 18, University of Texas at San Antonio Libraries Special Collections.

by WOAI to work on its transition from radio station to television station. Rosita recalled the early days of television when there was no technology to manipulate camera angles and varied shots: "They had a very, very small studio. I remember they used to do all sorts of tricks. They would hang a mirror, as if the camera was up on top focusing down."[80] Rosita was always self-managed, never bound by contracts to one television or radio station. Subsequently, she performed on a weekly basis for KTSA-TV and KCOR-TV. By the mid-1970s, she had worked for the three major television stations in the city and more than eleven different radio stations. Her representation was inseparable from San Antonio's public media culture.

The early 1960s marked a significant shift from Rosita's early years of performance. At this point, she made a conscious choice to move away from recording and touring: "I decided even though I knew I could make more money if I toured that I wanted to stay close to my family and not have to travel."[81] This point in her career marks the moment that she began to establish a livelihood performing for city-sponsored entertainment projects such as conferences and conventions. This moment represents the "Rosita" most often captured in the few biographies of her life and certainly in the marketing histories of the city. Her desire to continue singing in public while fulfilling the gendered role of primary caregiver to her children signaled her transition from recording and radio personality to a similarly gendered labor of being the public face of the city. Rosita felt fortunate that she had so many opportunities at so many contracted performances per year:

> Luego nos dio por poner shows, todo en variedad, pero variedad mexicana y española. Entonces tenía yo como ochenta y tantos convenciones por año y con eso, era muy bueno. Porque San Antonio era siempre de turismo.[82]
>
> Then we got this idea to put on shows, variety shows that were diverse, but all pertaining to Mexican or Spanish culture. Then I had about eighty or so conventions per year and that was really good. Because San Antonio always was a tourist town.

Rosita's voice further contributed to the cultural nationalist project of representing San Antonio as the "home of the Alamo" and the "cradle of Texas independence."

Cinematic narratives are key to nation-making projects, and they have certainly been key in the continued perpetuation of Texas cultural nationalism. Some of these films include *Martyrs of the Alamo* (1915), *Giant* (1956), and *The Alamo* (1960). In fact, *Martyrs of the Alamo*, directed by Christy Cabenne and supervised by D. W. Griffith, can arguably be understood as the "Mexican" version of Griffith's *Birth of a Nation* (1915), representing Mexicans as invaders in a world of "liberty-loving Texans who had built the Texas colony."[83] Rosita's public persona would become linked to three key cinematic narratives that reinscribe the hegemonic symbolism of Texas and the production of Anglo Texan masculinity, namely, *The Alamo* (1960), *Sancho the Homing Steer* (1962), and *Seguín* (1982).

In 1960, John Wayne as Davy Crockett (along with Richard Widmark as David Bowie, Frankie Avalon as Smitty, and Linda Cristal as Flaca) celebrated the Battle of the Alamo and its one-dimensional narrative by hailing movie audiences to "remember the Alamo." A national premiere of the movie of that name was held in San Antonio, and San Antonio was once again filled with the battle cry to "remember the Alamo." Although Rosita had only a very minor appearance in the movie, she received a great amount of coverage in the local media. Moreover, her minor appearance was a representation of *mexicana* gender and sexuality that has been central both to a racist Texas nationalist imaginary and sexualized *meixcanas* in Chicano cultural production. Rosita's appearance as a cantina dancer symbolically represents how racialized women are marginal and yet necessary figures to Texas nation building and how certain gender subjectivities must remain marginal to Chicano/Tejano cultural nationalism's codes of heteronormative gender and sexuality constructions of mother and daughter.

In her second cinematic appearance, Rosita is again aligned with another significant narrative production of the Texas nationalist imaginary, the narratives of folklorist J. Frank Dobie. *Sancho the Homing Steer* was a 1962 Disney made-for-TV movie based on Dobie's 1941 novel *The Longhorns*. In the movie, Rosita plays the wife of the central protagonist, the owner of the farm, played by Bill Shirley. At first glance, this film seems little more than a simple narrative of a farm couple caring for a lost baby longhorn. However, *The Longhorns* represents a significant contribution to the construction of the Texas imaginary proposed by Anglo folklorists and historians such as Dobie and Walter Prescott Webb. Dobie's writings represent a narrative force for the grandeur of Texas; in particular, his grandiose images of Texas cowboys, cattleman's culture, and the Texas longhorn are key images in the film's construction of hegemonic Anglo Texan masculinity. Dobie's narratives depended on subordinate representations of *mexicanos* in Texas. Chicano cultural theorist José Limón describes Dobie's writing as "ideologically constructing Mexicans in ways that comedically masked their social treatment."[84]

The figure of Rosita Fernández represents both the racialized *mexicana* señorita who upholds the racist masculinist imaginary of Texas generated by the battle cry "remember the Alamo!" and the dissonant gender representation typical of authentic working-class constructions of Tejano music. Both representations—the racially gendered subordinate as well as the classed inauthentic—are necessary to uphold both cultural nationalist projects. Chicano/Tejano music, or what I refer to as *la onda*—a sonic imaginary of the borderlands—has been one site of cultural production for *mexicanos* in Texas and one that foregrounds racialized working-class masculinity. Rosita's musical ventures and racialized gender representation do not fit easily on one side of the Alamo as signified through binaries of victim/hero and Anglo/Mexican. Throughout her career, Rosita's career choices and song selections consistently, both literally and discursively, align with the city's Alamo nationalist imaginary.

From the 1970s forward, Rosita becomes the city's cultural ambassador. For example, in 1976 she recorded the "official" song of San Antonio, not coincidentally titled "San Antonio." The song was written by Walter Jurmann, who was "so moved by the beauty and charm" of San Antonio that he felt it deserved a song of its own.[85]

San Antonio
(Walter Jurmann)

Los pajarillos cantan en su canto
relatan la historia
Ellos quieren que yo sepa del
Álamo y de su gloria
En el mundo me puse a buscar
un lugar que pudiera comparar
San Antonio, Cuidad de encantos

y fervor
Estrecho a ti mis brazos con amor
San Antonio, tú haces sueños
realidad
Al corazón me das felicidad
A la orilla del río guitarras se
oyen cantar
El azul de tus cielos, estrellas
ceden brillar
San Antonio, bella cuidad
del Álamo
Te recordaré a donde vaya yo
[musical interlude]

The birds sing and in their song
they tell the history
They want me to know about
the Alamo and its glory
In the world I tried to find
a place that could compare
San Antonio, city of wonders
and passion
I extend my arm to you with love
San Antonio, you make dreams
come true
And you give happiness to the heart
At the edge of the river
you can hear guitars singing
The blue of your skies, stars
yield their shine
San Antonio, beautiful city
of the Alamo
I'll remember
you wherever I go
[last verse repeats]

The 45 rpm single was released in two forms, as a postal "musicard" and as a single with a specially designed record sleeve.[86] The two versions represent Rosita in traditional Mexican costume, the musicard with a trio and the record sleeve with a mariachi band.

Rosita Fernández pictured in "San Antonio" musicard, early 1970s.

The musicard is an ideogram that literally plays the sonic imaginary of San Antonio and Texas; the musicard features numerous recognizable landmarks. At center top, Rosita is pictured with her trio at the Governor's Mansion. Right below her is a picture of the Alamo. On the left side, pictured one atop the other, are images of Mission San José and the Riverwalk. To the right of Rosita and the Alamo, also pictured one atop the other, are the Rose Window at Mission San José and the Sunken Gardens. The Rose Window was designed by Pedro Huizar, a carpenter and surveyor from Mexico, and built into the Mission in 1790. Although there is no official government/state/church documentation to verify Huizar's motivation for creating the window, various tales reference his love for a woman named Rosa. San Antonio cultural institutions have adopted this story, for example, on tourist Web sites. In fact, the window is arguably more of an attraction for visitors to the Mission than the

Mission itself. The Rose Window, like Rosita, can be thought of as "San Antonio's Rose," for it intertwines desire and passion and *mexicana* gender with the violent processes of colonization. Finally, displayed at the very top right of the musicard are the six "national flags" of Texas.

The two largest, most central images on the musicard are Rosita and the Alamo. Certainly, one could interpret Rosita's image on the musicard as interpolated into Anglo Texan colonialist symbolism. But her image also interrupts the coherence of hegemonic histories perpetuated by the images that frame hers. As the most prominent image on the musicard, her likeness offers a representation of San Antonio more diverse than that embodied by the typical(ly) subservient/silent/nameless *mexicana* subject.

The overarching circle metaphorically suggests that Rosita herself signifies another recording of memory. The musicard format doubled as a 45 rpm record and a postcard that could be mailed far and wide. Rosita intervenes in and intersects with the hegemonic narratives of Texan cultural nationalism, especially those symbolized by the Alamo.[87] The physical prominence of Rosita's image within the musicard collage reinforces the centrality of a racialized gendered "other" in Texas, positing a remembrance of Texas through Rosita. In fact, Rosita's racialized gender representation hovers over the interconnectedness of the iconic institutions. The eye works in normal progression to see Rosita first before moving in clockwise motion to the other frames. One could argue that the individual institutions depicted do not augment but rather constitute Rosita's image as re-historicized and re-membered. The postcard literally and discursively "plays" a hegemonic narrative of Texas even as it forms a replay that opens possibilities of alternative conception of such institutional monuments and the making of San Antonio. The Mission San José is not merely a fortress site but a symbol of the Christianizing and genocide of indigenous populations present long before the construction of Texas as a nation or the U.S.–Mexico nation-state border. Similarly, Sunken Gardens can be historically "replayed" to symbolize its original name of "Japanese Tea Gardens," thereby acknowledging the racist hostility toward Japanese Americans during World War II that prompted city officials during that era to change the name to Sunken Gardens. The Riverwalk can be "replayed" as one of many sites on which *mexicano* labor literally built the San Antonio infrastructure.

The second form in which the song "San Antonio" was released was as a 45 rpm single. The record sleeve pictures Rosita in a *china poblana* dress with the Mariachi Chapultepec standing atop one of several bridges along the San Antonio Riverwalk. The back of the record describes the song and its singer:

> La histórica y romántica cuidad de San Antonio es más bella cuando por la noche se oye la dulce voz de la "primera dama de canción" de San Antonio. Ella es la diminuta Rosita Fernández. Su estilo tan especial con las canciones románticas es reconocida por muchísimas partes, desde Hollywood donde filmó para Walt Disney en el rol estelar de la película "Sancho the Homing Steer," hasta México y Nueva York donde ha actuado con mucho éxito por televisión y los mejores clubs. Con frecuencia, Rosita ha deleitado con su voz al Sr. Presidente de los Estados Unidos Americanos, Lyndon B. Johnson, y en su famosísimo rancho, ha actuado para el presidente de México y para otros dignatarios de naciones Europeas. En sus viajes, Rosita siempre ha recibido atenciones finísimas pero ella siempre regresa a su cuidad adoptiva, San Antonio, Texas. Rosita y San Antonio son inseparables.[88]
>
> The historic and romantic city of San Antonio is more beautiful at night when you hear the sweet voice of the "first lady of song" of San Antonio. She is the petite Rosita Fernández. Her very special style with romantic songs is widely recognized, from Hollywood where she performed in the starring role of the film *Sancho the Homing Steer,* to Mexico and New York where she has been hugely successful performing for television and at the best clubs. Frequently, Rosita has delighted the President of the United States, Lyndon B. Johnson, and in his very famous ranch, she has performed for the president of México and for other dignitaries from European countries. In her travels, Rosita has always received the best attention, but she always returns to her adoptive city, San Antonio, Texas. Rosita and San Antonio are inseparable.

All of these cultural landmarks, when taken together, are contingent upon the centrality of Rosita's representation, the centrality of the racialized woman in the Texas nation. The combined image creates a map marking a nation-making process all the while intertwined with the image of Rosita.

For *mexicana* public performers in Texas during the early decades of the twentieth century, it was tremendously challenging to strive to carve out a livelihood; moreover, doing so was made more difficult in the face of rigidly constructed societal norms of gender and sexual propriety. Throughout her career, Rosita used singing and performances to move beyond the conventional racial and class audiences commonly associated with Texas Mexican music. Unlike her singing peers, she sang in Spanish as well as English and to working-class and middle-class and Anglo and *mexicano* audiences. Unlike the rural public sphere often associated with Texas Mexican music, most of Rosita's public life was lived in the energetic urban space of San Antonio. In many ways, her career and cultural work transformed as the city's cultural history changed according to the vicissitudes of media, politics, and demographics. Throughout her decades as a public performer, she continually negotiated her representation and iconography as "San Antonio's rose" and "la rosa de San Antonio."

Rosita's cultural labor and diverse racial and class audiences complicate the iconic model of Tejana representation in music most often symbolized by Lydia Mendoza. Although their careers span the same decades, Fernández and Mendoza took different routes in establishing their singing careers. This disparity is evidenced by how little Fernández's career—despite her vast circulation in various media—has been remembered outside of local commercial documentation. If, as I assert in the introduction to this book, Lydia Mendoza's public iconicity has been crafted in canonical music histories to fit within hegemonic borderlands parameters of working-class gender, Rosita is certainly "no Lydia Mendoza." In fact, Rosita's cultural labor challenges us to consider that seemingly contradictory middle-class musical representations are equally worth analyzing as part of borderlands imaginaries because they have much to teach us about how Chicanas/os create modes of forgetting, remembering, and negotiating the residue of violent pasts.

In 1999, Rosita Fernández, motivated by a desire to leave a legacy that her family and San Antonio fans could remember her by, released a self-produced compact disc containing some of her favorite songs.[89] The compact disc, *Rosita Fernandez La Legendaria: San Antonio's First Lady of Song,* was subtitled "San Antonio Rose/La Rosa de San Antonio." Along with Agustín Lara's "Granada" and Narcisco Serradel Sevilla's classic "La Golondrina," the compact disc includes the Spanish tune "Cuando vuelva a tu lado," written by María Grever, that is subtitled "What a Difference a Day Makes," which was an English-language version of the song that remains a popular American tune. All of these songs exemplify the competing variability and predictability of Rosita's *mexicanidad* as channeled through a mixed use of English and Spanish language as well as her choice to draw from both traditional Mexican songs and Americanized Mexican tunes.

Especially revealing is the song Rosita chooses to end her compact disc with, "Despedida" (Farewell). The song title is actually subtitled, in parentheses, as "intro," thereby double "mistranslating" the term's

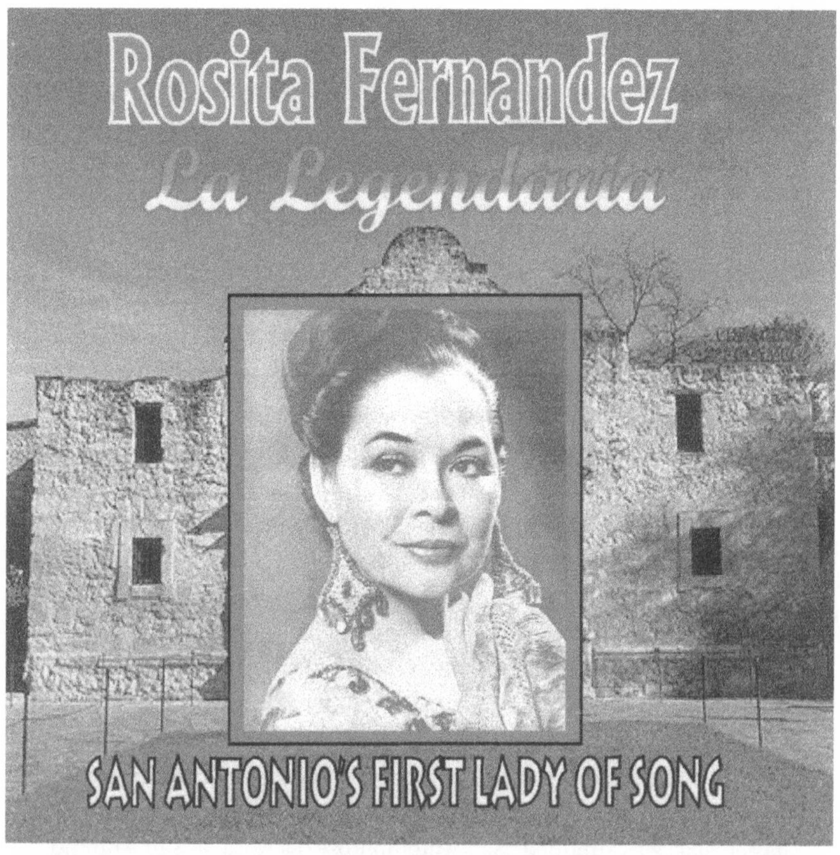

Front cover of Rosita Fernández's self-produced CD, 1999.

meaning and language. "Despedida (intro)" reverses the temporality of the meaning of *despedida* as ending, farewell, finale. Rosita's "Despedida," listed last on her compact disc, is represented as an introduction or beginning; her bidding farewell is not closure but rather a potential opening, a misdirected introduction, a disruption to the beginning of Texas and therefore a call to remember. Rosita's "Despedida" is a Spanish rearticulated version of Bob Wills's original hit "New San Antonio Rose," sung and accompanied by a traditional Mexican trio. Rosita and her trio hum the first several stanzas and then sing the following lyrics:

Despedida
(Rosita Fernández)

ay su amor, capullito en flor
cantar de mi San Antonio
su recuerdo fiel en mi corazón
mi Rosa de San Antonio *[repeat]*

oh, the love budding like a flower
to sing of my San Antonio
the loyal memories in my heart
my rose of San Antonio *[repeat]*

Wills's version centers its attention on the corporality of a racialized woman's body—"lips so sweet and tender like pedals falling apart"—to express desire for the courageous, albeit sexualized, woman hero situated alongside, yet obscured by, the grandiosity of the Alamo. In contrast, Rosita's version renders a differently configured love, for it is an emotion expressed by her that induces a different imaginary of San Antonio as opposed to a notion of love (*my* Rose of San Antonio) constructed through racialized codes of desire imposed on *mexicana* bodies.[90]

Rosita's version professes love for her beloved San Antonio, inscribing her body with an imagined San Antonio that can no longer be idealized by merely *mexicano* resistance against racist Anglo Texans or through monolingual language constructions. Fernández's reinterpretation occurs in two ways. First, the lyrics are different. Rosita does not merely translate Wills's version; instead, she inserts her desire and agency as primary. In other words, the focus is not a racialized woman's body but the connection between memories, history, and remained notions of her imagined "home," between Rosita and San Antonio. Second, Rosita spends most of the song humming, not singing, the lyrics. This humming, I contend, activates a sonic erasure of Wills's original rendering of "lips so sweet and tender" as a literal signifier of the "San Antonio Rose." This muting of Wills's original lyrics with humming creates a possibility for the listener to imagine love, place, and the rose of San Antonio rather than a predetermined subordinate racialized *mexicanidad*. Rosita's "Despedida" exemplifies Flores's claim (drawing on the work of Marita Sturken) that cultural memory is an act of remembering and forgetting: "Forgetting is not a passive experience, it is an active process that involves erasure."[91] This song recording propels possibilities for new interpretations of and engagement with San Antonio's "rose." As such, Rosita's re-versed version of the song interrupts the musical correlation between racialized femininity and the rose's symbolism. In "Despedida," Rosita, becomes "la rosa," displacing the object desired through an Anglo colonial gaze, an agent who expresses her own fondness and love for San Antonio by reimagining the place through her musical legacy and her self-proclamation as "la legendaria." "The rose" is replaced by "la rosa," who calls on the listener to remember San Antonio as we remember Rosita.

Rosita's choice for the front cover design of *La Legendaria* symbolizes her complicated, complicit, and conflicted representation and musical career. The cover overlays a large photo of Rosita's face on the image of the Alamo, thereby distorting its hegemonic iconic imagery in the eyes of the viewer that discursively mutes the call for us to remember. The superimposition of her face decenters and destabilizes the Alamo rather than erasing or forgetting its persistent echoes of commotion. Rosita simultaneously splits and erases part of the structure with her face. By leaving enough of a visual presence of the Alamo in place, Rosita's face functions to subsume it as if to symbolize her musical legacy as an imposing force. This Rose (Rosita) is a differently constructed metonym for San Antonio than the "rose of San Antonio." Instead of merely attempting to forget the Alamo, Rosita's image and CD playlist sounds a re-membering of the Alamo. Rosita's grandiose cover image represents a disturbance that troubles the ideogram of the Alamo and reminds the public of more than six decades of her public performance, cultural production, and media participation in San Antonio.

The call to remember Rosita is a high-stakes project because, as with any critical engagement with histories and cultural productions of strident figures, we may not find assurance or uncomplicated resolutions with what is revealed. Rosita's social experiences represent a career trajectory imbued with strife, structural inequalities, and dynamic identity formations. Rosita's negotiations of her self-representation, language, gender, and commercial success reveal the complexities and tensions symbolic in the complex process of negotiating the identity of Tejana/*mexicana* in Texas. Rosita spoke often with me about a desire to retain "lo mexicano" (Mexicanness)—defined by Laura Gutiérrez as "all things Mexican"—in San Antonio.[92] Her notion of "lo mexicano" in performances and aesthetics challenges equating "lo mexicano" as entertainment novelty and that which is not authentically Chicano or Tejano cultural production. It is certainly arguable that Rosita's notion of "lo mexicano" (or Mexicanness)—in Mexican song and costume—often coincided with the commercialization of an exoticized Mexican "culture" as a fixed commodity. That being said, it is important to contextualize how, where, by whom, and for whom "lo mexicano" is produced and how it is engaged.

Rosita's self-stylization of "lo mexicano" was often through her favorite costume, that of the *china poblana*. On May 5, 2001, the Smithsonian Institution acquired one of Rosita's *china poblana* dresses as part of its recognition of significant Latina/o singers and musicians in U.S. history.[93] The ceremony to commemorate the acquisition, held at the Teatro Alameda in downtown San Antonio, in many ways enacted a "coming home" for Rosita, for she appeared on that very stage scores of times throughout her career.

When I asked Rosita how hard it was to decide what dress she would offer the Smithsonian, she said it was not difficult at all. If there was one other symbol that was so closely tied to her throughout her career, besides the Alamo, it was this traditional Mexican costume. She recalled early versions of this dress being made by her family especially early in her career: "It was truly a family event to sit and sew the details of the dress. I recall my sisters and mother taking so much time. Gracias a dios. Mamacita, ella se dedicaba mucho para coser [Thank God. My mother was so dedicated to sewing]."[94] Rosita understood the style and color of what she wore as being central to her presentation as singer. It

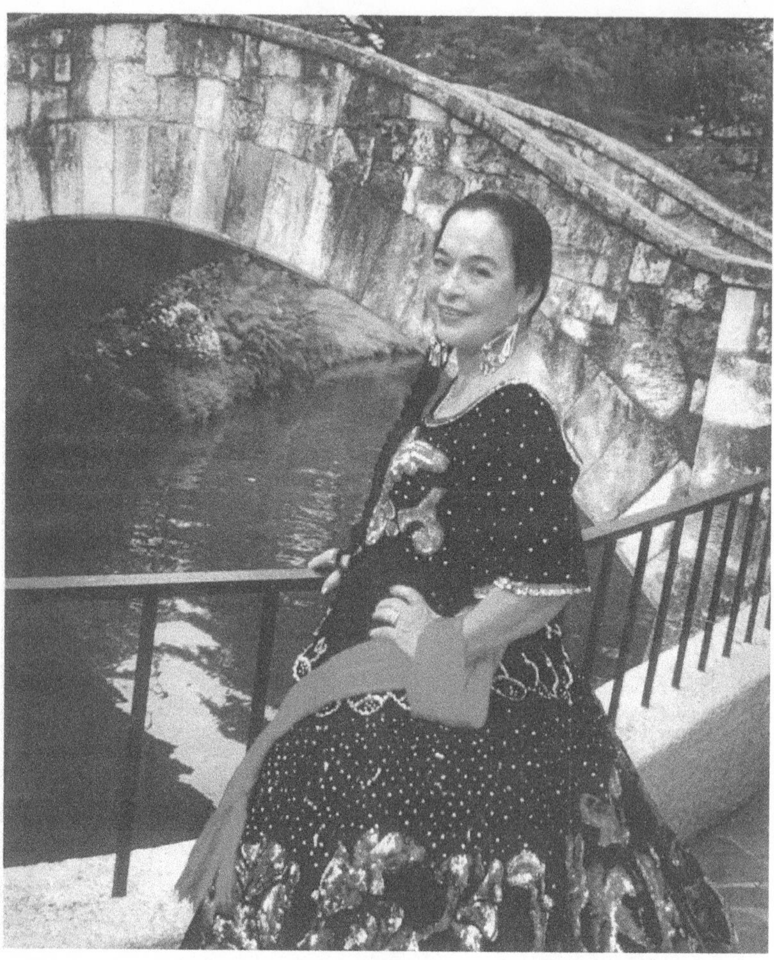

Rosita Fernández's *china poblana* (traditional Mexican costume) was acquired by the Smithsonian Institution in May 2001. Rosita Fernández Papers, MS 18, University of Texas at San Antonio Libraries Special Collections.

was, in many ways, her musical instrument as a singer: "Para nosotros era el vestuario. Quiero decir la mitad de tu actuación [For us it was the costume. What I mean is that it was half of the performance]."[95] Rosita wore the *china poblana* dress consistently to special engagements, performances at Fiesta Noche del Río, and photo shoots like the one for the 45 rpm record sleeve of *San Antonio*. Thus, the dress represents many of her travels and key public appearances throughout her career.

Rosita Fernández pictured with mariachi along the San Antonio Riverwalk on the cover of her 45 rpm single "San Antonio." Produced by Mirador Records.

Although the traditional colors of the *china poblana* dress match\ the colors of the Mexican flag—red, white, and green—Rosita's *china poblana* dresses were never composed of these colors. The one she donated to the Smithsonian was black with gold trim decorated with a gold sequined eagle appliqué. Gold and black convey formality and stature. A review of the dress's history provides a different lens through which to understand Rosita's gender and race representation that was often conveyed through the *china poblana*. Any mention of the *china poblana* in contemporary times invokes images of a dark-haired, dark-eyed señorita dancing to traditional music: the ubiquitous figure literally labels cans of Rosarita food products and provides service at Mexican restaurants. At a very general level, the dress has come to identify the performance of Mexican cultural nationalism. The costume was officially adopted as the iconic figure of Mexican womanhood in 1941 when the city of Puebla declared "China Poblana Day" with the commissioning of a statue and the underwriting of a movie starring María Félix. Nonetheless, the costume proffers a much more complex rendering of *mexicana* gender and sexuality within and outside the long-contested borders of Mexico.

Contemporary scholarship underscores much of the incongruous details surrounding the details and history of the *china poblana.* Jennifer Gillespie's work on the *china poblana* reveals a conflation between the seventeenth-century figure of Catarina de San Juan—said to be a young Indian girl sold into slavery in New Spain—and the sartorial style that emerged among indigenous and mulatto populations around the region of Puebla. Catarina de San Juan represents the often elided presence of young Asian women in the village of Puebla during the seventeenth century.[96] Relying on travel notes and artist renditions of women wearing the costume, Gillespie estimates that it evolved in the late eighteenth to early nineteenth century. Moreover, the word *china* referred to a female servant or slave throughout seventeenth-century Spanish colonial rule over Mexico. The word also came to designate a "well-dressed, independent mestiza woman" in the eighteenth and nineteenth centuries.

Thus, not surprisingly, lost in Mexican nationalist ideologies of this costume have been the complex constructions of gender and sexuality associated with women of subordinate as well as "well-dressed independent" race and class status throughout Mexico's colonial history.

For instance, the *china poblana* is described in personal narratives as representing a free-wheeling liberated womanhood: the women also contributed to the exploitation and exoticization of mestizas within criollo societies. In fact, one can trace the lineage between the early *china poblana* dresses of eighteenth-century Mexico to the fandangos in South Texas—public dance spaces that were held regularly and filled with the sensuous movements of Mexican women—and *mexicana* singers in the early decades of the twentieth century. Some 1836 lithographs by Carlos Nebel "exemplify some of this complexity regarding gender, class, sexual agency, race, and power, showing poblanas smoking and talking unchaparoned." Kimberley Randall suggests, "whether or not the character of the *china poblana* was a respectable one, the images of them in paintings and prints are typically imbued with an overtly sexual character. Free from restraints imposed upon women from fashionable society, the *china poblana* would dress as boldly as she pleased."[97]

Eventually, the *china poblana* dress became conflated with the virtuous figure of Catarina de San Juan, known as an advocate for the education and manumission of poor and native populations, as well as being associated with independent, self-sufficient, often scandalous women. Moreover, Gillespie adds that eventually the representation of Mexican womanhood through the *china poblana* dress converged with characteristics of the Virgen de Guadalupe to exemplify the ideal Mexican femininity that also extended to the figure of the *soldadera* as caretaker for soldiers during the Mexican Revolution.

The multiple and often incongruous narratives of the *china poblana* designate a contested racialized femininity that has worked to stitch together women's racialized bodies and race and class subordination. Moreover, what much of this recent exploration of the *china poblana* acknowledges is that the costume also represents a much more complex and contested construction of Mexican femininity represented by the costume in its eventual Mexican cultural-nationalist project. The material cultivation of the *china poblana* dress represented a contestory site for subordinate racialized women within the regulations of the Spanish caste system that implemented laws to regulate the color and cut of garments in order to discourage indigenous and mulatto groups from adopting European styles.[98] As the following quote describing an elite Spanish woman in the early nineteenth century demonstrates, the *china poblana* dress marked the power differences embedded in the racialized class formations of mestizas and Spanish women, as Pedro Calderón de la Barca once expressed it in the 1830s: "The dress of a Poblana is that of a woman of no character. The lady of the Spanish minister is a lady in every sense of the word. However much she may have compromised herself, she ought neither to go as a Poblana, nor in any other character but her own."[99] What is insightful about most narratives of the *china poblana*–adorned woman is that she consistently appears as a public subject rather than a domestic figure represented by symbols of motherhood or family. In this regard, the *china poblana* is a public instantiation of femininity that reaffirms and complicates dominant constructions of gender.

Although it is arguable that the representation of the *china poblana* has been exploited within Mexican nationalist cultural production, especially beginning in the early twentieth century, it is also important to consider the key sex, gender, class, and race systems that shaped the emergence of this costume during the eighteenth and nineteenth centuries. Artists, regardless of their medium, have always reworked aspects of aesthetics and style to craft new interpretations of their social world. Therefore, to interpret Rosita's *china poblana*–adorned body as merely a commercialized reproduction of "lo mexicano" dismisses the ways in which this material canvas discursively sounds a much more dense history—racist as well as subversive—through racialized female bodies that compel us to remember.

In 1977, Rosita, along with a five-member mariachi troupe, rode on the official "State of Texas" float in the inaugural parade of President Jimmy Carter in Washington, D.C. The float, titled "A New Spirit from an Old Heritage," contained arguably the most nationalist symbol of Texas, the Alamo. The float also included the lone star state flag, a mariachi band, and front and center, Rosita Fernández, dressed in the symbol of *mexicanidad,* the *china poblana.* This image of Rosita on the city's official parade float includes haunting traces of a previous event, in the early decades of the nineteenth century, where racialized gender, nation, and territory came to bear upon the body of a *mexicana* to represent nation. Raúl Ramos recounts the last Mexican Independence Day parade held in San Antonio de Béxar on September 16, 1835: "[Erasmo] Seguín's committee selected 'a beautiful young girl,' a beauty queen or *reina,* to ride on the float. The committee chose an ornate gown for her, 'of a manner alluding to the dress of indigenous people, our progenitors in the Americas.' By including these symbols in the highest celebration of their nationalism, Bexareños acknowledged the indigenous aspects of Mexican identity. It is unclear from the description of that parade what specific style of dress the *reina* wore: it was probably modeled on the clothing of a local indigenous group of *indios civilizados* (civilized Indians), or a variation of Tlascaltecan clothing."[100]

Certainly, one interpretation of Rosita's inseparable link to the Alamo and the symbolism while wearing a *china poblana* perpetuates the romanticization of Mexico, thereby eliding the histories of violence and racial oppression of *mexicanos* and indigenous peoples in Texas and Mexico and what Richard Flores refers to as the cumulative representation iterations of racist symbolism in public and popular culture.[101] Moreover, Ramos's documentation of attempts by Bexareños to acknowledge "indigenous aspects of Mexican identity," as well as historical analyses of the *china poblana,* also prompt more complex considerations of Rosita's representation while adorned in the *china poblana,* as continually the embodied tension between Anglo Texan racist ideologies as well as Chicano/Tejano cultural-nationalist fictions that embrace Mexicanness. Although it is not clear, as Ramos asserts, what type of clothing was worn by the "beauty queen" in 1835, descriptions of it sound quite similar to what we now refer to as the *china poblana.* Such histories of the *china poblana* costume and the racialized bodies associated with it reimagine the costume as a discursive canvas that disrupts its function to represent an easily consumable heteronationalist notion of Mexicanness by displaying an often elided history of racist violence imposed upon indigenous and Asian women's bodies. The *china poblana* discursively recalls that both Texas and Mexican nation-making projects have been built through and upon the bodies of racialized women. Moreover, Ramos interestingly notes that the last Independence Day festivities on September 16, 1835, in which the parade and the costume of the "beauty queen" were so prominent was the same day Bexareños decided to join the Anglo-American–led secession movement to establish the Republic of Texas that occurred months later.[102] There is an eerie similarity—with Rosita sitting atop the city of San Antonio parade float—in the manner in which her *china poblana* makes comparable moves to unsettle varied cultural-nationalist projects (one side of the Alamo as Tejano, the other side of the Alamo as Texan), with her ambivalent representation at the center.

Rosita has asked her listeners to remember. "Remember?" (as she asks in the subtitle to her compact disc) is both a question and an active prompt—just as Rosita's recollection of earlier times when laborious attention was given to details of costumes symbolizes the politics of cultivating style. Moreover, to speak of cultural nationalism, one must simultaneously speak of racialized gender and sexuality. It is profoundly ironic, then, that Rosita's *china poblana* dress is now a public representation in the "nation's museum," the Smithsonian. It is my contention that the

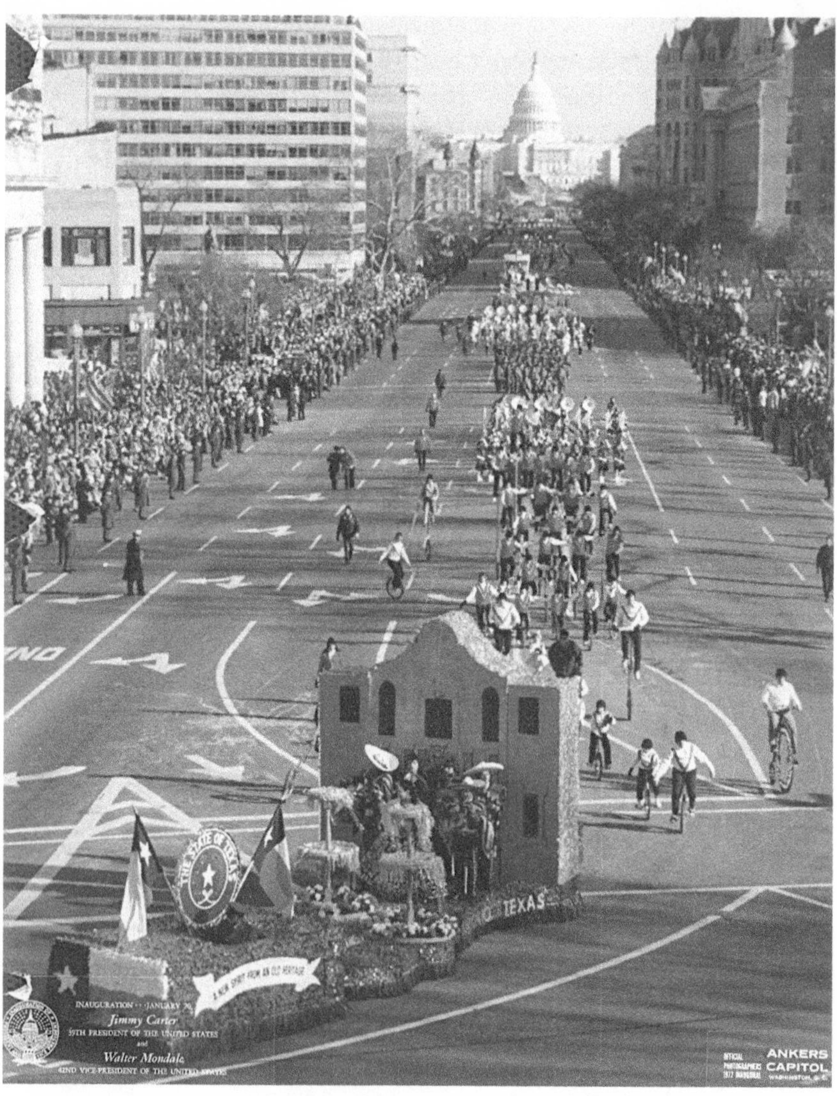

Rosita Fernández rides the City of San Antonio float in the presidential Inaugural Day parade, January 20, 1977, Washington, D.C. Rosita Fernández Papers, MS 18, University of Texas at San Antonio Libraries Special Collections.

china poblana recalls an embattled as well as a defiant racialized femininity. Rosita's gender and sexuality have been shaped not only by a reductive exotic *mexicanidad* (like the one found on the cans of Rosarita food products) but by a costume whose historical stitching exposes the racist ideological project of Mexican *mestizaje* that continues to perpetuate racist distortions and elisions of African and Asian people's exploitation, as well as public performing femininities who have been defiant to containments of sexual and economic agency.

This Bridge Called "Rosita's Bridge"

Bridges have always enabled transitions from here to there, the unifications of opposing sides, and the vagaries of self-exile and displacement. It was with similar appreciation of such symbolism that the bridge became a trope for the social experiences and political acts of women of color writers in the foundational text *This Bridge Called My Back: Radical Writings by Women of Color*, published in 1981. As Norma Alarcón argues in her articulation of the theoretical subjects of this pivotal anthology, the notion of a bridge symbolizes a multiplicity of differences and positionalities within and outside racial-ethnic communities.[103]

In 1982, three Tejano narratives intersected in the life of Rosita Fernández. First, she was honored by the modern-day incarnation of Juan Seguín, Mayor Henry Cisneros—the first Mexican-descended mayor elected in 1980 to serve as mayor in San Antonio since Seguín was mayor of San Antonio de Béxar; second, Rosita appeared in the role of Juan Seguín's mother, Josefa Augustina Becerra, in the Public Broadcasting production of *Seguín* directed by filmmaker Jesús Treviño; third, 1982 marked the 150th anniversary of when the town council or *ayuntamiento* of Béxar endorsed a petition that identified a series of political problems in Texas (what was then the Mexican state of Coahuila y Tejas).[104] This petition marked early tensions between Tejanos and Anglos and signaled the battles over a call for Texas independence. One item was clear in the petition: that Tejanos differed with Anglo Texans in that they "did not ask for a separation of Coahuila y Tejas" from Mexico.[105]

These three narratives combine to represent a discursive commotion symbolized through competing historical narratives of Texas, Tejano cultural nationalism, and the contested legacy of Tejano Juan Seguín;

they constitute a much more complicated assessment of the city's proclamation to name a bridge in Rosita's honor. The city proclamation read by then Mayor Henry Cisneros declared the bridge from the side of the San Antonio River where the Arneson River Theatre stage is located to the other side of the river as "Rosita's Bridge." Cisneros and Rosita had an extremely close friendship that was often displayed by the protective and favored attention given to Rosita, who became a motherly figure to the mayor. Playing the role of Josefa Becerra was thus not a huge representational leap for Rosita; she had built close relations with a figure who represented many of the characteristics of the historical Juan Seguín. Cisneros was, like Seguín, a cultural and political broker, a class-privileged son of San Antonio whose biography has been constructed—to borrow from Rosa Linda Fregoso's assertions about Seguín—"as that of a common man who shared similar interests with non-classed elite and mestizo Tejanos."[106] Fregoso refers to this mythology, which I argue similarly surrounded Cisneros, as the "mystification of the Tejano community."[107] By extension, historians make clear that Seguín can be slotted neither into a construction of Tejano common man nor into the representation of a Texas independence hero, as traitor to Tejanos who fought alongside Mexican forces led by General Santa Anna. There was, after all, no ideal "home" for Tejanos in either the call for Texas to secede from Mexico or Mexico's shift toward a centralist government. Thus, the representation—as captured in cultural production, such as the movie *Seguín*—of Juan Seguín as either Texan hero or Tejano traitor leaves no room for what Fregoso and Arnoldo De León refer to as acknowledging a heterogeneous Tejano population in the nineteenth century.[108]

The Arneson River Theatre was Rosita's central performance stage for decades. The city passed a resolution initiated by Cisneros stating that Rosita "has been an ambassador of good will in every section of our City, throughout the country, and in Mexico."[109]

For Rosita, the dedication was the city's most public recognition of her professional contributions to San Antonio's cultural history. Her connection to the Riverwalk goes all the way back to her childhood. She recalled that her father worked on the Riverwalk as part of the Works Progress Administration during the Depression. For Rosita, it meant coming full circle from her father's workaday life to the establishment of her own professional livelihood on that very site.

Rosita Fernández with Mayor Henry Cisneros at the naming ceremony for "Rosita's Bridge" in May 1982. Rosita Fernández Papers, MS 18, University of Texas at San Antonio Libraries Special Collections.

In one of our interviews, Rosita indicated what the naming of the bridge meant for her: "We usually think of bridges as things to transport people from one side to the other side, but Rosita's Bridge, I think it stands for uniting two sides, two cultures, the *mexicano* and the Anglo Texan."[110] Certainly, Rosita's description can be referred to as acculturated or even as a "multicultural" response. Yet, I propose that Rosita's definition of a bridge—as not merely symbolic of travel or transport but as a merging—holds a much more nuanced and ambivalent borderlands imaginary, one that does not easily align with the dominant cultural-nationalist narratives of Tejanos on either one side or the other, as victims or oppressors, as heroes or villains. Rosita's definition of her bridge represents Chicana feminist theorizations of "third space" borderlands subjectivities.[111]

Rosita's own cultural work represented by this notion of a bridge does not easily fit the competing sides of the call to "remember the Alamo." "Rosita's bridge" is a call to remember the Alamo as overlaid with a commotion of contradictions and complicities, especially for the legacies it left *mexicanas* like Rosita to negotiate. "Rosita's bridge" illustrates the complicated realities Rosita struggled through, responded to, and conceded to in order to make an economically fruitful life for herself and to fulfill her desires to sing publicly. Interestingly, the bridge is also a metaphor for similar negotiations proposed by Tejanos 150 years before the naming of Rosita's bridge: Weber reminds us that "the Béxar *ayuntamiento* was neither 'perfidious' toward Mexico nor overly 'friendly' toward the Anglo-American colonists. Remaining loyal to Mexico, but agreeing with the Anglo-Americans on the pressing need for reforms in Texas, Béxar leaders did not include separating from Coahuila, much less severing ties with Mexico."[112] Thus, one might understand the legacy concretized by Rosita's "bridge" as a symbol of negotiating, mediating, and occupying two sides.

The memory of Rosita is now marked by this historical "monument" in her honor, a bridge whose large arch connects one side of the Riverwalk to another, metaphorically disrupting the discourse of two opposing sides of the Battle of Texas Independence that has both reproduced Anglo Texan and Tejano cultural nationalism and is central to the musical soundscape of *la onda*. Throughout her career, Rosita was dedicated to maintaining the Arneson River Theatre that became so central to her public image. In 1958, she helped initiate the most recognizable public performance associated with the Arneson River Theatre, the annual summer program Fiesta Noche del Río. For the next quarter century, she performed at this nightly entertainment ensemble that features mostly mariachi music and Spanish flamenco. Fiesta Noche del Río caters to both tourist and local audiences and stands in stark contrast to music programs deemed more "roots" music or "música de la gente," best exemplified by San Antonio's Tejano Conjunto Festival or cantina spaces that draw a mostly working-class local audience.

In a general sense, Fiesta Noche del Río symbolizes much of Rosita's lifelong negotiations of English-speaking and -listening and *mexicano* Spanish-speaking and -listening publics and middle- and working-class audiences. Fiesta Noche del Río also epitomizes the various and sundry histories and populations of the geopolitical space of San Antonio. In other words, to dismiss Fiesta Noche del Río as simply nonauthentic because the show includes Spanish as well as Texan folk-song cultural traditions simplifies the multiple sides/sites of nation-building projects that *mexicanos* have experienced and inhabited.

Rosita's career and images of her representation remind us of the unique ways in which race, sexuality, and gender converge in the lives of *mexicana* public performers in Texas. Her experiences and career remind us of the complexity and contradiction within the relationship between woman and nation. As a racialized/gendered subject, she is never completely free to move outside of hegemonic exploitative racist symbolism. Nevertheless, her becoming "Rosita" in San Antonio represents a dissonant public cultural history that has carved out space distinct from and at times in compliance with a commercialized music industry and an Anglo Texan colonialist public sphere. For some of her *mexicano* audience, Rosita's inseparability with San Antonio offers the possibility to reimagine their own relationship to the Alamo and Anglo Texan culture.

At the close of John Sayles's film *Lone Star* (1996), the central protagonist, Pilar Cruz, speaks one of the most memorable lines in the film: "Forget the Alamo." Albeit pained by the news that her lover is actually her half brother, Pilar speaks these words with an ease and commitment to which many Tejanas/os can relate. Pilar makes us all believe that the act of forgetting the Alamo is possible. But Pilar's imperative to break with the past captures the realization that Tejanos can never fully forget the Alamo. Tejanos can surely curse the *pinche* Alamo or even hold a demonstration on top of it,[113] but Tejana/o subjectivities cannot simply forget, for their contestations to racist Texas history classes, as well as their joyous participation in Fiesta Week's annual celebration of the Battle of San Jacinto, are reverberations of the battle cry to "remember the Alamo." Similarly, Rosita's representation never represented an option for her audience to forget: she was too ever-present and vastly audible within "the cradle of Texas independence."

"Remember the Alamo" is a persistent echo within *la onda*'s sonic imaginary of the borderlands; it is an echo that maintains a racist narrative of Texan independence—in folklore song, heroic iconicities, monuments, and holidays—as much as it sustains the centrality of a cultural-nationalist canon of figures and histories of Chicano/Tejano music.

Feminist queer-of-color scholarship in cultural studies, popular culture, and cinema (among others) has revealed that cultural resistance strategies are imbued with a politics of representation that often replicates structures of increased violence and marginalization for nonheteronormative gender subjects, often reducing women of color to normative genders and sexualities in order to solidify heteronormative racialized masculinity.[114]

The proposition to simply forget the Alamo is ultimately an impossibility because forgetting requires remembering: it is what, who, and how one remembers that form possibilities for new social identities and heretofore unimaginable pasts. As such, forgetting the Alamo requires *mexicanos* to remember questionable figures such as Juan Seguín and critically engage with Tejanas like Adina de Zavala, granddaughter of Lorenzo de Zavala—first vice president of the Republic of Texas—who helped to start the Daughters of the Republic of Texas, a republic that was in actuality never formally recognized by Mexico, "the other side."[115] Institutional memory projects have slotted these figures as examples of Tejanos who remain on one side of the battle. Yet, like the representations of Adina de Zavala, Juan Seguín, and others, Rosita Fernández is an irresolute figure; she has created a great amount of musical sound and formed an abundant presence, but is too elusive and inconclusive to indisputably fit within the Chicano musical canons. According to racist Anglo Texan ideologies, Rosita symbolized the racially exotic *mexicanas* that easily assimilate into heroic Texas history. According to normative Chicano music ideologies, Rosita represents a palatable *mexicanidad* that can be claimed as a good example of middle-class musical formations. These are the cacophonous racialized gendered discourses that have operated to literally and discursively forget the complexity of Rosita's cultural labor and that, I contend, present the methodological challenges posed by such dissonant divas—that is, the challenge to avoid simply recovering disharmonious figures from Chicano historical neglect, but rather to reimagine the borderlands through their contentious musical lives.[116]

Rosita's cultural work is the ever-present reminder that racialized women in the borderlands have always moved between and against social and culturally constructed sides and limits because of the uniquely inharmonious ways race, class, sexuality, and gender converge in their lives. To be sure, Rosita Fernández could have made choices to establish a career not as closely aligned with hegemonic exploitative racist symbolisms like the Alamo. However, doing so would not have resulted in a career free of sexist Chicano and English-language American music industries.

Tejana/o social identities emerge from histories of contested struggles, troublesome desires, and active engagements with tumultuous social-structural commotion. Rosita Fernández's representation exemplifies the cultural labor of a *mexicana* musical figure who engaged with Texas commotion and has left scholars, public historians, and fans with much to reckon with. Her life experiences and musical career represent a Chicana musical reflection of contradiction and complicity—desires for class autonomy, negotiations of language politics, and a determination to remain connected to her contrived *mexicano* imaginary.

Dominant narratives and counternarratives of Texas history have most often been constructed through two opposing sides. My call to remember Rosita is thus a prompt to engage the racist and sexist legacies of *mexicanas/os* in Texas, not only as counternarratives to the perpetual cry to "remember the Alamo," but as sonic circuit breakers that allow for an interruption to Texan and Tejano cultural-nationalist binaries that have limited representations of *mexicanas* to either racist sexually subordinate or accommodating inauthentic gender constructions. Remembering Rosita requires us to listen through a career signified by dissonance: her vast presence across decades and media that continually moved through and against racist logics of *mexicanas* in Texas, her desire to never relinquish a public career solely for marriage and family, as well as her strategies to commercialize herself and to align herself with Alamo symbolism. Remembering her presence is a challenge for Chicano/Tejano music narratives constructed within cultural-nationalist limits of masculinist race and class constructions. Yet, Rosita calls on us to remember her and not just forget the Alamo. Musical figures such as Rosita call us to remember: not merely the resistance strategies that serve as powerful mechanisms for challenging and surviving racist and sexist legacies, but also the troubling, problematic, and disturbing, because they too offer critical insight for ways of formulating powerful acts to contest, to sing, and even to succumb.

TWO

Borders, Bullets, *Besos*

The Ballad of Chelo Silva

REMEMBERING ROSITA represents an alternative sonic imaginary of San Antonio, one that is in neither complete opposition nor submission to the battle cry to "remember the Alamo." Having argued that Rosita Fernández's call to remember insists that contradiction and ambiguity are central to listening through dissonance, I now turn to Chelo Silva, who, like Fernández, is situated at variance with heteromasculinist constructions of cultural resistance in Chicano music. In 2008, I attended the Sixth International Corrido (Mexican Narrative Ballad) Conference at the University of California and was reminded once again of how powerful corrido music continues to be to the construction of Chicana/o subjectivity and a central musical form in the sonic imaginary of the borderlands. The conference, dedicated to singer and composer Lalo Guerrero and Professor Guillermo Hernández, included performances and presentations reaffirming the centrality of the corrido for addressing themes such as immigration, *las adelitas,* and the post-9/11 era.[1] The corrido, as popular music, as folklore, and as a grand narrative of Chicanos/Tejanos, has sounded a history of injustice, resistance, and survival for well over a hundred years. Since the late nineteenth century, the corrido—or what Américo Paredes referred to as a "border ballad"—has allowed its authors, singers, and scholars to sound the borderlands imaginary into being. Although there is much debate and discussion in the vast amount of scholarship devoted to corrido studies, there is no denying the power of Paredes's corrido scholarship in the formation of Chicano cultural studies, Chicano narrative, and in the sonic imaginary of *la onda*.[2] Thus, Paredes's corridos are of interest in this chapter. A key example of the power held by corridos for representing *mexicanos,* Mexican American history, and borderlands culture is *Corridos sin Fronteras: A New World Ballad Tradition,* sponsored by the Smithsonian Institution Traveling Exhibition Service (SITES). "In Mexico and parts of the U.S., stories of triumph, defeat, and determination are preserved by narrative songs called corridos. Whether recounting the adventures of 19th-century rebels or addressing modern social problems, corridos embody the values of bravery, loyalty, compassion, and generosity."[3]

This chapter analyzes Chelo Silva, nicknamed "la reina Tejana del bolero" (the Tejana queen of the bolero) as a dissonant figure who establishes an alternative "border ballad." In *Feminism on the Border,* in her analysis of Gloria Anzaldúa's *Borderlands/La Frontera,* Sonia Saldívar-Hull asserts that *Borderlands* resists "genre boundaries as well as geopolitical borders." The book, she says, creates "a new corrido of the mestiza with a political analysis of what it means to live as a woman in a borderland."[4] I follow Saldívar-Hull's feminist call to imagine "new corrido" forms—to turn our ears toward voices having sung outside the resounding power the corrido has held in the sonic imaginary of the borderlands. I propose that Silva's boleros are feminist "border ballads" that are filled with differently conceived power dynamics and memoryscapes of what it means to live and to love in the borderlands. Although Silva sang and performed since the mid-1930s, she reigned supreme in the genre of the bolero during the 1950s and 1960s, becoming one of the several Chicana artists—along with Eva Garza—to garner enormous success among U.S., Mexican, and other Latin American publics. With a focus on gender and sexuality, this chapter argues that Chelo Silva's subjectivity as a *bolerista* rings dissonant within the cultural-nationalist construction of Chicano borderlands music. This chapter is an invitation to listen to the ballad of Chelo Silva.

I situate Silva's bolero productions and multiple life narratives to exemplify their unique gendered cultural productions often elided in analysis of Chicanos/Tejanos. The borderlands imaginary configured through the corrido is a heteromasculinist formation of "home" and community configured through battles over territory, interethnic conflict, and *mexicano* cultural resistance against Anglo-Texan racism. Moreover, my attention to gender and sexuality considers Silva's music and performance as intertwined with what I refer to as "un archivo de chisme" or an *archisme* of knowledge-in-production. In other words, utilizing the Spanish words *archivo* (archive) and *chisme* (gossip), I propose *archisme* as a way of acknowledging hearsay, murmurs, and silent gestures in Chicano communities as another base of knowledge production, in the Foucauldian sense, that is, both deposited into and withdrawn from in the construction of subaltern subjects and histories. *Archismes* follow in the spirit of Ann Stoler's assertion that Foucault's work on archives stresses the political forces, social cues, and moral virtues that produce "qualified knowledge" while simultaneously disqualifying other knowledge formations. Moreover, Silva's *archisme* serves as a queer methodology—as "ever vigilant to the fact that sexuality is intersectional, not extraneous to other modes of difference"—intended to expose regulations of gender normativity in canonical constructions of Chicano music histories.[5] With a focus on Paquita la del Barrio, whose predecessor was Silva, I close by asserting that Silva's bolero "border ballads" have created a space to cultivate nonnormative gender and sexuality registers heretofore unauthorized in the corrido-constructed borderlands imaginary.

Chelo Silva's cultural production symbolizes a differently configured "border ballad" constituted by traces of bodily desires, submission to tragic love, and nongender-normative representations. I position Silva's bolero figure in relationship to the corrido musical imaginary of the borderlands because although each song form is a unique musical construction, each comes to embody Silva's and Paredes's lives. I regard Silva and Paredes as embodied representations of each music in order to consider music not as a reflection of the social world but as a social-structural mechanism of "difference." As I worked to construct this chapter I was overwhelmingly invested in separating Silva from Paredes. And yet, Silva consistently grazes Paredes's corrido-constructed borderlands. She simultaneously associates and disassociates with him. Silva was his first wife and mother of the first son who bears his name. She is an echo in Paredes's life narrative even as she is disconnected from the heteronormative gender constructions of wife and mother.[6] Silva, that is, is audible and legible enough only to verify a social world that Paredes—himself and his scholarship—turned away from. Accordingly, the musical imaginaries of Paredes's corridos and Silva's boleros symbolize, respectively, gender and sexuality politics of mother and wife as well as the *sinvergüenzas* (women "with no shame") and *escandalosas* (scandalous and dramatic figures) too often muted.

Silva is but one dissonant diva who encourages attention to gender and sexuality analysis in Chicano music. This "reina Tejana del bolero" requires us to take risks when listening to what she has to say through the singing of her border ballad, the bolero. Moreover, Silva's life has taught me that there is much to be heard about her life through the gossip and silences that shaped her persona. Multiple "truths," fragments of secondhand information, and embellishments of her crude behavior figure right alongside Silva's boleros as part of this narrative. Silva's *archisme* encompasses traces and empty spaces filled by the snippets of musical texts or memories with fuzzy borders. Yet, her musical void reveals a great deal about the politics of gender and sexuality that have shaped the corrido borderlands imaginary.

Consuelo "Chelo" Silva was born the eldest daughter of seven children in Brownsville, Texas, in 1922. Silva was raised mainly by her mother because her father left the family when she and her siblings were very young. Her mother worked two or three jobs at once in order to make a living, sometimes working very late nights at cafés like La Casa Blanca, often arriving home at two o'clock in the morning.[7] According to Silva's sister Angélica, Silva was a gifted vocalist from the time of her childhood, often demonstrating her talents at the Guadalupe Catholic church, with her family, and at various social events.[8] During her teenage years, Silva began to garner attention for her powerful voice, and often appeared at public festivals and church services. Her popularity increased in Brownsville when she began singing with the popular local Orquesta Típica Mixteca founded by Vicente Tito Crixell, and eventually in more formal settings where she received accolades for her strong voice.[9] "Parishioners celebrating Kermesse at Our Lady of Guadalupe Church listened awestruck as the young (fifteen-year-old) Silva poured her heart into a glittering selection of familiar Mexican songs."[10] Vicente Crixell was so thrilled with her voice that he composed a song for Silva titled "Los Días del Charro," which she later sang in order to promote Charro Days, Brownsville's annual cultural event, where many local singers gained popularity.[11]

From an early age, Silva garnered the adoration of fans. In the 1930s, Carlota Cuellar wrote the following verses honoring the musical impression Silva was able to convey through her music. "Cancionera de emoción" was one of the first songs Silva sang on her inaugural KGFI radio broadcasts when she was about sixteen years old. KGFI transmitted her voice from its Corpus Christi home base throughout various regions of South Texas. Silva also performed at the first Charro Days festival in Brownsville in 1938 that at the time was one of the biggest cultural attractions in the city.[12] The original piece of paper where the lyrics were written by Cueller states the following at the top: "Esta canción es dedicada a Chelo Silva por su inolvidable amiguita Carlota Cuellar" (This song is dedicated to Chelo Silva from her unforgettable friend Carlota Cuellar):[13]

Cancionera de emoción
te traigo en el alma mía
canta un huapango y un són
con todita tu alegría

Admirable eres Consuelo
Eres humilde y sencilla
Siempre tienes alegría
Porque cantar es tu anhelo

Cuando cantas ese tango con
todo tu corazón
Se te oye una voz tan dulce
que nos llena de emoción

Ojos negros y graciosos
Tienes tú linda poblana
Y tienes el alma grande
Como noble Mexicana

Los jóvenes mexicanos
que se encuentran a tu lado
cantando puras canciones
de nuestro México amado

Song of Emotion
I have you in my soul
it sings a huapango and a són
with all your happiness

you are admirable Consuelo
you are humble and sincere
always full of joy
because singing is your desire

when you sing that tango with
all of your heart
we hear a voice so sweet
that fills us with so much emotion

eyes so dark and graceful
you have, pretty country girl
and you have a huge heart
like a noble Mexicana

Mexican young people
who find themselves at your side
singing pure songs
of our beloved Mexico

The song written in dedication to Silva exemplifies the emotional core her voice tapped into among her audience, even as a teen. It is not clearly known what place the composers Carlota Cuellar or Mrs. Flavia O. de Gutiérrez had in Silva's life other than as fans of her singing. Nonetheless, the song represents an early indication of the impression her music would have on her women fans.

Singer Rita Vidaurri, Silva's *comadre,* once stressed in an interview that Silva was especially good at leaving an impression on the audience with her bolero songs or what Leticia Del Toro has referred to as Silva's true mastery at substantiating each song with depth and realism.[14] Despite the inconsistency of her career—owing to the difficulty of balancing marriage and raising children—Vidaurri emphasized that Silva remained a compelling figure because of her unique performance style. Vidaurri recalled that in the late 1970s—well after the peak of her career—she organized a concert that included herself, Chelo Silva, and other local artists. "We sold out of everything . . . the place was full . . . and Chelo . . . oh, people loved Chelo Silva, they always loved her."[15] Even popular presses covering Silva's recordings and performances noted a unique approach and connection to her audience primarily through her boleros. In an interview with the Mexican newspaper *Excelsior,* Silva commented that she had never received formal training for vocals, an admission that seemed awkward when admitted publicly but that nonetheless emphasizes the power of a singer's interpretation skills and not solely vocal skills:

> Consideró Chelo que sus discos han tenido éxito gracias al tipo de boleros que le han tocado grabar. "Mi voz no tiene nada de particular—subrayó—simplemente se acopla al tipo de canciones que gustan a las mesas."[16]
>
> Chelo suggested that her records had success thanks to the kind of boleros she was fortunate to be able to record. "My voice is nothing special," she emphasized, "it simply connects to the kind of music that the public desires."

For Silva, the power behind her song interpretation was not the product of institutional rigor but of her rigorous life experiences. This is the kind of power the public charges singers like Silva, whom they have entrusted with such power, to create a suspended imaginary of what sometimes cannot be spoken. Singers like Silva declare the words and connect the emotion to convey a meaning, the kind of meaning about love and vengeance that lingers outside institutional training in a dissonant echo chamber of alternative desires and knowledge.

In the 1930s, Silva garnered attention from a local notable who would come to symbolize—through his musical compositions and scholarship on the corrido—the antithesis of bolero song discourses of love and despair: Américo Paredes. The host of a local radio program in Brownsville called *El músico y poeta,* Paredes offered a new public arena for the interpretation of Silva's boleros. The musical fusion of Paredes and Silva on radio resulted in a passionate personal union, one institutionalized through marriage the same year they met in 1939. Ramón Saldívar described Silva's voice as born to sing on radio because of the musical enchantment of her "low sultry voice":[17] "Silva could tease her radio audience into romantic rapture" and cause many listeners to "test the imaginary borders between male and female sensuality, and rumors of her crossing them existed."[18] The marriage, which produced Paredes's first son, Américo Jr., ended after several years even though their divorce was not final until 1947, by which time Paredes had already enlisted and departed for World War II.[19] The rupture of their union was a symbolic prelude to the unique journeys each would take. As Saldívar explains, "Paredes wanted to develop and amass his own original repertoire; Silva desired to explore broader musical horizons, perform songs by other composers, and tour with other bands. Consuelo Silva, it seemed, was not going to offer either the consolation or comfort promised by her name. Paredes, in turn, was not able to deal with a woman like Silva."[20] Silva's sister, Angélica, similarly stressed that Paredes loomed large in Silva's life when they were married: "He was a power, but he couldn't contain her."[21]

During the 1940s, Silva established her career through recordings and live performances from the Southwest of the United States into northern Mexico. In the late 1940s her career was in a slump and she worked odd jobs, including dressing mannequins at a locally owned clothing shop. The mid-1950s marked the peak period of her musical career as her boleros circulated in jukeboxes and on the radio waves in the U.S.–Mexico borderlands and throughout Mexico, as depicted in an

Chelo Silva and Américo Paredes, Brownsville, Texas, late 1930s. Photograph courtesy of Américo Paredes Jr. holdings.

Advertisement featuring Chelo Silva in Villahermosa, Tabasco, Mexico, mid-1950s.

advertisement featuring Mexico's popular performers of the 1950s. Angélica Silva shared that Chelo Silva's daughter Garnette once told her, after seeing her mother perform in Mexico City: "Oh, tía, you should have seen, when she was done singing the floor would be full with flowers. Hundreds and hundreds of flowers. '¡Otra, otra!' They wanted her to keep singing all night."[22]

Silva was a significant voice within the *bolerista* generation that was extremely popular in Mexico and Spanish-speaking communities across the United States.[23] Around this same time, in 1958, Américo Paredes appeared on XEO radio in Brownsville to speak about his recently published book, *With His Pistol in His Hand: A Border Ballad and Its Hero,* the culmination of years of research on the music and cultural politics of the corrido that had begun as a doctoral dissertation.[24] Paredes's book came to epitomize the scholarly achievement of Chicano studies' presence in the U.S. academy and articulated a popular figure of *mexicano* cultural resistance. Paredes, in fact, chose to focus on the corridos of Gregorio Cortez because he was drawn to "those border stories" that held an element of protest or a counterposition to "the peaceful Mexican who is goaded into violence by Anglo injustice."[25] Moreover, as José David Saldívar reminds us, Paredes was a trained composer, guitarist, and singer himself and saw the corrido "as what it patently was: a unit of musical sound—a performance-oriented genre sung mostly by men, but also, occasionally, by women."[26]

As borderlands subjects, Silva and Paredes have come to literally and discursively embody two unique cultural modes of knowledge production in the borderlands: the bolero and the corrido. After the breakup of their relationship, "while Silva's musical career rose to star status, Paredes's musical aspirations declined to the point that he soon ceased to perform publicly altogether."[27] Silva chose the microphone. Paredes chose the pen. As sonic texts, the bolero and the corrido offer distinct configurations of power and empowerment. Historical narratives of Paredes's life and scholarship[28]—that empirically documented corridos in order to legitimize modes of cultural resistance by Tejanos—have been impeccably documented, as opposed to Silva's fragmented and rumor-filled life narrative.

Although this chapter is not about the corrido or Américo Paredes, I find myself turning toward them both as I attempt to turn attention toward Chelo Silva.[29] Silva turned away from the corrido and toward the bolero to locate her voice. At the same time, she was literally turned away by Américo Paredes as wife, and ultimately her music has been mostly tuned out by a generation of Chicano music scholars and institutional histories attempting to analyze and display borderlands music. As much as Silva is a cultural icon in her own right, her representation is most often situated at the margins of Paredes's corrido imaginary. Silva is dissonant within public and scholarly canonical music narratives.

What if we turned on Silva's story through her music and consider the bolero as a "border ballad"? If *With His Pistol in His Hand* is, as Saldívar argues, a "socially symbolic text that engages the reader in an alternative reconstruction of Texas border history,"[30] then it is imperative to hear what Chelo Silva's boleros have to say. If we follow Richard Bauman's reminder that Paredes theorized the corrido as a tool to reflect "conflict, struggle, and resistance," to what or to whom might we turn to in order to think about power as conflict, struggle, and resistance configured not merely through battles over geographic territory, men's heroic deeds, and racial subordination?[31] I contend that it is critical to listen to a reconstruction of Texas border history through an alternative border ballad that illuminates the politics of women's bodies as contested "territory" or racial subordination as differently shaped by gender and sexuality. What might we find in a Texas border history narrated through the bolero? Perhaps that *besos* are as power-ridden as bullets; that there is truth in what is not said; and that the power of music is not so much in its function as a mode of cultural resistance as in a mode of submission to inappropriate desires and sexual acts.

I turn now to a brief overview of musical and discursive characteristics of the corrido, accounting for what Paredes and other scholars distinguished as the Tejano corrido or "border ballad" of *mexicanos* in South Texas. I then briefly review some of the history and characteristics of the Mexican bolero as the main musical repertoire of Chelo Silva. I suggest finally that because Paredes's border ballads have powerfully narrated racialized *mexicano* bodies in the borderlands as embattled, heroic, and resistant, it is equally imperative for further critical considerations of a borderlands imaginary to contemplate the racialized gendered bodies, experiences, and histories of those whose struggles and subordination are also shaped by moral ambivalence, heartbroken vengeance, and unbridled desires.

Bullets and *Besos*: Corrido and Bolero

When we consider the sonic imaginary of the borderlands as constructed by Paredes's corrido or "border ballad," it is one constructed along heteronormative spatial and temporal configurations of masculinity, namely, through conflict (privileging race and class conflict between Anglo and *mexicano* men) and territory (as a defended "homeland"). Sandra Soto describes this focus on conflict and territory as "Paredes's insistence on the cultural authenticity and geopolitical specificity of the corrido tradition of the Lower Rio Grande border."[32] I find Daniel Chamberlain's assertions about the relationship between community as identity and peripheral positionality useful when thinking about the construction of masculinity in corridos. Chamberlain argues that "the corrido situates its listeners in the traditions, habits, and values that configure a shared sense of shared character while it simultaneously draws the borders that outline the community as an identity that is distinct from others. As a narrative activity rooted in popular culture, the corrido has stubbornly defended its position on the periphery because it is only here that it can fully be itself."[33]

Within the Chicano borderlands, no other genre of song has allegorized *mexicano* cultural resistance against Anglo white racist supremacy more profoundly than the corrido and what Sandra Soto refers to as the performative acts of "corrido masculinity."[34] While numerous scholars have analyzed and compiled discographies of Mexican corridos pertaining to their symbolic relevance for Chicanos, arguably no other scholar or text has come to signify the corrido more prominently than Américo Paredes and his book *With His Pistol in His Hand: A Border Ballad and Its Hero*. Paredes's scholarship on corridos and his life story represent a vanguard for illuminating the injustices and violence by Anglo Texans against *mexicanos* in Texas. As noted by José Limón, Paredes's scholarship was primarily concerned with "the form of class and racial subordination, the latter evidenced in part in the rough and ready lynching 'justice' often administered to Mexican-Americans accused of crimes."[35] Scholars who have followed Paredes have succeeded in canonizing the corrido in Chicano studies by reflecting decade after decade on the contributions of Paredes's writing and his corrido analysis ranging from literary to musicological assessments.[36]

Paredes suggested that the corrido was a musical narrative device of *mexicanos* in South Texas, making a distinction between corridos that emerged in northern Mexico and those from Mexico City. According to Paredes, border corridos often pertained more to border conflict, while Mexican corridos pertained more to national patriotism.[37] Notwithstanding these distinctions, the "epic heroic corrido of Greater Mexico," as Paredes referred to it, can never be completely disconnected from corridos south of the border.[38] Limón asserts that, "the corrido of border resistance to Anglo-capitalist encroachment both predates and prefigures the heroic stance and function of the truly epic corridos of the revolution."[39]

As a general trend, corridos incorporate mostly heteromasculine-oriented themes and strongly patriarchal ideology. While the corrido centers a narrator who "is anonymous as is the author" who sings of a protagonist, event, or social-injustice theme recognized by a community collective, the bolero's authors are most often notable figures whose songs center anonymous and morally ambivalent protagonists who are often nongender-specific.[40] María Herrera-Sobek notes that while some women such as Lydia Mendoza did become renowned corrido singers, the genre is mostly male-dominated, with men having written and sung the majority of corridos.[41] In addition, she argues that corridos adopt a heteromasculinist perspective and tend to extol the exploits of male protagonists, while women play secondary roles in the narratives.[42] Although it is true that throughout the past century corridos have covered a range of themes, events, and persons, corridos overwhelmingly center representations of "great men" ranging, for instance, from Gregorio Cortez to Cesar Chávez. Mark Pedalty's description of the broader Mexican corrido tradition is certainly applicable to Paredes's "border ballads" such that we can characterize "El Corrido de Gregorio Cortez"—both the corrido itself and as embodied through Paredes—as a "bold promotion of great men, great horses, enduring love, epic betrayals and strong moral convictions."[43]

The corrido most often does not merely center men protagonists and masculine vocals but also consistently figures the male protagonist as a race- and class-subordinate subject. The battles of these embattled subjects are over social injustices, or what Ramón Saldívar refers to as "subaltern Mexican American opposition to Anglo-American state apparatuses and assimilationist pressures."[44] According to Paredes, "to investigate the corrido's rhetoric is to unfold its complicated critique of white supremacy as ideological performance."[45] The corrido's musical and scholarly function, as a form of cultural resistance, has served to authenticate Chicano identity within very limited gender, sexuality, and class parameters.

Considered by some as the "most influential book in Chicana and Chicano cultural studies," *With His Pistol in His Hand*—published on the eve of the Chicano civil rights era—prompted critical attention within the academy to Mexican American cultural production as a site of strategic opposition and resistance.[46] Chicano scholars have argued that *With His Pistol in His Hand* was the first Chicano text to counter racist discourses about *mexicanos* in Texas, in part by disclosure of systematic violence of *mexicanos* by Texas Rangers.[47] Paredes's analysis of "El Corrido de Gregorio Cortez" recovered the heroic legend of Cortez from the margins of Texan folklore studies, and, more significantly, contradicted the legends of Texas Rangers as daring and courageous.[48] Paredes's book represents multiple levels of heroism: Cortez's escape from the white-supremacist Texas Rangers, Spanish-Mexican folklore in South Texas as a form of cultural resistance, and the heroic feat of Paredes himself, whose research and writing validated the corrido's emergence along the Lower Rio Grande border within academia as a "literature of resistance."[49]

So strong is the link between author, scholarship, and the production of Texas Mexican subjectivity and folklore that at moments Paredes himself becomes a later-twentieth-century academic version of the heroic Gregorio Cortez, central protagonist of both the ballad and book that bear his name. In fact, José Limón states of Paredes that "in offering Cortez as refutation of such racist characterizations, in standing up as an assistant professor to his powerful senior Anglo colleagues at [the University of] Texas in the late fifties and early sixties, not to mention the Texas Rangers, Mr. Paredes and his book become like a corrido and its hero for a new generation of Chicano social activists of the sixties, who recognized the legendary fighting qualities of the two men, Cortez and Paredes."[50] Although Limón's comments are a compliment to Paredes's scholarship and his "fighting qualities" in the academy, they exemplify the heroic representations produced during civil rights social movements analyzed and critiqued by Chicana/feminist of color scholarship as heteromasculinist nationalism.[51]

Especially toward the end of the twentieth century, a pattern emerges in narratives of Paredes's life similar to the tales of battle, survival, and climactic endings characteristic of Texas Mexican corridos. A significant example of this parallel is the contemporary song by Tex-Mex folk songstress Tish Hinojosa titled "With His Pen in His Hand" (an obvious homage to Paredes's book). Hinojosa sings this corrido in tribute to Paredes and calls his writing a "weapon" for cultural resistance. The following lyrics exemplify the strong links among Paredes as a heroic figure, the corrido, and the influence of his scholarship on Texas Mexican corridos and folklore:

> *Con su pluma en su mano (With His Pen in His Hand)*[52]
> (written and sung by Tish Hinojosa)
>
> Con su pluma en su mano
> Corazón de fiel chicano
> México-americano
> Muchos cuentos fue a cambiar
> Con su pluma en su mano
> Con paciencia y sin temor
> Escribió muchas verdades
> Y respeto nos ganó
>
> With his pen in his hand
> Heart of true Chicano
> Mexican American
> Many tales he changed
> With his pen in his hand
> With patience and without fear
> he wrote many truths
> and won respect for us

Tributes such as this one by Hinojosa, along with the canonization of Paredes's scholarship, memorialize his significant legacy in borderlands studies. In this vivid example, the corrido serves as a powerful narrative form for mapping Paredes's life as a scholar, public intellectual, and heroic figure. In fact, Hinojosa's song can be said to symbolize a formal farewell—the corrido's *despedida*—on behalf of Paredes's imagined Chicano community.

The corrido continues to be considered one of the quintessential musics that sound a Chicano/Tejano borderlands imaginary. Despite Paredes's assertion that the heroic border ballad no longer had powerful resonance after the 1930s, the prominence of the corrido, and especially the film *The Ballad of Gregorio Cortez,* continues to reproduce a heteronormative masculine-centered iconic imaginary of the borderlands. According to Ramón Saldívar, "In the end the unresolved legacy of Gregorio Cortez, dramatized explicitly in Paredes's Chicano narrative . . . is still part of our world, more than eighty-five years after the death of this border hero."[53] Introductions to Chicano cultural studies and folklore still prioritize Paredes's scholarship on the corrido. In 1982, at the beginning of what film scholars refer to as a golden era of Chicano cinema, there was no more iconic text to turn to for constructing "community" and "cultural resistance" than *The Ballad of Gregorio Cortez.*[54]

The corrido musical soundscape has constructed a "partiality of representation," a construction of Chicano subjectivity that does not "encompass the complexity of Chicana/o cultural and social identities,"[55] a narrative glaringly devoid of women's cultural practices and nonheteronormative sexualities. "The strong link between the corrido and temporal borders, social frontiers, and gender difference, as well as international boundaries," argues Chamberlain, constitutes the corrido's function to configure identities.[56] Although critical attention has been given to constructions of gender and sexuality in the analysis of Paredes's literature and folklore studies, it might also be argued that this exemplifies how difficult it is to move beyond Paredes and his corrido-imagined borderlands. The corrido is so powerfully centered in the Chicano musical soundscape that it has been difficult to hear anything or anyone else in analyses of Chicana/o cultural politics and borderlands subjects.

Equally powerful but less audible in the Chicano musical soundscape has been the bolero. Analytic attention to power and subjectivity in bolero music has occurred more often in Latin American, Boricua, and Latino studies fields. In Chicano music, the bolero is distinguished from working-class music and often framed narrowly along middle-class cultural registers represented as *jaitón* (high tone or middle-class) or "sophisticated."[57] Although the bolero is considered an urban bourgeois cultural product of Mexican modernity, this assertion has worked as a foil to equate working-class musical production as Chicano/Tejano "authentic culture." In general, the bolero is mentioned as an example of Mexican music that has migrated from Mexico and often integrated into the musical repertoire of Mexican American orquestas.[58] Anthony

Macías has argued that while scholars such as Peña have identified the bolero as "acculturationist," it is important to acknowledge that musical taste, class, and cultural identity are far less deterministic; we cannot assume that only middle-class Mexican Americans were drawn to boleros.[59] Moreover, what such class emphasis has elided is the politics of gender and sexuality of boleros for Chicanas. Dionne Espinoza provides a noteworthy counterpoint in her analysis of the bolero "Sabor a mí," as interpreted by lead vocalist Ersi Arvizu of the band El Chicano.[60] Following Steven Loza, Espinoza analyzes the song's meaning as "the eastside anthem" of East Los Angeles music.[61] Moreover, Espinoza's analysis includes a rare focus on gender and sexuality as power in the bolero, positing that "'Sabor a mí' signaled a shift in the heterosexual race and gender politics of romance."[62]As such, the bolero within borderlands music has received much more attention with regard to social class distinctions but less analysis with regard to gender and sexuality. A sustained analysis of gender, class, and sexuality in bolero performances by Chicana/Mexican American singers remains a highly unexplored area.

The bolero song tradition represents a powerful staging of public testimony about love, pain, and desperation as critical sites of inquiry on sexuality and power. The bolero turns our ears toward love as the site of conflict and injustice. Attention to the bolero bears witness to sexual and gendered subjects historically left dissonant by the corrido's prominence in Chicano music scholarship and cultures of self-representation.

The bolero's temporal structure, lyrics, and performative affect create possibilities for the production of nonnormative genders and sexualities, expanding the meaning of borderlands music for border subjects. Chelo Silva, "La Reina Tejana del Bolero," whose music, like her life, was full of broken hearts, dramatic rumors, and sexual innuendo, embodied the aesthetic of boleros. Pablo Dueñas writes of her:

> De alguna manera los boleros de sufrimiento y desengaño que ella cantaba eran reflejo de su propia vida y de los lugares donde ella cantaba; canciones como: *Imploración, Ponzoña, Vete, Cheque en Blanco, Hipócrita* y *Como un perro,* integraron el ámbito de bares y cabarets fronterizos, donde ella era "la reina del bolero".[63]

> In many respects, the boleros of suffering and disappointment that she sang were a reflection of her life and of the places she sang;

> songs such as "Imploración," "Ponzoña," "Vete," "Cheque en Blanco," "Hipócrita," and "Como un perro" integrated the ambiance of bars and cabarets along the border where she was "the queen of the bolero."

Chelo Silva used her interpretations of songs in recordings and public performances to generate alternative knowledges and subjectivities, enacting women's sexual agency and reminding us that passion, in all of its contradiction, complication, and rage, is as much a historical modality as an emotional one. Particularly for racialized women, enactments of sexual passion engage with historically situated systems of power as much as they reflect intimate power relations. With particular attention to Chelo Silva, I consider the possibilities bolero music offers to Chicana gender and sexuality—often reduced to scandal, inauthenticity, and ridicule—for staging alternate schemes of power and representation.

Most music historians trace the bolero to the streets of Santiago de Cuba, where Afro-Cuban rhythms were central to its formation. In the 1920s, bolero music traveled to Mexico via the Yucatán. The Cuban bolero was transformed by the romantic rhetoric of poets and singers in the Yucatán such that "when Cuban rhythms arrived in the peninsula, they were smothered by romanticism."[64] The bolero received its biggest exposure in Mexico City, where it was transformed and urbanized by composers such as Agustín Lara. Important idiosyncratic interpreters included Lucha Reyes, Toña la Negra, Pedro Vargas, and Agustín Lara, whose voices could be heard across the Southwest, broadcast on XEW radio in Mexico City. Key to the bolero's transformation in Mexico City in the 1920s was the explicit sexuality manifested in its lyrics and form. The frank sexual references were in part a product of the venues Agustín Lara drew on for his music, the bordellos and brothels of Mexico City.[65] As Pineda Franco explains: "Lara was defying social and moral codes, as well as musical patterns, through a lyrical homage to prostitutes and chorus girls through his urban musical style."[66] Lara observed the prostitute as "an ambivalent female figure who could have pure and licentious connotations at the same time."[67] Certainly, the space of the bolero was not a site of untainted liberation. Agustín Lara's demeaning lyrics about the "mujer de la calle" ("woman of the streets") and his many songs about prostitutes and *perdidas* (lost ones) are notable examples of his ambivalent representations of women's sexuality.

Songs highlighting "inappropriate" women must certainly be situated within the shifting gender relations produced by Mexican modernity and changes to gender systems during urbanization in postrevolutionary Mexico, as Frances Aparicio has suggested.[68] Simultaneously, Lara's lyrics became symptomatic of ways men had become defensive about women's circulation in new public spaces and their subversion of conventional social values that had restricted women to the household. However, it is precisely at the site of this oppressive and liberatory possibility that the bolero has constituted a cultural and political terrain for staging gender and sexuality as systems of power.

Songs such as "Noche de ronda" (Night games) came to represent "the apotheosis of what [is] 'prohibited' and 'desired' in everyday life."[69] What has always been interesting to me is that while Américo Paredes was studying and writing about corridos in South Texas, boleros were circulating in the musical soundscape around him. With radio broadcasts from Mexico City radio stations XEW and XEB, Mexican Americans in the borderlands heard and engaged with boleros and their singers regularly. Mark Pedalty asserts that with "broadcasting to all of Mexico, Cuba, and parts of the southern United States and occasionally places even farther afield, XEW greatly affected the bolero's spread."[70]

Certainly, gender and power shape and are shaped by bolero music, with its lyrical attention to female sensuality, and on emotions ranging from derision to despair.[71] Referring to the shift from corrido to bolero in the context of Mexico's modern musical milieu, Pedalty notes

> [a] move from heroic male protagonists . . . to anonymous, abstracted, and quite often, non-gender specific subjects . . . Corridos communicated contemporary events, normally emphasizing the deeds of great men . . . Conversely bolero subjects are usually either gender neutral or decidedly female.[72]

Moreover, women have participated more frequently as writers and singers of boleros. Thus, it is critical to think about the bolero within the broader context of Americanized cultural codes that Mexican American women, like Silva, had to negotiate with regard to their gender and sexuality during the early decades of the twentieth century.[73] The recording and circulation of Spanish-language recordings and transnational radio broadcasts based in Mexico City throughout most of the Southwest during the early decades of the century were musical sound waves that shaped Chicana and other racialized subjectivities as much as such musical logics were shaped by them.[74]

Paredes's "weapon" for constructing subaltern knowledges of *mexicanos* in greater Mexico was his cultural production and analysis of corridos. Lest we forget, Paredes was not only a scholar of folk songs and border music, but also a musician, having authored and sung corridos himself. Silva's tool was the microphone and her voice. Her performative interpretation of boleros produced a differently gendered borderlands subject, one who draws our attention to structural conflicts narrated through desire, vengeance, and bitter heartache where "the abstract protagonist is locked in existential combat with love, not war."[75]

Considering the bolero as an alternative border ballad with different gender and sexuality contours of a musical borderlands imaginary also directs attention to the etymology of each term. Paredes's asserts that the corrido is what the "Mexicans call their narrative folk songs, especially those of epic themes, taking the name from correr, which means 'to run' or 'to flow,' for the corrido tells a story simply and swiftly, without embellishments."[76] The bolero "is derived from the Spanish term 'volar' (to fly)."[77] The bolero personifies "the utopian or searching aspects of culture, not just the material conditions of the present but also what the social collectivity imagines beyond them."[78] The bolero's etymology from "to fly" is often referenced by scholars as a way to describe the music's ability to transport and elevate its listeners to places outside material reality that I contend has the possibility of destabilizing Chicano identity from a place so rigidly linked to ballads of interethnic conflict. This is, in fact, what Vanessa Knights alludes to when she describes bolero music as "a fluid space created for diverse subjectivities to be expressed, thus queering the normative, heteropatriarchal constructions of gender and sexuality."[79]

"Que Murmuren" (Let Them Whisper)

THE CORRIDO as the quintessential border ballad has worked to musically enunciate a hegemonic heteromasculinist borderlands imaginary.

Américo Paredes's pen has delineated clear boundaries and social relations in the borderlands for well over half a century. And yet other borderlands imaginaries and nonheteronormative subjects have lingered dissonantly in the space of the de-enunciated and de-legible. Such is the case with the *bolerista* Chelo Silva. With no other Chicana singing artist did I encounter such awkward silence or lack of detail in the personal tellings of her life and lack of photos that captured her image. The extent of rumors about her "inappropriate" gender behavior and the elision of her representation in photos contrasted with the vivid grandness of her iconicity.

My construction of Silva's life is based as much on interviews with family and conversations with fans as it is on the murmurs and awkward silences that formed self-edits in recollections of her. Silva lived her life as an embodiment of bolero songs, a life characterized by vengeance, lost love, and nonheteropatriarchal constructions of gender and sexuality. Oftentimes scrapping up the pieces of Silva's life made me feel as tortured as some of the themes in boleros.

No in-depth oral history was ever conducted with Silva, nor has she left a clear traceable narration of who she was through material artifacts.[80] Even in her hometown of Brownsville there is no institutional memory of her. Juan Montoya noted in his *Harlingen News* article "Chelo Silva, like Her Story, Shunned in Bordertown," that Brownsville has hardly any mention of Silva in the city's institutional history. Montoya says that Silva's history is marked through her music and through her fans' connection to her music. Willy Garza, owner of Willy Garza's Border Lounge, commented that "a few bars in her old neighborhood [including Garza's bar] have Silva's recordings on their jukeboxes . . . many people in my generation remember Chelo . . . we kind of grew up on her music."[81]

Like the bolero, her life narrative is not easily charted along a normative temporality of marriage and reproduction. I quickly learned that, against the process of documenting "truths" and substantiating rumors, Silva's legacy is a feminist-of-color project of enunciation. I contend that the paucity of images and whispers surrounding Silva's life have actually worked as a knowledge-producing receptacle for cultivating nonnormative subjectivities that have hovered around the sonic edges of the borderlands.

Que murmuren (Let Them Whisper)
(Rafael Cárdenas, Rubén Fuentes)

Que murmuren
No me importa que murmuren
Qué me importa lo que digan
Ni lo que piense la gente
Si el agua se aclara sola
Al paso de la corriente
Que murmuren
Que digan que no me quieres
Que digan que no te quiero
Que tú me estás engañando
Que vienes por mi dinero
Riete de pareceres y de lo que se figuren

Let them whisper
It doesn't bother me if they whisper
It doesn't matter what they say
Nor what people think
Because the water clears on its own
With every passing current
Let them whisper
Let them say that you don't love me
Let them say that I don't love you
That you're deceiving me
That you come to me for my money
Laugh at their opinions and whatever they assume

By 1952, Silva was recording boleros on the regional Tejano label Falcon Records, and on Columbia Records (Mexico) by 1955. At the height of her career, Silva traveled quite a bit, sometimes unaccompanied by a male companion, and thus faced sexual harassment and sexism in the music industry. Angélica Silva made an important distinction about the music industry, distinguishing between women's attempts to be independent wage earners and gifted singers and the institutional mechanisms of opportunity. In other words, it didn't matter how hard a woman like Silva was willing to work or how strong a signer she was; facing sexism in the industry often required that she be brash and aggressive in response to sexual harassment: "I don't think she had a hard time [as a woman] creating a career or being able to sing, but in terms of [men being] disrespectful, yeah, she would tell us stories about going someplace and they [the men] would just be nasty."[82] Navigating the musical spaces of performance and sociality was extremely challenging at times, especially when *mexicanas* were unaccompanied by a male partner. Sofía Rodríguez, a longtime club owner and local music promoter in South Texas, was a good friend of Silva's and often traveled with her—once going through twenty-six cities in two months—when she performed with Mexican trios such as Los Dandys.[83] Rodríguez witnessed the challenges women faced when unaccompanied by men when they came to her bar to dance.[84] She said that single women appreciated coming to her bar because she wouldn't let men harass them: "If they want to dance with you [men], fine. If they didn't want to dance with you, there was no reason for you [men] trying to make them [women] dance. They're paying their own way, you know what I mean?"[85] Traveling on one's own, as well as being seen in public social spaces without a male partner, left *chisme* (gossip) spaces opened to be filled with murmurs and innuendo.

Chelo Silva recorded "Que Murmuren" in 1957 in Mexico. By this time she had also gained a questionable reputation for already having been divorced and for having younger lovers. One example of such rumors is a recollection by Peter Gonzales Falcón, who recalls meeting Silva when he visited the Million Dollar Theater in Los Angeles: "Chelo had this blond bouffant hairdo, a comfortable dress and was drinking liquor. She was onstage, in her flip-flops. She was surrounded by young men. She would motion to them and say, 'Ven, mis hijos! Todos son mis *boyfriends*!' I said to her assistant, 'She's just joking, right?' Her assistant laughed and said, 'No.'"[86] "Que murmuren" was released, coincidentally, around the same time as Paredes's corrido book *With His Pistol in His Hand,* published in 1958.

The protagonist in Silva's song is at once disclosed and contained by such whispers; for whispers as hushed commentary concurrently work to expose a subject's actions and to contain and discipline. "Que murmuren" also serves as a metaphor for the way in which Silva is simultaneously an acute presence and a concealed representation. Murmurs—hushed comments that cannot be clearly discerned—leave open curiosities about perhaps what is forsaken, unspeakable, and thus unimagined by a person's own projections. Murmurs are thus the muddled counterpart to explicit *chisme* (gossip) and what Niko Besnier refers to as "hidden transcripts" that form Silva's unique *archisme* of knowledge.[87] Following Foucault's notion of the "archive," such hidden transcripts, I contend, have shaped "the specific regularities of what can and cannot be said."[88] In this setting, the *chisme* (gossip) that circulates around Silva is composed of murmurs, awkward silences, and tangential transitions that I often encountered when speaking to family, friends, and fans.

If the archive is "the series of rules which determine in a culture the appearance and disappearance of statements, their retention and their destruction, their paradoxical existence as events and things,"[89] *chisme* represents a site of knowledge production that reflects gendered rules and regulations that have at times contained Silva's representation and life narrative to the space of dissonance. Thus, I also consider Silva's "archivo de chisme" (archive of gossip) or what I call her *archisme* to function as a feminist project for historicizing nonnormative Chicana/o genders and sexual desires. I believe Lisa Lowes's theorization of gossip is worth citing at length. Gossip is

> a popular discourse that interrupts and displaces official representational regimes. Extravagant and unregulated, gossip functions as an "unofficial" discursive structure—or perhaps we might better characterize it as an antistructure or a destructuring discourse—running distinctly counter to the logic of verisimilitude and the organized subordination of written narrative. Though gossip is unofficial, I do not mean to imply that it occupies a terrain that is separate or discrete from official narratives; rather, gossip is peculiarly parasitic, pillaging from the official, imitating without discrimination, exaggerating, relaying. In this sense, gossip requires that we abandon binary notions of legitimate and illegitimate, discourse and counterdiscourse, or "public" and "private," for it traverses these classifications so as to render such divisions untenable.[90]

In the spirit of Lowe's assertion about the knowledge production of gossip, I draw from Silva's *archisme,* or the unofficial discourses of her "inappropriate" gender and sexual relationships. Moreover, I argue that Silva's *archisme* is not simply a space from which previously unrecorded truths are recovered and finally legitimized. My attempt here is to acknowledge the power of Silva's *archisme* while attempting to not merely uncover what Besnier refers to as that talk that occurs "off-stage."[91] Such an act of exposing on paper what has remained mumbled destroys the subversive potential of an *archisme.* It is within the hidden transcripts "of stories, songs, rituals, or gossip that subordinates reflect on their subordination," according to Besnier.[92] Precisely. Silva's *archisme* remains a dynamic knowledge-in-making for the *sinvergüenzas* (those without shame) and *indecentes* (the indecent) in the borderlands.

When people I spoke with recalled Silva, it was obvious that her music represented a powerful force of love, pleasure, and desire.[93] Yet, almost consistently in the background were the awkward references to her inappropriate behavior of having younger lovers as well as gestures hinting at her "improper" womanhood. Silva's *archisme* is filled with stories of extramarital lovers, drinking, and crude talk that so often correlate with characteristics of heterosexual masculine singers. For Silva, such *chismes* created a hyperimpression on listeners of her music. Yet, Silva's *archisme* has remained difficult to reckon with when it has come to institutionalizing her presence. Silva's life narrative is itself a murmur in *la onda,* a barely audible trace of a defined offering of a presence never clearly or normatively discernible enough to narrate fully.

Roland Barthes has argued that the body in the voice is "the grain" of the voice.[94] "[The] voice comes from [the] body, it can tell you about [the] body."[95] The discursive connection between voice and body has particular significance when it comes to *boleristas* like Silva, whose songs are characterized by bodily emotions and articulations of pain, desperation, and emotional torture. For example, Silva's mid-1950s recording of "La Huella de mis Besos" speaks the way a kiss forever lingers on the body. No matter what effort is made to erase the kisses of a lover or how many other kisses come after, the kiss of this lover remains eternally etched on the body.

La Huella de mis Besos (Bolero)
(Severo Mirón)

Podrás cambiar de nombre
de patria, de todo
modificar tu rostro
tu historia, tu modo

Pero por más que borres
que limpies, que cambies
la huella de mis besos
tendrás en la cara

Llegarán otros besos
que tapen los míos
mas por debajo de ellos
los míos lucirán

Y hasta que cuando en la tierra
otra tierra te tape
ahí estarán mis besos
pegados siempre a ti

You may be able to change your name
change where you're from, change everything
change your face
your history, your way

But the more you erase
you clean, you change
the trace of my kisses
will always remain on your face

There may be other kisses that arrive
that cover mine
but underneath those other kisses
mine will remain vivid

Even when you're buried in the ground
and more ground covers you
there shall remain my kisses
stuck on you forever

For listeners of Silva, boleros mark memories and historical moments through *besos* and through the caresses between bodies. Silva's vocals hold narratives of gender and power in the borderlands as well as memories of class struggles and race relations; her listening audience is able to fill in a past sometimes otherwise unobtainable. Ironically, Silva's body—as presented through professional or personal photos—hardly exists in print culture.[96] By my own estimation, there exist few photos of

Silva in comparison to those of other artists who had similar success in music. It is estimated that only about five images of Silva—ranging from publicity promotions to formal album covers—circulated in her lifetime.[97] LP album covers are the most striking when it comes to the elision of Silva's "body" from the voice you hear singing. When Silva's image has appeared on album covers, she appears only partially or her image appears as animated. Certainly, the practice of "stand-ins" for album cover shots likely occurred for various reasons, including financial cost. Yet, in the case of Silva, the combination of rumors and murmurs about the ways she lived her life and the limited, distorted images presented with her recordings represent part of her musical dissonance.

In the case of Silva's album covers, her body is not "covered," not fully featured on the album cover. These representations of Silva elide her body as both desired and desiring. The album cover image of *Chelo Silva* shows her displaying a passive pose, glancing downward. Her name appears prominently in capital letters on top. Her upper body is the only part of the entire front album cover enclosed by the color red, the symbol of hot-blooded passion. The color red and the lamp above her signify "the red-light" districts of prostitution and public sex work.

In the albums *Mis Favoritas* (My favorites) and *Ponzoña* (Poison), Silva's image is a cartoonish replica. In *Mis Favoritas,* Silva is pictured with the chin-length bob popular at the time. She appears smiling, full-face forward in a nonthreatening girlish demeanor. The feminine image projected is nonassertive and signified as friendly by the colorful flowers that surround her. This friendly female figure does not appear sexualized and thus easily renders the Chicana mother or wife representation.[98] There is a gender distortion between the lyrics of love songs—such as "Fichas negras," which pertains to a lover who has been dealt away like a deck of poker chips, or "Como un perro," a bolero about someone so heartbroken and desperate for the lover to return that she or he is willing to wait at the person's feet like a dedicated dog—and the "respectable" woman's image on the cover.

The album cover for *Ponzoña* features a similar cartoon creation showing Silva's nondescript head hovering over the landscape. A venomous snake emerges from the desert to meet up with her head. It is not clear whether the snake's poison is targeting Silva or perhaps that Silva's close proximity symbolizes that she is also a venomous subject. Either

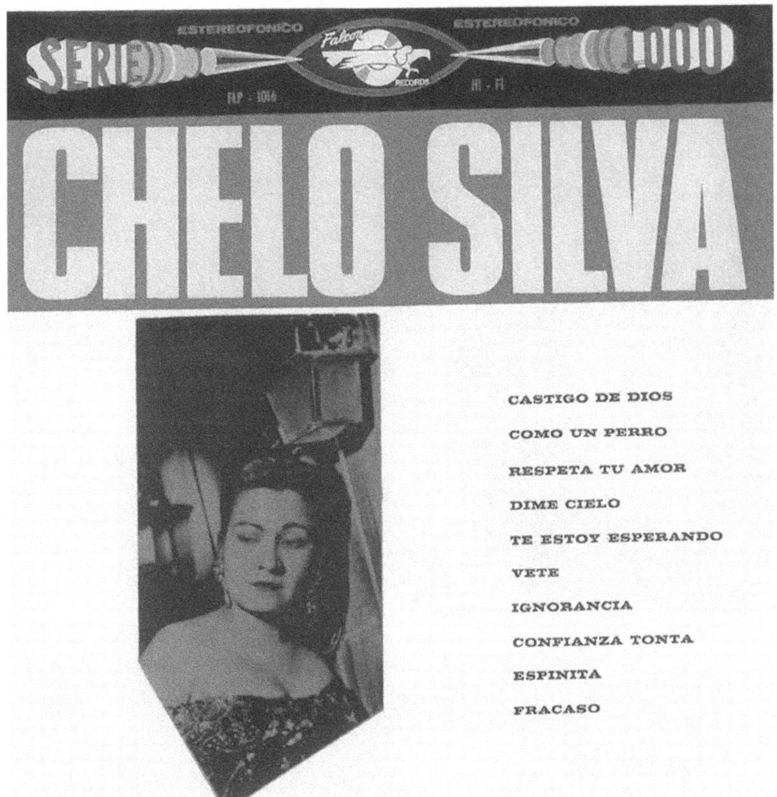

Front cover of the album *Chelo Silva,* 1960s. Produced by Falcon Records.

way, her body is cropped out, split from the torture and emotions in her songs.

On some album covers, Silva is not present at all—not even a bodiless or cartoon version of her appears. Instead, she is replaced by completely different female figures. For example, in *Nomás lo que soy* (Just what I am) and *¿Sabes de qué tengo ganas?* (You know what I desire?), images of unidentified women replace Silva's body. Having a studio model or other image appear on album covers is in and of itself not significant, but it becomes critical to note when combined with the archive of gap-filled narratives and *chismes* persistently murmured about Silva's "inappropriate" gender acts. The lack of Silva's images must be considered with the very images that "cover" her albums of recorded songs.

Front cover of the album *Mis Favoritas,* 1960s. Produced by Falcon Records.

Front cover of the album *Ponzoña,* 1960s. Produced by Falcon Records.

Front cover of the album *Nomás lo que soy.* Produced by Falcon Records.

Front cover of the album *¿Sabes de qué tengo ganas?* Produced by Columbia Harmony Records.

Nomás lo que soy features a woman with long, flowing blond hair sitting topless, a breast peeking through under her right arm, in an inviting, seductive position on a stack of hay. Similarly conveying seduction, *¿Sabes de qué tengo ganas?* shows a blonde woman holding a drink close to her lips and looking up in a gesturing pose toward a partially visible male figure. The question is written right above the male's lips, as if he is asking the woman, "You know what I desire?" Both of these examples represent the antithesis of how Silva is portrayed—as a sexually contained feminine subject—when she appears at all on album covers. The few images of Silva—hardly ever of her full body—on albums literally and figuratively serve to contain her sexuality as disconnected from the body and its registers of love about which she sings so much.

Representational practices matter when it comes to constructions of gender and sexuality, especially with regard to ways listeners connect to a body and to a voice. Album covers have always played a significant role in conveying the visual imagery of music as well as the commercial representations of artists themselves. Thus, erasures and reconfigurations of Silva's image, at times through someone else's image, must be understood as another mechanism that constructed Silva's representation, especially for the ways that eclipses, gaps, murmurs, and elisions played such a significant role in who the Silva that we have come to know is. Eclipsed versions of stories, just as embellished twists in rumors about Silva, are the sonic counterparts to the visual erasures and reconfigurations of her image.

For a Chicana *bolerista* (bolero singer) like Chelo Silva, boleros presented possibilities for "displacing" the self, both literally and discursively, through travel and tour circuits, as well as through recorded music and emotionally charged performances that became a circuit for sexual agency. As Carlos Monsiváis writes of the movement of the bolero: "Although the corrido contains a plebeian poetic which moves, it possesses no cultural aura and does not 'elevate' or 'transport' its interpreters and listeners. In contrast, how can one resist transportation when one is caught up in songs that both intensify and affirm sentiment?"[99]

The album cover "body doubles," I argue, are simultaneously an elision of Silva's physical body and another representational gap, in this case visual. The voids of visual images of her, as well as the murmurs and rumors, are the gender contours of Silva's bolero representation.

Silva's *archisme* cannot be made legible within the confines of heteronormative gender in the canon of Chicano music. Yet, I believe that there is a great deal of history and knowledge that has been filled in and worked out in those hushed spaces of Silva's life stories and by her bolero border ballads. For women who desire(d) to take flight *(volar)* to destinations where they could recall the kisses that still linger on their body, as well as for nonheteronormative sexual subjects who recognize the kinds of desire and passion that sometimes exist in the voids of visibility and murmur, Silva's bolero songbook and the *archisme* of her life story represent key articulations of gender and sexuality too often deemed dissonant.

During the last half of the twentieth century, Paredes's cultural and intellectual labor that focused on the corrido has propelled this musical song form to an unprecedented prominence within Chicano studies as well as a central narrative in public cultural institutions that historicize Chicana/o experience. In contrast, Silva's renditions of boleros have produced gender and sexual representations that burst the limits of heteronormative gender boundaries. Through a close analysis of what I consider her public *despedida* (farewell), I demonstrate that the bolero represents both a transformative discursive apparatus for representations of nonheteronormative gender and sexual subjects and an alternative historical narrative of Silva's life.

Ask Me! *Despedida* (Farewell)

Journalist Abel Salas once stated, "If you have not heard Chelo sing, you have only heard rumors about her."[100] In 1983, Chelo Silva, "La Reina Tejana del Bolero" (the Texas Mexican queen of the bolero), stepped onto the stage at the annual Tejano Conjunto Festival in San Antonio where she was honored with the "Golden Zarape" award for her contributions to Tex-Mex music. A disc jockey for KCOR took the stage to introduce her:

> Estamos transmitiendo en estos momentos aquí en presencia al público a control remoto por KCOR . . . esta transmisión está llegando en todo San Antonio Tejas y hasta donde alcance nuestra sígnal de KCOR . . . esta transmisión está llegando para que todo el mundo se dé cuenta del homenaje que se está brindando con

> cariño. A nombre del público de San Antonio . . . a nombre de KCOR . . . yo creo . . . creo sinceramente que para ella merece no una cosa así . . . si no un mar . . . un cielo de gratitud porque nos ha dejado en su canción . . . en su trayectoria . . . en su romanticismo . . . a nombre de KCOR y para los artistas premiados brindamos el zarape de oro otorgado a doña Chelo Silva por su brillante trayectoria artística musical hasta el momento.[101]

> At this moment we are transmitting to the public via remote control from KCOR . . . this transmission is reaching all of San Antonio, Texas, and as far as KCOR's signal can reach . . . this transmission is reaching you so that all the world will note the tribute that we are saluting with love. In the name of San Antonio's public . . . in the name of KCOR . . . I think . . . think sincerely that for her she deserves not something like this . . . but rather an ocean . . . a heaven of gratitude for what she has left in her song . . . in her career . . . in her romanticism . . . in the name of KCOR and for awarded artists we salute you with the Golden Zarape bestowed on Doña Chelo Silva for her brilliant musical artistic career to date.

Chelo Silva's last major live performance exemplifies the bolero's staging of some of the explicit sexualities and undisciplined genders that have been written out of history. Through her interpretation of bolero songs at her formal *despedida* (farewell), including "El Cheque en Blanco," "Soy Bohemia," and "Pregúntame a mí"— songs that testified to aspects of her own life—Silva responded to rumors and accusations of indecent behavior. Singers like Silva who moved beyond the normative and acceptable gender and sexual codes of her generation are granted only brief or edited references in music histories; such is the case with 1970s–80s singer Laura Canales, who has yet to receive sustained analytic attention in Chicano musicology. Silva has resided in the margins of the grand narratives of Chicano music, constantly spoken of but herself inexpressible, displayed as spectacle and still underanalyzed. As her fans have consistently reminded me, Silva's true presence and essence are in the bolero songs that allowed her listeners to transport themselves to other fraught imaginaries, those "interstitial spaces where differential politics and social dilemmas are negotiated."[102]

Love and power framed Silva's life. Among her play list on the evening of her *despedida* was the famous bolero "El Cheque en Blanco" written by Mexican composer Emma Elena Valdelamar, who drew on personal experience to write the bolero.[103] Nicknamed "la clave del corazón" (the key to the heart), the bolero's power for conveying emotion and passion outside conventional moral parameters of public display quite predictably was the musical form Valdelamar drew from to express her fury.[104] A brief review of how Valdelamar came to write the song exemplifies the sexual agency and self-possession afforded to women within the performative space of the bolero. After a love affair gone wrong with a very well known Mexican public figure who had mistreated and disrespected her after years of companionship during which she was devoted to him, Valdelamar decided that her main motivation in writing the song was "para venganza personal . . . y dije . . . me la va pagar" (for personal vengeance/revenge . . . and I said . . . he will pay). Moreover, it was the combination of song and space that provided Valdelamar with the opportunity to testify to her pain and bitterness. She chose to debut her song "El Cheque en Blanco" at a public social event where she knew her ex-lover would be present.

El Cheque en Blanco (Blank Check)
(Lyrics and composition by Emma Elena Valdelamar)

Yo, yo no soy letra de cambio
Ni moneda que se entrega
Que se le entrega a cualquiera
Como cheque al portador
Ay, me decepcionaste tanto
Que ahí te dejó un cheque en blanco
A tu nombre y para ti

Es por la cantidad que quieras
En donde dice desprecio
Ése debe ser tu precio
Y va firmado por mí

Me, I'm not a financial transaction
Nor currency that is exchanged
That is payable to anyone

Like a check made out to "cash"
Oh, you disappointed me so much
That I left a blank check for you there
Made out in your name and for you

It's for whatever amount you want
Where it says contempt
That should be your price
And it's signed by me

After her performance, Valdelamar recalled that her ex-lover threatened to kill her—holding a gun to her head—for having embarrassed him at the public event. Not intimidated, she responded, "Go ahead, but now everyone has already heard the song."[105] Valdelamar's performance of "El Cheque en Blanco" bears witness to her exchange with her ex-lover, its story retold by fans and reorchestrated in every performance thereafter, and its importance is exemplified by its nickname, "el himno de las mujeres" (women's hymn).[106] Unlike the corrido's musical mechanism, there is no hero in this bolero; resistance is not embodied through heroic masculinity. The song's powerful lyrics destroy any notion of love as anything but a socially constructed system of transactions. Rather, boleros such as this remind us that love is fraught with deceitful kisses and unrequited promises, illuminating erotic fervor as a constituent of power. Boleros such as "El Cheque en Blanco" emphasize that love is always conditional, a mode of transaction and exchange where, at any moment, a foreclosure on one's sexual agency, faith in love, or trust may come due. "El Cheque en Blanco" would become one of the most popular Mexican boleros and one of Chelo Silva's most notable signature songs.

As Valdelamar's bolero composition and performance make clear, it is the connection between personal experience and musical narrative that marks performers like Silva not just as singers, but also as interpreters of song. Particularly within the *bolerista* tradition, there is a key musical distinction between the Spanish terms *intérprete* (performer) and *cantante* (singer).[107] In the documentary *Las que viven en ciudad bolero* (1993), the women *boleristas,* including Consuelo Velázquez and Emma Elena Valdelamar, identify themselves as *compositoras* (composers) and *intérpretes,* but never as *cantantes.* Herein lies a key distinction that is significant particularly as it pertains to gender, sexuality, and power in bolero performance. *Intérpretes* of boleros are more than mere conveyers of lyrics, more than simply *cantantes* or singers.

Intrepretando el bolero—performing one's own interpretation of a song's significance and meaning—is not just a matter of the singer's voice and the lyrics. Vocal inflections, pauses, and bodily gestures during live performances, together with lyrics, constitute a singer's mark on a musical text. In her description of the magical performance style of Chelo Silva, Del Toro notes that Silva strongly exemplifies the "emphasis on what the individual can bring to a song or a performance."[108] The *bolerista*'s signature comes through in her unique performance of a particular composition.

Emotional experiences relived in song, on the part of audience or singer, "transport and elevate" the listener to an otherwise unattainable imaginary, be it an imaginary of bitterness, ecstasy, or countermemory.[109] The performer does more than move her audience by the raw emotion of the song and her performance; she also invokes informal but "common" knowledge such as rumors or public criticisms. Songs and musical performances do not merely trigger the listener's memory of another place and time; a recording or a song performance is itself a memory engram. Like gaps between musical tracks, songs and specific performances offer possibilities for the listener to draw on for alternative modes of desire or as a form of public testimony.

Silva's public recognition at this popular music event was quite at odds with the neglect of her musical contributions in borderlands music histories. During the 1980s and 1990s, the Tejano Conjunto Music Festival in San Antonio was one of the more significant live music stages for borderlands music, particularly for Texas Mexican music audiences. The festival was considered a showcase of "who's who" in Tex-Mex conjunto music, although it was always dominated by men performers. Aired on San Antonio's most notable Spanish-language station, the public "stage" encompassed not only the live audience but all who listened within the reach of KCOR's radio waves. The size of the live and radio audiences, the imposing stage, and the fragility of her health all came together to produce a pivotal performance for Chelo Silva. On this day, she was the central protagonist and the narrator of her own history and the producer of her own subjectivity. As this focus on Silva's live radio performance testifies, her choice of song, the effort in her strained voice, and her impromptu lyrical shifts audibly mimicked the sexual expressions of nonnormative gender subjects, "las mujeres indecentes" (indecent women), whose battles are not located within heteromasculinized narratives of gender and resistance, overburdened by the scholarly prominence of corrido studies.

The corrido as heroic "border ballad" has not merely sounded a Chicano borderlands imaginary profoundly established by Paredes—"con su pluma en su mano, corazón de fiel chicano" (with his pen in his hand, heart of a proud Chicano)—but also established protagonists and events in corridos as foremost voices. The musical components of this song tradition have afforded *corridistas* (corrido singers)—as well as corridos dedicated to those who have studied them, such as Américo Paredes—a formal farewell to their public. According to Dan Dickey, of the six conventional parts that compose the corrido, the *despedida* or farewell of the *corridista* is the more vital component in Tejano border corridos.[110] Moreover, the *despedida* in one form or another is almost never neglected by the *corridista*.[111] The *despedida* represents a unique figuration that allows for a narrative's closure as well as a singer's own performative farewell. Discursively, it operates as the self-initiated act of departing, ending, transitioning on one's own terms, and, moreover, bestows a formal deference to the *corridista* and his or her narrative performance.

A farewell is not merely a closing or good-bye, it also figures discursively as a point of departure and a historical notation of presence, sealing or signaling a place and time from which one departs. A farewell forms a recollection to someone or something to play back, like what we experience when we replay a record. I contend that Silva's last major live performance was her self-crafted *despedida,* one that, as a *bolerista,* she has not been granted by the power of the pen.

Chris Strachwitz, founder of Arhoolie Records, fortunately recorded the live performance on a cassette tape recorder as he drove to the site of the Tejano Music Festival where Silva was performing. The songs appearing on the compact disc *Chelo Silva: La Reina Tejana del Bolero* were included in the Tejano Roots series that Strachwitz produced, a major recovery project of foundational Texas Mexican/borderlands music artists. A few songs are missing from the live performance because Strachwitz turned his recorder off once he entered the festival grounds. Nonetheless, his rare fragment of Silva's live performance is a cherished complement to fans' recollections of her unique performance style. It is significant to note that this image of Silva is the only one I have come across on a record cover that displays her full body. With that said, Silva's representation in this image does not fit her persona. Here she is dressed in a full formal gown looking rather matronly, safe, and graceful in front of the band.

Silva's live performance captures her defiance of normative-gendered standards onstage, as in her life choices. Over the course of decades of performance, Silva refused to alter her lifestyle or performance antics. Friends and fans knew Silva to use sexually explicit language,

Chelo Silva on front CD cover of *Chelo Silva: La Reina Tejana del Bolero* from the Tejano Roots series. Produced by Arhoolie Records.

someone who "liked to party" and "loved to curse and drink beer."[112] Leonardo Quiroz of Johnny Herrera's House of Music record shop in Corpus Christi once told me that Chelo's reputation for sexual promiscuity and for being a foul-mouthed drinker overshadowed historical attention to her life, over that of talented vocals and unique performance style.[113] Silva's border ballads, such as "Borracha," were not about heroic protagonists or themes of social injustice, but they do convey tragedies and destruction that can never be delinked from structural systems of power.

> *Borracha (Drunken Woman)*
> (José Vaca Flores)
>
> Borracha yo he nacido
> Borracha yo he crecido
> Y sé sinceramente que borracha he de morir
> No culpo ni al destino que me marcó un camino
>
> I was born a drunk
> I was raised a drunk
> And I'm sure I will die a drunk
> I do not blame the path that destiny has charted

This live performance shows that even after decades of performing and recording, she continued to endow each song with her signature. Here Silva accomplishes what Monsiváis refers to as a "social pact" between singer and listener: "you listen to me with devotion, and I will change your state of mind."[114] During the live radio performance, Silva's age and waning health are evident. Her strained voice embodies the pain of boleros. The hoarse voice labors to reach notes marking years of public performance and personal challenges in her life. Listening to her strained voice allows us to imagine her worn body onstage. Her performance indicates that, unlike the geographic trope that is central to much of Chicano music analysis— that of nation-building projects marked by territorial wars—the geography of the body is a topography with surface and depth that represents a different terrain of knowledge and historical memory.[115] Yet, her story has always been there in the despair and passion of her boleros, waiting for scholars to simply "ask her" about her life.

Vanessa Knights has argued that it is not merely the linguistic content that conveys meaning in song but the "bodily, sonorous, element of vocality." During this performance, Silva's labored body strains to transport her audience to another place, a differently gendered topography that draws attention to different features of what constitutes borderlands music and its subjectivities. According to her dear friend, singer Rita Vidaurri, Silva was aware that her health was fragile, and she acknowledged to Vidaurri that this would likely be one of her last grand live performances.[116] Leticia Del Toro also notes that at the KCOR live performance, "she confessed to her audience that she had felt ill that morning and she wondered if her last days might be spent in San Antonio."[117] To my knowledge, this was the last grand live performance she would give. Silva passed away on April 2, 1988, less than five years after this performance. In her opening words to the audience, she says:

> A KCOR, no tengo palabras con qué, que feliz me han hecho este día de hoy . . . les voy a decir una cosa . . . me puse un poco enferma. Y yo dije, yo creo que aquí en San Antonio voy a quedar yo, como dice mi canción . . . esto nunca se me olvidará.
>
> I do not have the words for KCOR, how happy they have made me today . . . I am going to tell you something . . . I'm a little sick. And I said, "I think I am going to stay right here in San Antonio, like my song says" . . . I will never forget.

Silva's statement to her audience goes beyond expressing mere gratitude for KCOR's recognition. She reminds the audience of the ways in which song performance can be a compelling form of autonarration. Songs bear witness and form a public record. In expressing her intention to "stay right here in San Antonio," she discursively sets in motion the constitutive relations among place, memory, and time. A self-declaration to "stay right here" is also a testament to her public that, through her songs, she is here to stay. These words not only staked her claim to the geographic place of San Antonio—a historical focal point for borderlands music and cultural production—but also acknowledged the way memories of such performances preserve someone's continuing presence. As Deborah Paredez asserts, "performance accumulates much of its ower as a spatial practice. Live performance, by its localized and ephemeral nature, offers a way to account for the specificity of historical, geographical, and political location: a play or a concert takes place in this venue in this city at this moment in time."[118] Paredez continues: "While performance only ever occurs in the present, it simultaneously lifts us out of this present, haunted by the ghosts of the past . . . and gesturing toward future possibilities."[119] In that geographic place, at that time, as much as in this time, Silva remains "right here" voicing a musical rebuttal to the rumors that plagued her life. Her performance that evening etched a memory groove into the multiple and contested records of her life, a groove that deepens and widens the capacity for inquiries every time the song is heard. This time, in this place, the groove was cut on her terms. After all, just as songs form a conduit for memory, live interpretations have the power to disrupt apparently seamless narratives of public truths.

Silva's play list during this live radio broadcast included some of her most popular renderings, including "El Cheque en Blanco" (Blank check), "Imploración" (Appeal), and "Soy Bohemia" (I am bohemian). However, Silva's most notable performance that evening was "Pregúntame a mí" (Ask me). Unlike the corrido, whose protagonist or event is proclaimed by the singer, these boleros allowed for Silva to become the subject of her own musical *despedida*. The *intérprete* performative tradition afforded *boleristas* like Silva to infuse life into songs in such a way as to represent various truths and realities, about themselves as much as about the changing social world. The set of live songs that appear on the CD compilation of Silva's boleros includes one of her popular rancheras, "Pregúntame a mí" (Ask me). The performance exemplifies Silva's bravado *bolerista* interpretation of this song—and what might also be considered a form of melodrama, according to the feminist analysis of ranchera music posited by Olga Najera-Ramírez.[120]

Silva's live rendition of "Pregúntame a mí" emphatically responded to decades of hushed commentary that shaped her gender and sexual subjectivity as nonnormative. With a microphone in her hand, Silva's live performance produces a self-justifying narrative of her life by directly addressing the haunting questions that framed her "inappropriate" social behavior and shortcomings as a wife. Angélica Silva shared that Chelo "liked to sing songs of deceit . . . como hacina *[sic]* de decepción . . . decepcionada." Recall that Silva married at age seventeen. Before she was even twenty years old, her first marriage had ended. "I think the first marriage . . . the breakup of her first marriage with Américo. I think that hurt her. I think that was . . . que estaba decepcionada [that she was disillusioned, disenchanted with love]. She was really in love with her first husband. After they broke up . . . she went through hard times. Having to go to work and then sing and, you know, having to leave her baby with my mom while she went to sing."[121]

Interpreting the lyrical narrative of "Pregúntame a mí," Silva chastises those who have listened to rumors of "unsuitable" behavior when they assessed her achievements. The lyrics of "Pregúntame a mí" symbolize the contradiction that is Silva's life: the more successful and popular she became as a singer, the more she was excluded from the canon of borderlands music, a process strangely reminiscent of what Pedalty refers to as the simultaneous process of "social climbing and moral decline" described in boleros.[122]

Silva's *interpretación* of "Pregúntame a mí" emerged from the places she had been, loves she lost, and the rumors and judgments that framed her life.

Pregúntame a mí (Ask Me)
(Performed at the 1983 Tejano Conjunto Festival in San Antonio)[123]

Que no te cuenten mi historia
No indagues qué es de mi vida
Si quieres saberla, pregúntame a mí
Que no vengan con cuentos
Si tienes valor para oírlo,
Yo puedo decirte por qué me perdí
Se sufre mucho en la vida;
Y nunca nunca se aprende que
Cuando un cariño nos paga mal
Es fácil equivocarse,
Pensando que entre las copas
Está el remedio para olvidar

Don't let them tell you my story
Don't ask what has become of my life
If you want to know, ask me
Don't let them tell you any stories
If you have the courage to hear it
Let me be the one to tell you why I strayed
One suffers much in this life;
And one never ever learns that

When love treats us badly
It's easy to make the mistake,
Of thinking that between one drink and another
Lies the cure to forget

The song's lyrics are direct and explicit. Like her predecessor Valdelamar, Silva uses song lyrics, public performance, and interaction with her audience to respond to those who continually asked what had become of her life. As with any singer performing live, creativity is not simply the ability to reproduce a recorded version or the vision of the song's composer. Rather, musical magic emerges in the command of breaks, the extension of a note, and the impromptu recital and reinterpretation of the original song lyrics. *Boleristas* don't merely work the lyrics, they work the space, the stage, and the audience as well.

In the liner notes to *Chelo Silva: La Reina Tejana del Bolero,* Strachwitz makes reference to Silva's reputation in his preview of some of the lyrics: "[T]he KCOR performance best exemplifies Chelo, audaciously addressing the questions of her life."[124] Moreover, the Arhoolie Web site states: "Many of the boleros that Chelo Silva performed and included in her repertoire also reflected a certain nontraditional, almost rebellious image, generally not adopted by female singers. Her songs spoke of love affairs gone awry, betrayals, and desires that could not be subdued."[125] The inclusion of a partial transcript of Silva's "Pregúntame a mí" in the liner notes of the compact disc affirms the significance of this song's selection for the KCOR event and justifies its inclusion on this music compilation compact disc. And yet, it is the lyrics that are *not* reproduced in the liner notes that symbolically capture the spirit of Chelo Silva:

Yo (ja) yo como muchos me equivoqué
Y entre copa y copa también te olvidé
Pero soy inútil ahora lo sé
Porque el día siguiente te volví a querer
Y te buscaba y no te encontraba
Y para olvidarte volví a beber
Y me gustan grandotes
Aunque *[pausa]* que me rompen el . . .
digo . . . la boca
Por eso es ahora que tomo tanto

Ten por seguro que ya te olvidé
Por eso ahora que tomo tanto
Ten por seguro que ya te olvidé

Like many I was mistaken
With drink after drink I also forgot you
But I am useless, now I know
Because the next day I desired you all over again
I searched for you but I couldn't find you
And to forget you I went back to drinking
[At the end of this lyric Chelo gives a grito *(Mexican-style yell): "Ahh ja ja," then proceeds to say the following to her audience:]*
I love big ones
Even if they/it tears the . . .
[pause and screams by audience]
I mean . . . my mouth
[fans cheer again and the music proceeds, Silva sings . . .]
That's why now I drink so much
You can be sure I forgot you
That's why now I drink so much
You can be sure I forgot you

"Pregúntame a mí" has been recorded by various artists besides Silva, including Tony de la Rosa and Conjunto Ideal.[126] Chelo Silva recorded the song twice for Falcon Records accompanied by the Conjunto Los Principes.[127] Of these recorded versions by de la Rosa and Conjunto Ideal, it is only Silva's version that includes the risqué lyrics "Y me gustan grandotes, aunque me rompen la boca, ¡ihmm!, pregúntame a mí" (I like big ones, even if they tear my mouth). Thus, the original recording of the song is already injected with Silva's libidinous interpretation. Yet, in her live performance Silva shamelessly intensifies the already naughty lyrics by switching between *el* and *la,* thereby opening up the range of possibilities for what it is that comes in contact with her mouth. In the original recorded version, Silva steps outside the standard lyrics to say: "Y me gustan grandotes, aunque me rompen la boca, ¡ihmm!, pregúntame a mí" (I like big ones, even if they/it tears my mouth). While *grandotes* (big ones) could describe big masculine men, the phrase also informally refers to "big penises." Evoking *boleristas* of the past, as in the example of Valdelamar singing "El Cheque en Blanco" to her ex-lover,

Silva uses lyrics and live performance to launch a public directive: "ask me" ("pregúntame a mí") about my life choices and lived experiences, but be prepared for the response.

On the night of her *despedida,* Silva used live performance to make a minor yet significant change in lyrics. The live audience—some of whom can be heard singing along with Silva—is obviously anticipating the original set of risqué lyrics. Chris Strachwitz recalled that at this performance, "She looked stunning and the women were cheering her on."[128] When Silva arrives at a break in the music, just before the reference to "big ones," the audience's expectation that something risqué is coming increases. Silva says that she likes *grandotes* (big ones) "aunque . . . . me rompen el . . . ," even if they potentially rip or tear a part of her body.[129] Silva then briefly and coyly pauses as if she has accidentally blurted out something she should have concealed, or revealed a body part she desired to keep secret. The masculine pronoun *el* might be expected to refer to a body part such as (arm) or (eye), but given the context and Silva's flirtatious behavior, it does not take much effort to conclude that she is likely referring to *el culo* (the ass). In fact, even without coming to a conclusion about what Silva is referring to, we can deduce that it certainly is not *la boca* (the mouth). The possibilities are multiple, leaving the audience free to imagine women talking about sexual acts in a way that is usually forbidden. Herein lies the power of Silva's live performance, teasing an audience that is already familiar with the song at the precise moment when she is being honored for her musical contributions.

This shift from the originally recorded lyrics suspends the audience in anticipation of something scandalous and sexually nonnormative. After Silva sings "Aunque . . . que me rompen el" (even if they tear the), she then teasingly proceeds to correct herself by finishing with, "digo . . . *la* boca" (I mean—or I intended— the mouth). The transition between the masculine *el* and the feminine *la* opens up multiple possibilities for what she is referring to, generating suspense over what message the audience will finally receive. Silva's pause teases the audience, suggesting that something vulgar may be coming—hence the loud cheers, as if to encourage the latter—and Silva assertively delivers. Much like the narrative in "El Cheque en Blanco," Silva signs her name to this song through her unique performance. To roaring approval, she uses the live concert to transport her audience to the place where nonnormative genders and sexualities reside, at the limits of *la onda*. Silva's impromptu shift in lyrics represents a powerful technique for renarrating and reinterpreting her sexual subjectivity. In this moment, Silva chooses to transport herself and the audience beyond the already licentious lyrics she recorded long ago and into the sexual excesses where her subjectivity has resided.

Comparing Silva's original recording of "Pregúntame a mí" with her live version reveals how her extemporaneous changes in the live performance give the song new meaning. Silva's improvisation exemplifies the ways in which performance signatures can begin to build a counterhegemonic gender/sexual archive for Chicana/Latina gender and sexuality. "Pregúntame a mí" directs the public to ask Chelo herself about her life, to give her story a different kind of attention. This is but one example of Silva's performance of gender and sexuality that has been dissonant within the master narratives of borderlands music history dominated by corrido and conjunto musical forms.

In the Mexican documentary about the bolero *Las que viven en ciudad bolero,* the narrator notes that compositions by the acclaimed Mexican composer Emma Elena Valdelamar owed much of their musical life to *boleristas,* including "Los Bribones, Chelo Silva, Amparo Montes, María Victoria, Benny Moré, and Paquita la del Barrio." Songs by Valdelamar such as "Mil besos" and one of Silva's most notable, "El Cheque en Blanco," convey a different cultural practice of storytelling, one that runs counter to discourses of home, roots, and geographic territory central in the corrido song tradition. Subjects produced in corrido songs locate origins in geographic place. Subjects of the bolero locate origins in passion and conflict, perpetually in motion in attempts to re-create other configurations of love. Chicano subjects and protagonists of corridos are clearly written on the page, named, historicized, honored. Boleros have not been as prioritized as other musical forms in the pages of Chicano music studies and, by extension, have limited the multiplicity of genders and sexualities constructed in questions pertaining to race and power in Chicana/o borderlands experience.

Via performance tours and recordings, Silva figuratively and literally wandered from discursive place to geographic place telling stories, making love, and making a living. Her movement beyond the geographic and gender/sexual-normative parameters of "home" was socially risky; for working-class women of color of previous generations, the attempt to succeed in music instead of marriage was in and of itself viewed as morally reprehensible. Consistently, in my interviews with singers (and/or family) there was an emphasis on how being a wife and mother was equally important to a singing career.

Silva's knowledge production by means of the stories her songs tell is forever etched in vinyl records and in memories of her performances that counteract Chicana/o knowledge-production systems penned as narratives of resistance and through masculinized tropes of valor. In her analysis of bolero singer La Lupe, Frances Aparicio argues that La Lupe has until recently been underappreciated by scholars of salsa music. Similarly, I contend that, like La Lupe and other licentiously lyrical singers, Silva too "transgressively eroticized herself as a feminist act of resistance [and thus] possibly remains one of the most central motivations behind the masculine silencing to which she [is] subjected."[130]

Silva's boleros, *archisme,* and fragmented life narratives represent the ballad of Chelo Silva; this border ballad is a sonic testimony of those Chicana subjectivities relegated to the margins of grand narratives of the borderlands. Through her decades-long worn voice and the ravaged memories included in each song, Silva's KCOR performance and her recordings still replay her claim to her "unsuitable" behavior. Nonnormative Chicana subjectivities produced in music and other realms of cultural production offer alternative historical imaginaries that complicate the structural dimensions of power. Silva demonstrates profoundly that narratives of power struggle are located in musical sites other than those still sounded loudly in corrido heroic narratives of Cortez or Paredes.

Power struggles have been conveyed through the microphone, through the velvet sound, dramatic gesture, and unapologetic declarations of Chelo Silva. Despite the lack of sustained attention to Silva in Chicano music studies, her songs still exert a powerful force against *la onda* for Tejanas/Chicanas. Take, for example, the following poem dedicated to Silva written by Brownsville native Rosa Canales Pérez:[131]

Bohemian Rhapsodies

Bohemian Rhapsodies
Seldom find their place in
Mexican-side of town cantinas

More beer than wine cantinas
Heavy with cigarette smoke

"El Monkey Lounge"
"El Mante Bar"
"El 1-2-3"

Troubadours strapped with
Acordeón and bajo sexto
Wander in and out
But thumping wails
from stereophonic jukebox prevail
En el 1-2-3
A hard-living barrio poet
Stands back turned toward the rest
Hands upon the jukebox
Selecting his music
Like pulling a cork
From a bottle of vintage rare
Until the voice of
Chelo Silva fills the air

Chelo Silva
Self-avowed Bohemian
Passionate
Elegant
Rebellious
Bending notes from
Shades of Mexican blue

One bolero after another
Torch songs aching with
Heartbreak, talent and
Never-ending hometown due

Chelo Silva
1950s Texas bolero queen
yet to be replaced
reigning from the grave

Caste in a cantina scene
With a hard-living barrio poet

Secure within the
Tolerance zone where
People don't ask
Too many questions
When the Bohemian
Rhapsodies of an
Errant soul find
Their way back home

Pérez's poem highlights many of the discourses that shape Silva's representation, including heartbreak, passion, cantina culture, and her errant soul, still lingering in the shadow of "el músico y poeta."

As a distorted representation on album covers, a subject of hushed commentary, and a marginal reference in Américo Paredes's grand life, Chelo Silva has represented a figure of unbefitting and licentious acts. The eclipsing of Silva's image is symbolic of her dissonance. Yet, this has not resulted in the disappearance of her presence; for, if we consider her song "Pregúntame a mí" as a metaphoric response to mechanisms of containment, then we can ascertain how through her music Silva is continually filling out the *archisme* of her life stories and the imaginaries of her public and singers who follow her musical path.

I suggest that Silva's boleros form a queer temporal genealogy that moves back and forth across time and across genders. It has long been recognized that Paquita is the successor of Silva, a reincarnation, if you will, of Silva's bolero bravado spirit.[132] As music journalists have asserted, "La cantante mexicana Paquita la del Barrio forma parte de una tradición de cantantes rebeldes del despecho femenino como Chelo Silva o Chayito Valdés" (The singer Paquita la del Barrio forms part of a tradition of rebellious singers of feminine rancor such as Chelo Silva or Chayito Valdés).[133] In an interview on *El Show de Cristina,* Paquita once said that her musical inspiration was Chelo Silva. Angélica Silva has observed that Paquita sings many of Silva's popular songs and has the same singing style, "like perhaps Paquita is imitating her," as Silva's other sister, Margarita, has stated.[134] As a contemporary incarnation of Silva, Mexican bolero and ranchera singer Paquita la del Barrio is best known for songs that convey brash commentary on heterosexual masculinity and describe men as *inútil* (useless) womanizers. On any given Saturday in the Guerrero district of Mexico City, Paquita "holds court"

Paquita la del Barrio singing at her club La Casa de Paquita in Mexico City, July 2006. Photograph by the author.

in her club, La Casa de Paquita, singing her most notable songs, including those made famous by Silva such as "Como un perro" (Like a dog) and "El Cheque en Blanco" (Blank check).

Paquita has stated in numerous interviews that it was in fact during a tumultuous time with a lover that she came across Silva's music, specifically the song "El Cheque en Blanco." Paquita was married at the time to her second husband, Alfonso, who she found out had been cheating on her. Ironically, she found a cassette tape of Silva's music in her lover's car. "Recuerdo que me subí a su carro y encontré un cassette de Chelo Silva, una cantante tejana, y ahí estaba la canción 'Cheque en blanco.' La escuché y con dolor que tenía y sentimiento empecé a llorar, me la aprendí y la empecé a cantar en mi negocio" (I recall getting into his car and I found this cassette of Chelo Silva, a Tejana singer, and there was the song "El Cheque en Blanco." I listened to it and with the painful sentiment I had, I started to cry. I learned the song and I started singing it in my club).[135] "El Cheque en Blanco" was Silva's and is one of Paquita's most recognized songs.

Paquita is considered central to the tradition of those singers considered "the abandoned but tough woman who scornfully trashes no-good former lovers, exposed as worth less than a cigarette."[136] "It sounds like to me that Paquita also (like Silva) is kind of *decepcionada* (disillusioned, disenchanted)," says Angélica Silva.[137] So powerful is Paquita's chastisement of men who are unfaithful and abusive that it is not uncommon for her to find herself the object of hostility, as in this news story:

> Como la ven que hace unos días Paquita la del Barrio fue agredida con naranjas en Zamora Michoacán ya que algunos de los caballeros presentes se ofendieron con ella cuando interpretó uno de sus recientes temas "Chiquito". Los hombres empezaron a arrojarle naranjas que por fortuna esquivó Paquita. Ella siguió cantando pero algunos de los hombres, siguieron agrediéndola y finalmente después de decirles unas cuantas palabras altisonantes, La del Barrio se retiró prometiendo no volver a ese lugar.[138]
>
> As you can see, several days ago, Paquita la del Barrio was pounded by oranges in Zamora Michoacán when some of the men in the audience were offended with her when she sang one of her recent hits, "Chiquito." The men started throwing oranges that, fortunately, Paquita was able to escape. She continued singing, but some of the men continued throwing oranges, and finally, after saying a few pompous remarks, La del Barrio vowed never to return to that place again.

Paquita is hugely popular among women, particularly those who see themselves as coming from the same "lower" social and economic strata as her—represented by the location of her club in what is often characterized as a "rough neighborhood." She has also garnered a significant fan base among Latino gay men. Similar to a typical Saturday at La Casa de Paquita, a drag performance of Paquita will take place at any given local Latino gay bar in cities like Los Angeles, San Francisco, El Paso, and Laredo. Chelo Silva drag performances occur, for example, in Latino gay bars in the broader Los Angeles area, at El Calor in Anaheim, the Lion's Den in Costa Mesa, and the Frat House in Garden Grove. There is certainly nothing unique about such drag performances of Silva and Paquita; they are usually part of a show featuring staple Latina singing icons such as Celia Cruz, Shakira, and Paulina Rubio. Ann Cvetkovich, asserts in her analysis of queer culture archives that queer fandom archives include, for example, photos, gossip, and other memorabilia that serve as material evidence of such fan culture.[139] I consider drag performances of Silva and Paquita as part of a queer archive. To borrow from Cvetkovich, drag performances of Silva and Paquita are such historical practices where "fan cultures queer certain stars."[140] It is not solely the drag performances or personas themselves that are inherently queer, but they are made so through an archive assembled through gossip, performances channeling nonheteronormative desire, and alternative histories of the fans.[141]

Interestingly, it is not only the brash bolero renditions condemning abuse and adultery by Mexican men but the body of Paquita herself that makes for what Catherine Ramírez refers to as an inadequate or aberrant femininity.[142] Unlike other Latina singing icons popularized in drag form such as Shakira or Thalia, Paquita is a large, full-figured woman with a deep voice. She is not the hyperfeminine Latina with the prototypical long, dark, flowing hair. Paquita's haircut is actually short, bleached, and combed over. In lesbian-speak, her haircut is quite "butch." "Alejandro," a Mexican drag queen "Paquita" I interviewed in Mexico City, stressed that as a fan of Chelo Silva, he performed as Paquita because of her body size. As a tall, heavier, full-bodied male, Alejandro could easily fit into Paquita's femininity while having access to Silva's bolero songbook.

Paquita la del Barrio and drag queen performances of Silva and Paquita sustain a queer genealogy of the ballad of Chelo Silva. In this borderlands, the queer feminine body is the marked territory of desire as well as violence. Silva's queer genealogy offers no clear Chicano ontology. The musical sound of songs like "Como un perro" or "Hipócrita"—whether sung by Silva on one of her recordings or on a random Saturday night by a drag queen Paquita—constitutes Silva's dissonance along with the murmurs, hearsay, and moral indictments that have worked to contain nonheteronormative gender and sexuality in the imagined "home" of Chicano music.

A Chicana Butch Tribute to Chelo Silva

The simultaneity of illegibility and legibility of Silva, as in the acts of erasure on album covers and in canonical Chicano texts, as well as her queer genealogy through figures like Paquita la del Barrio, remind us that we must seek alternative sites of knowledge for exploring systems of power and music in the borderlands. As an undergraduate student at the University of Texas, I was educated quite well on scholarship by Don Américo in my Mexican American studies courses.[143] Simultaneously, I was fully confused with making sense of my own desire to cultivate a butch lesbianism, a masculine-presenting, same-sex-loving, nonnormative gender subject that "your mothers warned you about."[144] Butch Chicanas are those ever-present figures who sit in the corner of a cantina or show up as the "friend" of your cousin at a family wedding, the hypervisible bodies that are contained by hushed hearsay and rumor captured by the Spanish phrase "de eso no se habla" (we don't speak of that).[145]

Similar to gender queer masculine subjects who are hypervisible but ambiguous and indistinct, Chelo Silva has been an acute sonic presence with a concealed and disciplined representation in the few borderlands musical narrations of her. In her "femme tribute" to Chavela Vargas, Yvonne Yarbro-Bejarano "queers" the heterosexual codes of legendary Mexican ranchera singer Chavela Vargas to "provide femme identifications and engage butch desire."[146] Yarbro-Bejarano's now-classic analysis of Vargas's song lyrics, her masculine presenting, self-fashioning, and public declarations as an "out" lesbian illuminates both an articulation of Vargas's "butch" masculinity and Yarbro-Bejarano's self-identified femme desire of Vargas's butchness. The "femme tribute" honors not only the radicality of Vargas to publicly proclaim her lesbianism but also her masculine gender presentation within a highly patriarchal Mexican musical public sphere.

I close this chapter with a "butch tribute" to Chelo Silva, yet one that is different from Yarbro-Bejarno's project because Silva is not a self-identified "lesbian" subject. In the spirit of Yarbro-Bejarano's analysis, I have intended to illuminate the politics of gender and sexuality in Chicano music while also reflecting upon the possibilities of alternative desires and historical narratives that Silva enables via her boleros. My "butch tribute" to Silva argues that her border ballad—constitutive of her fragmented life narratives, exemplified in her last performances and her bolero songbook—generates constructions of gender and sexuality that have been indecipherable within dominant Tejano heteromasculine configurations of power in the borderlands. Moreover, it is the potential of the bolero to convey that which has gone unspoken and the power of *besos* to mark unspeakable lingering desires that, too, are decipherable in Silva's *archisme*—as knowledge-in-production—that is symbolized by this "tribute." "La Reina Tejana del Bolero" is a representation inscribed by social structures that continually worked to contain her sexual agency, desire, and self-representation.[147] The dissonance of Chelo Silva within *la onda,* the torturous attempt to coherently trace her life during my years of multisited research, and stories given life in Silva's *archisme* come together to form the border ballad of Chelo Silva. Silva's boleros, her border ballads, are where she deposited and withdrew enactments of passion, erotic scenarios, and memories of betrayal; those boleros have held the stories and *chismes* of the antiheroes, "los otros" (the others), and the vengeful, and they still serve as historical conduits for alternative knowledges and histories and draw attention to the ways in which *mexicanas* bear witness to different configurations of "conflict" and "subordination." In the early decades of the twentieth century, a unique musical sound would emerge to impel the sonic imaginary of *Tejas,* and "a popular type of accordion music commonly known as conjunto, began to appear, raising the serious issues of race, class, gender, ideology, and cultural hegemony in a new musical form."[148] With this new musical form would come different configurations of power and empowerment through the sound of the accordion, and discord, in the shape of a female body.

THREE

Tex-Mex Conjunto Accordion Masculinity

The Queer Discord of Eva Ybarra and Ventura Alonzo

On any weekend night, in some dance hall, ice house, or music festival across Mexican Texas, the first riffs of an accordion will sound to form a sonic compass of *Tejas,* leading listeners to tap their feet and bob their bodies in a familiar motion. The high-pitch piping notes of the accordion music sounds *Tejas,* sonically mapping the discursive imaginary of a Texas distinctly claimed as *mexicano.* The accordion sounds *Tejas* in multiple genres, from the patent Tex-Mex conjunto to accordionist Flaco Jiménez's riffs in "The Streets of Bakersfield," to the punk tunes of Piñata Protest by Álvaro del Norte, to the cover of "Purple Haze" often squeezed out by accordionist Esteban Jordan (nicknamed el "Tex-Mex" Jimi Hendrix). *Tejas* looks like dancers moving cumbias and polkas in a counterclockwise circle, tastes like flour tortilla breakfast tacos washed down by a cold Big Red, smells like the frosting on top of a pink cake, and sounds like the accordion.[1]

Tex-Mex accordion sound cannot be fully appreciated, comprehended, or explored exclusively as audible. It is my contention that the Tex-Mex accordion's unique sound, as well as its function as a narrative trope of Texas-Mexican history and Tejana/o identity formations, works with its visuality—the scenes of dancers propelled into a counterclockwise circle, the image of the accordion instrument in public history projects, and the visual representation of musical performance—to constitute the sound of *Tejas* as a borderlands imaginary. In other words, accordion sound is most certainly audibility akin to harmonic breaths of inhaled and exhaled whistled vibrations. The Tex-Mex accordion also sounds the intense territorial identity shifts; Mexican, Texan, Texas-Mexican, Texian, Tejano, Tex-Mex are squeezed in and out, out and in. Yet, accordion sound is also the master *visual* representation of brown masculinity in Texas. Tex-Mex accordion sound can be captured by listening as readily as by looking at the artwork of Carmen Lomas Garza's *Baile en 1958*. Moreover, to consider questions and analyses of Tex-Mex accordion sound as purely audible, as if devoid of racialized gendered bodies, is to remain uncritical of the ways this unique sound has been shaped and configured audibly as well as visually. Accordion sound is not only the audible instructive force propelling dancing bodies on the dance floor; rather, the visuality of the bodies themselves complete the sonic imaginary as twirling torsos and shuffling feet reverberate the beats and form a concentric circle of Tejanas/os that seems to increase the volume.[2]

A number of narratives and scholarly analyses centering the accordion address the instrument's relationship to subjectivities and historical narratives. Martha Mockus asserts in her feminist analysis of accordionist Pauline Oliveros that "the accordion occupies an odd, marginalized position in American musical culture. Perhaps more than any other instrument the accordion always sounds its connections to ethnicity, on the one hand, and schlocky kitsch on the other."[3] Although my focus is a Chicana feminist consideration of Tex-Mex accordion sound, there is a similar connection, as Mockus conveys, between the instrument's symbolism of marginal ethnic histories and working-class culture. Similarly, in E. Annie Proulx's novel *Accordion Crimes*, the accordion emblematizes a multifarious and complex ethnic history in the United States.[4] As the novel suggests, the accordion itself is the narrator of U.S. ethnic history as the instrument passes through the hands of German immigrants in Iowa, Mexican Americans in Texas, Franco-Canadians in Maine, African Creoles in Louisiana, Poles in Chicago, Scots–Irish ranchers in Montana, and present-day Norwegians in Minnesota.

Recent scholarship has theorized Latino music, space, and place through audiotopias, nation, and hybridity, for example, effectively establishing the ways in which borders, transnational migration, and race reflect musical melding, cultural politics, and new subjectivities; this chapter further considers the borderlands sonic imaginary of *la onda*, with a focus on *Tejas* as sounded through the Tex-Mex conjunto accordion.

Tejas is explored through a Chicana feminist analysis of accordion masculinity, and, by extension, gendered bodies, instrumentation, and visual representation in conjunction with Chicano/Tejano cultural-nationalist discourses of home and gender.[5]

Chicano music historiography charts borderlands Tex-Mex accordion-driven conjunto music as emerging at the beginning of the twentieth century, particularly in the context of postrevolutionary Mexican social and political dynamics in Texas.[6] Various types of accordions have circulated in the Southwest, such as the piano accordion, but the distinctness of the Tex-Mex conjunto is represented by the diatonic button accordion.[7] So central is this button accordion to Tex-Mex conjunto music that the history of the instrument's arrival in the Southwest has itself become a narrative "instrument" in the historicization of its borderland subjects.[8] Most generally, Tex-Mex accordion sound is represented as interconnected with the brown male body, itself a physical topography that is sculpted by laboring the Texas terrain. The accordion has also musically sounded heteronormative gender relationships such as in *George Washington Gómez* by Américo Paredes. In a key scene in the novel, the young protagonist, Guálinto, returns home to his working-class culture. In one passage, heteronormative gender, working-class masculinity, and race in South Texas are metaphorically spun into motion by the accordion-driven Tex-Mex conjunto music of Paredes's "greater Mexico." Paredes writes:

> The music was a fast, shrieking polka, played so fast that the tune was barely recognizable. The men streamed in and took the girls out on the floor, where they danced furiously in a hop-step-skip fashion. The little house trembled on its slender foundations to the scraping and stamping.[9]

In Paredes's passage, sound is conveyed by the author's description of vibrations and beats, but also through visual descriptions of normatively gendered social relations. Examples of the accordion as central to fictional narratives, the representation of iconic musical masculinity, and Tex-Mex documentary films have sounded a distinct heteronormative *Tejas*.

Having been raised in the geopolitical *transfrontera* zone of South Texas, I still recall the sound of accordion-driven conjunto music. I find the accordion intriguing precisely because of the ways its sound links heteromasculinity, canonical narratives, and the body; these linkages become especially fraught in Chicano musicology, which often tends to reduce analyses of the music to discourses of authenticity and working-class masculinity. Music and cultural studies scholarship by Manuel Peña, José Limón, and Guadalupe San Miguel, for instance, foreground Tejano masculinity as the subject of cultural resistance to Anglo Texan hegemony. Furthermore, numerous historical narratives and video documentaries situate the accordion as the foremost musical symbol of *Tejas*.

According to Chicano musical canons, the origins of and key contributions to conjunto music can be traced solely and unproblematically to male accordion players. In fact, we can trace the music's history and transformations alongside the histories of specific individuals. The scholarly focus on the origins and time lines of musical transformation and births of musicians reflects a heteronormative temporality within the cultural-nationalist imaginary of *Tejas* and its gendered and sexual subjectivities. Thus, most musical canons note that Bruno Villareal was the earliest recorded Tejano accordionist.[10]

Although Avelardo Valdez and Jeffrey A. Halley acknowledge that women accordionists like Eva Ybarra have obtained success and provided new "gender roles," their analysis of gender remains entrenched in a familiar and uncomplicated binary that occludes the specificities of how power and labor are organized in public spaces.[11] Thus, I suggest that in such attempts to account for women's place in *Tejas,* the accordion serves as a "medium for the simultaneous expression and construction of conventional notions of masculinity and femininity and situates performers and audience alike along clearly established gender lines."[12] Merely adding more women to the scene, as Valdez and Halley implicitly propose, does little to address gender as a system of social structural power, especially given the power that accordion musicianship has maintained for regulating economic agency, historical narratives, and constructions of female sexuality in *Tejas.*

I analyze Texas Mexican accordion-driven music for the ways it has sounded—audibly and visually—a heteronormative *Tejas* imaginary where women have been positioned as objects of desire in song lyrics, as fans, or as participants in dance. Since the turn of the twentieth century, the accordion sound has imagined the place of tradition, home, and identity—in short, the real—as the expression of the absolute essence of the group that produces it. Take, for example, comments about conjunto music by Manuel Peña: "In a sense then, conjunto is antithetical to pop music. The latter demands constant turnover, conjunto demands permanence. Pop music styles have shallow cultural roots, conjunto's roots are deeply entangled in tejano culture."[13] If we consider the ways in which Chicano music historiography, literary production, and documentary narrative projects fill the musical soundscape with discursive accordion reverberation, then, I contend, the accordion-playing bodies of Tejana accordionists create a dissonance within the heteronormative sonic landscape of borderlands music, thereby creating possibilities for alternative *Tejas* imaginaries.

In the case of Tex-Mex accordion-driven musical sound, there must be attention to how sound is constituted by body, instrument, and historiography. Whereas scholarship on audioscapes has established how sound reflects the emergence of new subjectivities and transforms the cultural politics of minoritarian cultures, a consideration of discordanat reverberations in the *Tejas* musical imaginary requires an engagement with the sonic that foregrounds the peculiarity of female accordion musicians. To theorize dissonance is to theorize the interconnectedness between looking odd and sounding odd, such as the cultivation of working-class color styles and excessive accoutrements. In other words, studying *Tejas* through Tex-Mex accordion sound requires an analysis of sound that incorporates its audible, physical, and discursive productions.

In this chapter, I argue that Eva Ybarra's accordion-playing body represents a dissonance within heteromasculinist discourses of Tex-Mex conjunto accordion music. I place my reading of Ybarra's queer discord within a queer conceptualization that I theorize as *curiosidad* (and, by extension, *la curiosa*) that emerged in interviews and conversations with those attending music festivals. My analysis of Ybarra is based on the discourse of the accordion as itself a female body and the widely circulated representations of male bodies playing the accordion; both of these have been central to the sounding of *Tejas*. I begin the chapter with attention to Ventura Alonzo, arguably the first Tejana accordionist to perform onstage and in recordings. I am not invested in celebrating Alonzo as the "first lady" of Tex-Mex accordion music—self-produced family biographies, public history, and Chicano musicology have amply achieved this—but rather in proposing that she represents and establishes, through her life stories, a Chicana feminist music analytic of *curiosidad* (or *la curiosa*). In other words, I argue that we cannot fully comprehend the complexity of power in borderlands music by merely analyzing Ybarra within canonical Tex-Mex musicology because she does not fully register the cultural codes, the bodily fit, and the working-class labor paradigms narrativized. In order to comprehend Ybarra's dissonance, we must move through Ventura Alonzo's discordant accordionist presence as *curiosa*, that is, as giving sound to the odd-looking, the strangely registered, the fun novelty, and the unusual spectacle, in similar spirit to what David Eng, Judith Halberstam, and José Esteban Muñoz define as "queer."[14] Alonzo's story represents *una curiosidad* in *Tejas* that is outside the bounds of the normative masculinist representation of Tex-Mex conjunto accordionists. Alonzo, as *curiosa*, allows for a Chicana feminist analysis of racialized sexuality that not only critiques stable notions of *Tejas* identities but locates the dissonance of racialized class knowledges not gendered masculine.

Like Ybarra, Alonzo remains dissonant within the cultural-nationalist soundscape of *Tejas*. Her narrative allows us insight into women's innovative acquisitions of playing skills, the balancing of musical production and child-bearing reproduction, and the manner in which working-class histories of Tex-Mex conjunto music have been overdetermined by racialized masculinity. A critical overview of Alonzo's life stories provides us with a Chicana feminist methodological apparatus for hearing Ybarra's dissonance by being attentive to gendered class, the female body, and the patrilineal reproduction of musical knowledge that together have produced a discordant sounding of *Tejas* by women accordionists like Eva Ybarra.

Ventura Alonzo: ¡Qué Curiosa!

"¿Qué QUIERES que le pongamos en el cajón cuando se muera para que nos recuerde de ti?" (What do you want us to put in your coffin when you die for us to remember you by?), asks Ventura Alonzo's daughter Mary from her seat nearby. Alonzo responds:

Ventura Alonzo with her accordion. Photograph courtesy of the Houston Metropolitan Center, Houston Public Library.

> Me ponen el retrato, ése que está allí. Ése me ponen en el cajón, así. Y donde están todos los músicos y no más yo de mujer entre todos, puros músicos, puros músicos y no más yo.[15]
>
> Place that portrait, that one there. Place that one in the coffin, like that. The one where there are all the musicians, and just me the only woman among all of them, all musicians, all musicians and just me.

Alonzo's instructions to her daughter to remember her as a woman among musicians demonstrates the ways in which masculinist discourses of musicianship gave her no access to the term "musician" and, moreover, shows the methodological shortcomings of Chicano music histories that have resulted in the illegibility of Tejana accordionists like Alonzo during the mid-twentieth century. In her response, Alonzo strives to take her place alongside *los músicos,* to make herself decipherable through her own story. To my knowledge, there are no recordings of Alonzo's accordion playing to listen to, so it is her stories that too must be considered a sounding of *Tejas.*

I listen for Alonzo's music through her self-representation as "musician" in ways that can only be conveyed by her everyday life. Her presence as symbolized by the phrase "yo no más de mujer entre todos, puros músicos" (just me, the only woman among all of the musicians) strikingly points to her *curiosidad,* her odd and peculiar presence in the masculine-gendered discourse of musicianship, especially in her time. As an accordionist, she was not representative of normative womanhood; neither was she decipherable, even to herself, as musician. Avelardo Valdez and Jeffrey A. Halley assert that women in the Tejano conjunto music scene have been highly visible as participants, dancers, girlfriends, wives, and sometimes even singers, but they rarely appear onstage as accordion musicians receiving the validation and adoration of fans.[16] Valdez and Halley explain the gender politics in Tex-Mex conjunto music by reminding us of the distinctions between singers and musicians: "When [women] are performers, they tend to be singers rather than instrumentalists."[17] In canonical tellings of Tejano conjunto/orquesta music, "musicians" are the central protagonists with complementary attention to women singers who may have accompanied them or even other accordionists whose stories have remained unheard because they did not play publicly. There is slight acknowledgment of Alonzo's musical life in Houston as "one of the first lady big band musicians in the state of Texas"[18] and a rich description of her in Peña's book *The Mexican American Orquesta.* And yet, what Alonzo's response to how she desires to be remembered demonstrates is that even when Tejanas like herself have managed to cultivate livelihoods as accordionists, their musical presence remains dissonantly marginalized as musicians; they are rather understood as *curiosas,* novel complements to and unusual versions of *los músicos* (the musicians). As Peña writes, "Ventura Alonzo stands virtually alone as a strong female leader in a musical landscape dominated by patriarchal figures."[19] Moreover, as this feature in the *Houston Chronicle* attests, Alonzo was an odd spectacle on the music scene:

> Alonzo created quite a stir when, in the 1930s, she entered the traditionally male Mexican music scene with an accordion strapped onto her tiny, 5-foot frame. But with a remarkable musical ear that had allowed Alonzo to play anything she heard since she was a child, she was accustomed to turning heads with her performances.[20]

Tex-Mex music scholars, including Manuel Peña and Guadalupe San Miguel, have acknowledged Alonzo's rarity within the mostly male-dominated Tex-Mex orquesta scene in the early decades of the twentieth century.[21] States Peña: "Alonzo was one of the few women instrumentalists in commercial orquestas—and possibly the only woman in a leadership position."[22] Although both Peña and San Miguel laud Alonzo's rare presence as a female accordionist, there is more attention to her band's class-based transitions between ranchero and orquesta music and less attention to the context of public performance, labor, and gender.

"In Houston, I was the queen of the accordion," claimed Alonzo.[23] Taking up the accordion was part necessity and part skill. Like Bruno Villareal, Alonzo played the piano accordion. Canonical music time lines mark Villareal as the first Tejano accordionist to record in 1928, whereas Alonzo is said to be the first Tejana accordionist to record during the early 1940s.[24] Alonzo y Sus Rancheros recorded "Magnolia (polka)," "Navegando (vals)," "Ojos Negros (polka)," "María Luisa (vals)," "El Campo (polka)," and "Matilde (vals)" for Falcon Records in McAllen in May 1950.[25] "They also recorded at Rio Records in San Antonio and Alameda Records in Houston in the 1950s" and for AC Records in the 1960s.[26] Alonzo remembers feeling self-conscious and odd at times because of the public's inquisitiveness, for many associated the accordion with cantina culture, drinking, smoking, and a lower-class lifestyle.[27]

Cantinas are generally described as working-class neighborhood bars that are often associated with seedy licentious behavior. Therefore, women who are seen as inhabiting that space are often viewed as promiscuous or of questionable morals. In my personal conversations with Alonzo, as well as in interviews, she stressed that she was not a smoker or drinker. Moreover, while Peña analyzes Alonzo y Sus Rancheros's transition from ranchero (or working-class "country" music) to *jaitón* (or "high-tone" middle-class music) along class lines, I believe Alonzo's self-identification as a nondrinker and nonsmoker, as well as the musical transition of her band to middle-class venues, reveals more about the politics of gender that Mexican American women had to negotiate in the mid-twentieth century.[28]

Ventura Martínez Alonzo was born on December 30, 1904, in Matamoros, Mexico, to José Martínez and María del Pilar Escamilla.[29] Alonzo's parents fled Mexico along with many others who feared the consequences of the Mexican Revolution. Not long after settling in Brownsville in 1914, the family moved to Kingsville, where Alonzo learned to read music and play those instruments she referred to as appropriate for girls, including the piano and the clarinet. She recalled learning to play the piano when she was about nine.[30] Alonzo was much better at learning to play by ear:[31]

> A mí me gustaba tocar el piano. Mi hermana, ella era maestra de música, pero yo no. Yo tocaba sin notas. Una vez una maestra me oyó tocar, y me acuerdo que dijo: "Esta muchachita no es de nota. Es de aquí de la cabeza."[32]

> I liked playing the piano. My sister was a music teacher, but not me. I could play by ear. One time a teacher heard me play, and I still remember her saying: "This girl is not a musician by notes. It comes naturally from her head."

Alonzo's father passed away in 1915 at the age of forty-nine. In 1917, Alonzo moved to Houston to live with her sister. Her life was characteristic of many *mexicanas* who were moving to urban areas during this time. When she arrived in Houston, she could no longer attend school because the family needed income. Thus, her formal education ended with the tenth grade. She worked for the National Biscuit Company for about two years before she married and was subsequently expected to work inside and outside the home.[33]

For Alonzo, there was never a question that playing the accordion meant playing in public—even despite the fact that it was so rare to see a woman accordionist onstage: "Tocaban no más puros hombres. No había mujer" (Only men would play. There were no women).[34] Alonzo enjoyed the fact that her musical skills garnered her the power to make an impact in her community, especially economically:

> Me gustaba la música. No más era toda, era no más. Tenía el pensamiento en componer. Sí compuse música. Le ayudamos a la iglesia, con jamaicas, mi esposo, mi hijo y yo, yo con la acordeón.

> Ayudamos y contribuímos mucho dinero para hacer una escuela para los niños. Siempre fue para ayudar. Nunca cobré. Por eso tengo esos *awards* que tengo allá.[35]
>
> I liked the music. That was it, it was. I had the idea to compose. I composed music. I helped at the church, with festivals, my husband, my son, me, me with the accordion. We helped and contributed lots of money to open a school for children. Always to help. I never charged a fee. That's why I have those awards that I have there.

Certainly, Alonzo played the more acceptable local social venues for women during that time, such as family gatherings. Eventually, she would play on radio stations, at dance halls, in churches, but not in cantinas. In her early years of playing, she met artists who would later come to be known as the "fathers" of accordion-driven Texas Mexican music, namely, Flaco Jiménez and Valerio Longoria.[36] Not surprisingly, Alonzo is never mentioned in narratives about these accordionists.[37]

Alonzo's first marriage was to Jesús Gallegos, but this marriage was short-lived because of Gallegos's attempts to keep her from being a musician. Alonzo was pressured to marry Jesús at age eighteen. "¡Me quitó los años!" (He took my best years!) she exclaimed. After divorcing Jesús, she married Francisco (Frank) Alonzo in 1931.[38] She had three children, Mario, Óscar, and Arnoldo, before divorcing. "Yo me tenía a mis hijos. Cuando me divorcié, yo pagué el divorcio. Yo los mantube a los tres" (I attended to my children. When I divorced, I paid for the divorce. I supported all three). Alonzo's spirit of economic independence supports Emma Pérez's assertions about Mexican American women in the 1930s whose working lives challenged dominant narratives depicting women as merely working in the domestic sphere.[39] "Both the census manuscripts and oral interviews confirm that by the time a Mexican American girl was fourteen, she was more likely working to contribute to her family's income."[40] Moreover, Alonzo represented another uncommon presence as a leader of her band and eventually co-owner of her club.[41]

Although historians credit Frank's love of music with initiating their joint venture into a music career, Alonzo claims otherwise.[42] Frank, Alonzo clarifies, was not as musically inclined; in fact, she herself takes

Ventura Alonzo with Alonzo y Sus Rancheros. Photograph courtesy of the Houston Metropolitan Center, Houston Public Library.

credit for teaching her husband to play the *bajo sexto* (sixth bass) and initiating the band's formation.[43] Furthermore, Alonzo recalled that when she and Frank considered recruiting others to form a band, there was tension over who would be its manager.[44] The figure of Alonzo as the accordionist strums discord in early decades of conjunto accordion music in documentaries as well as Tejano/Chicano canonical literature.

Two significant elements stand out when considering heteronormative gender and the accordion during Alonzo's time: public performance and travel. Alonzo stressed that she never drank or smoked and usually played in venues she considered appropriate for women, making explicit her constant negotiations when performing in Houston's urban public sphere:

> Él aprendió que yo sabía tocar la acordeón. Entonces él se animó. Empezamos a tocar en jamaicas, y así. Amistades me hablaban a mí y a mi esposo para tocar y *[sic]* íbamos y tocábamos, pero yo nunca probé de cerveza ni licor de nada, ni fumar, nunca en mi vida.[45]

> He learned that I knew how to play the accordion. Then he was encouraged. We began to play in festivals, and that was that. Friends would call me and my husband to play and we'd go and play, but I never drank beer or liquor or any of that. I didn't even smoke, never in my life.

Alonzo's band did not play in cantinas because "así me criaron mis padres" (that is how my parents raised me).[46] Alonzo's comments exemplify a constant negotiation between her nonnormatively gendered labor as an accordionist and the type of venues she played in.

Alonzo's band traveled to approximately fifty cities throughout Texas.[47] When her children Mary and Frank Jr. were young, Alonzo would leave them with her mother, but baby Alonzo used to travel with his parents. Alonzo recalled "allí lo escondía bajo del piano, y se dormía" (I would hide him under the piano, and he would fall asleep).[48] In her analysis of blues women during the early twentieth century, Angela Davis argues that travel and particular kinds of performance sites shaped gender and sexuality. The process of travel is individualized, secularized, and sexualized.[49] Thus, although Alonzo embodied a rare kind of gendered public figure, the types of spaces her band played in resulted in a tension over maintaining a gender-normative representation.

In 1956, Alonzo and Frank opened a nightclub called La Terraza (the terrace) in Houston. Alonzo pulled double duty, spending about half her time attending to domestic responsibilities before going to work at the club. She stated that as a woman musician, the public expected more from her, so she learned quickly, both as an entrepreneur and as a musician. For instance, she had to become diverse in her choice of tunes:

> Yo fui la única que tocaba corridos, conjunto rancheras, boleros y todo esos. Sí, me gusta y todo. Yo tocaba de todo, y me pedían porque tú tienes que darle gusto a la gente.[50]
>
> I was the only one who played corridos, conjunto rancheras, boleros, and all those. Yes, I like it, all of it. I played everything, and I'd get requests because you must give the audience what they want to hear.

These dual roles were often difficult to negotiate because, as the central figure in the band (the only woman and co-owner), Alonzo had to perform her role as a musician within the demands of marriage and motherhood.

As the self-appointed manager of the band, Alonzo often took requests from the public; however, her husband Frank would read her close contact with the audience as flirtatious. According to Alonzo, she was being a smart businesswoman who gave the audience what it wanted:

> Y tú tienes que darle gusto a la gente. Si tú no le das gusto, y no te hablan, "Tócame esta pieza. Sí, ahorita se la toco." ¿Y nunca se la tocan? ¿Por qué? Pues se enoja aquella persona, y ya no vuelven a decir. Y llega y decía mi esposo, porque mi esposo era un poco celoso, decía "¿Para qué le dices?" Pos, así es cómo traen la contela. Si no, ¿cómo le vas a hacer? ¿Cómo, pues si no te quieren?[51]
>
> And you have to keep the audience happy. If you don't, they won't come back and say, "Hey, play this. Sure, I'll play that." And if you never play it? Why not? Then they'll get upset and won't return to say anything at all. And my husband would say—my husband would get jealous—he'd say, "Why do you do that?" Well, that's how it is; otherwise, how are you gonna make money? How else would you handle them? How, if then they don't want you?

Alonzo y Sus Rancheros were the house band at La Terraza and opened for other bands as well. In fact, some of the early artists to play in the club included Valerio Longoria, who would often watch her play onstage, and a young Paulino Bernal. Bernal was actually the first one hired to play at La Terraza.[52] Alonzo's skill attracted other bands from far and wide: "Mira, Beto Villa, Beto Villa fue a Houston no más a conocer, para conocerme a mí. '¿Quién es la señora que toca la acordeón?'" (Look, Beto Villa, Beto Villa went to Houston just to meet, to meet me. "Who is the lady who plays the accordion?").[53] Santiago Jiménez Sr. was hired to play at La Terraza as well. For the approximately twelve years that she and Frank owned La Terraza, Ventura managed all aspects of the business:

> I would be the ticket taker at the door, play in the band, manage the accounting of the business, and even after a long set of playing onstage, I would return home and wash and starch all of the band members' shirts for the next day.[54]

It is obvious from Alonzo's recollections that, despite having crossed paths with early conjunto accordion "fathers," her accordion sounds a discord with the heteronormative narratives sounded in *Tejas*.[55]

"Who's Your Daddy?"

ACCORDIONIST PAULINE OLIVEROS has described the sensuous intimacy unique to playing the accordion, referring to the way the body hugs the accordion, itself a breathing body.[56] Accordionist Katherine Setar has observed that while playing the accordion, "the sound waves traveled through my upper torso, allowing me to easily experience the sound, not only through my ears but throughout my body."[57] Eva Ybarra has described how the push–pull motion of the accordion on her chest sometimes pinches her breasts, leaving bruises.[58] Ybarra's upper torso and arms are branded with the bodily traces of labor, including the sculpted muscle on her inner left forearm.[59] The left side of her upper body tends to carry much of the weight of pushing and pulling when she plays.[60] Ybarra plays the accordion—as is common practice among conjunto music accordionists—standing up with her left hand curled around the bellows, hovering over the bass buttons.[61] Ybarra's right hand arches over the button board, and this is the hand and fingers that push, glide, and jump across to create quick runs of high-pitched harmonic whistles. Ybarra has said that people often tell her that she caresses the accordion and that she makes it weep.[62] The descriptions by accordionists highlight the intimacy of the bodies of musicians pressed up against the body of the accordion. Moreover, it is an intimacy that in Tex-Mex conjunto music has been discursively shaped by the gendering of musicianship as masculine and the gendering of the accordion as feminine.

Avelardo and Halley assert that "the accordion in conjunto music is considered an archetypical male instrument within the Mexican American community" and that has discouraged young girls from learning the instrument.[63] I extend this assertion to argue that it is more precisely the dominant representation of a masculine male body intimately joined with a feminine-gendered accordion that induces public displays of *curiosidad* by Ybarra; that is, Eva Ybarra's female-playing accordion body registers as discordant in relationship to the normative masculine-body–feminine-instrument relationship.[64] Heteronormative temporality in *Tejas* has been sounded by the power of accordion patrilineal knowledge formations. Valdez and Halley found, in their exploration of a few women conjunto accordionists, that "the primary mentor-teaching of a young, aspiring male accordionist was a grandfather who, on the other hand, never encouraged his granddaughters to learn the instrument."[65] Valdez and Halley continue by stating that "even in those families with long musical traditions, such as the Farías family—whose members constitute La Tropa F, one of the most popular conjuntos in San Antonio—young females are discouraged from learning the accordion and bajo sexto."[66] An explicit example is that of the Jiménez family of accordionists. Santiago Jiménez Sr., father of Flaco and Santiago Jr., recalls the musical lineage for acquiring the accordion and passing it down to his (now) famous sons:

> SANTIAGO SR.: Well, I learned to play the accordion at the age of twelve. Back then, my father played at dances and I, watching him, started to learn the polkas, redowas, and schottisches. And then sometime later, well, maybe at the age of twenty, I began to make the first recordings here in San Antonio.
> JUAN: Your father, then, played the accordion?
> SANTIAGO SR.: Yes, my father played the accordion.

Later in the interview, Santiago Sr. names all of his children, six sons and two daughters.

> JUAN: And then, how many of them became musicians?
> SANTIAGO SR.: Almost all my children play a little, but the best known, best known was Flaco Jiménez and Santiago Jr.[67]

The interviewer, Juan Tejeda, a member of the Austin-based band "Conjunto Aztlán," the founder of the Tejano Conjunto festival, and coeditor of the book *¡Puro Conjunto!*, locates himself within this genealogy. After asking Santiago Sr. to talk about some of his early recording, Tejeda recognizes one of the songs, and says:

> JUAN: "Viva Seguín," I play that one myself. You see, I'm also following in your tradition. Your son taught me, Santiago Jiménez Jr.
> SANTIAGO SR: Is that so?
> JUAN: When I was ten years old. And I played with him too.
> SANTIAGO SR.: Imagine that. How nice![68]

The masculine body—as visual discursive mechanism physically squeezing sound from the accordion—has been a key representation for spinning a heteronormative temporality of gender and sexuality in *Tejas*.

Eva Ybarra at age five. From left to right: Flaco Jiménez, Pedro Ybarra, and Eva Ybarra at microphone. Photograph courtesy of Eva Ybarra.

A significant tool in the discursive production of *Tejas* during the last three decades of the twentieth century has been the historical documentary. As with canonical music scholarship, documentaries including *Chulas Fronteras* (1976), *Songs of the Homeland* (1995), *Accordion Dreams* (2001), and *The Big Squeeze* (2009) imagine the accordion in the role of storyteller, as a narrative tool. Whereas this chapter's analysis of accordion visuality forefronts music festival posters and film documentaries, various museums and exhibits from the Tejano Music Museum in Alice, Texas, to the Smithsonian Institution's traveling Corrido Exhibit similarly monitor the connections between the accordion as visual object, the instrument's musical sound, and Tejano masculinity. The history of the Tex-Mex accordion has become the history of Texas Mexican people, and its sound forms a connection to place. The following overview of video documentaries proffers another example of a historical teleology that links male bodies and geographic landscape through the accordion sound.

Chulas Fronteras (1976), directed and produced by Les Blanks and Chris Strachwitz, is arguably the most acclaimed documentary about Tex-Mex borderland music and culture produced by music historians. Filmed on location in South Texas and northern Tamaulipas in December 1975 and early 1976, the video documentary conjures a Tex-Mex subject through musical narrative. The project weaves songs around visions of rural landscapes, food, and public musical spaces, in particular cantinas and dance halls. Rural landscapes depict men as laborers tending to fields or cowboys on horseback. One can smell the warmth of landscape, taste the food, and feel the sound as it moves brown bodies. Food, especially *carne asadas* (Mexican-style grilling), provides the homosocial spaces of masculine bonding while cantinas and dance spaces allow for men's expression of desire and pleasure.[69]

Chulas Fronteras begins with the camera following a map of the Río Bravo and the Texas–Mexico borderlands, from El Paso/Juárez to Brownsville/Matamoros. The masculine body is displayed as a physical force that works the geographic terrain. The accordion-driven sound of conjunto music moves the viewer just as it moves workers along migrant paths while sonically mapping a borderlands imaginary already overdetermined by bodily labor and rural landscapes. Immediately, the viewer is prompted to make a connection between three elements: music, masculinity, and the land. These three elements are overemphasized in scene after scene as *Chulas Fronteras* constructs a rural-class subordinate *mexicano*/Tejano subject. At the same time, women are rendered invisible or as subjects to be desired in songs, as dedicated companions, dance partners, or background fillers for the frame. Women are the companions and guardians of family and the central caregivers in the domestic sphere. Lydia Mendoza makes an appearance as the only woman musician in the documentary. A gifted songwriter, singer, and guitarist, Mendoza once expressed to me in an interview that "Lydia no es Lydia sin su guitarra" (Lydia is not Lydia without her guitar). Although Mendoza is eventually featured singing and playing her most acclaimed song, "Mal Hombre" (Bad man), the viewer's first introduction to Mendoza is in the domestic space with family making tamales for Christmas.

Scenes that merge masculinity with accordion sound typify *Chulas Fronteras*. Such scenes cut across images of rural landscapes, barbecues, public performances, and heterosexual desire as expressed through the lyrics of such songs as "Mi Tejanita" (My little Tejana). The lyric's text in English is displayed on-screen as heterosexual couples spin around the dance floor: "Es mi tejana la más bonita. Otra como ella no vas a encontrar" (My Tejana girl is so beautiful. There is no one else like her).[70] For example, the documentary features Eugenio Abrejo, accordionist for Los Alegres de Terán, as he leaves home to play on the road with his conjunto. He is kissed by his wife and daughters as they bid him farewell. One only wonders who Abrejo will teach to play the accordion since he does not have a son. If tradition holds and Abrejo follows in the steps of his father, there will be no one to inherit the accordion. The final scene of the documentary focuses on the passing down of the accordion from one generation of men to the next. As the scene and the documentary close, we see an older man with a young boy on his lap, the very emblem of patriarchal teachings. This scene assures the viewer that conjunto accordion music will continue as long as there are sons, nephews, grandsons, and brothers in *Tejas*.

Songs of the Homeland (1995), *Accordion Dreams* (2001), and *The Big Squeeze* (2009) represent director Héctor Galán's accordion documentary trilogy.[71] The documentaries include interviews with musicians and typical scenes of live music nightspots, dancing, and wide-open landscapes. These documentaries endeavor to reproduce the heteronormative Tejano accordion subject by proceeding linearly through the century. Unlike *Chulas Fronteras*, Héctor Galán's documentaries include "official" spokespersons, including academic scholars and cultural arts directors, and are narrated by popular singers Freddy Fender and Tish Hinojosa.

All these documentaries share the similar narrative frame of *Tejas* as constituted by the centrality of the accordion in documenting the history, cultural milieu, and music of Texas Mexicans. For example, in his introductory narrative, Fender establishes a link between land, music, and history in *Songs of the Homeland:*

> A hundred years ago, a new music was evolving in South Texas. It was a land where people were caught between Mexico and the rest of the United States. The people here created a unique culture: their language was Spanish, their traditions were Mexican. They lived and worked in a vast area that was little known to the rest of America. The Mexican Americans struggling to form an identity here called

> themselves Tejanos for the word *Tejas*, the Spanish name for Texas. As they adapted to a new culture, familiar traditions began to change. Nowhere is that more evident than in the music. The music Tejanos created was a unique American synthesis of Mexican and European styles. The music reflected the spirit of the people and the land in which they lived. At the heart of the music is the button accordion, an instrument embraced by early Tejano musicians. It is still vital to the music today.

If, as George Revill argues, "national music gains cultural authority through properties of sound" that are "actively produced in the material/imaginary networks created by musical performance," then gender and sexuality are critical for analyzing the sounding of a *Tejas* imaginary that has been overly determined by racialized and classed male performing bodies.[72] In these documentaries, heteronormative discourses of gender and sexuality are often signified through a "holy trinity" of conjunto musical forefathers, typically some trio or combination of accordionists including Valerio Longoria, Ramón Ayala, Santiago Jiménez, and Narciso Martínez. So pronounced is the rhetorical discourse of fatherhood and family that the title of this section ("Who's Your Daddy?") is intended to emphasize a patriarchal accordion genealogy, that is, the practice of passing accordion musical training from father to son, uncle to nephew, grandfather to grandson. It is not uncommon to find three generations of accordion players within the same extended family. In Chicano musicology, a cultural-nationalist imaginary of *Tejas* is sounded through heteronormative temporalities of familial reproduction.

By extension, Tejano heteronormative masculinity is further stabilized by the accordion, whose discourses of reproduction, patrilineal musical knowledge, and as a symbol of cultural bearer signify the instrument as a female body. For example, consistent references by musicians and historians alike refer to the accordion as "the keeper of tradition," "the heartbeat of a people," and "the origins of *Tejas*." Embedded in such references is the notion of the accordion as a cultural reproducer of a unified community of "la gente."[73] According to musician Max Martínez, "not only does the accordion give to conjunto music its distinctive sound, it is the solar brilliance around which everything else revolves."[74] The accordion serves as a "medium for the simultaneous expression and construction of conventional notions of masculinity and femininity, and situates performers and audience alike along clearly established gender lines." The accordion is discursively produced as a female body that is fastened—by the strapping on of a heterosexual framework—to a masculinized body that, in turn, has sounded a heteronormative *Tejas* imaginary.

Another key visual production of Tex-Mex conjunto masculinity has been the annual poster contest for the Tejano Conjunto Music Festival. The following are but several examples of more than thirty posters representing the nearly three decades of music festivals held annually. The 1982 poster of the inaugural Tejano Conjunto Music Festival held in San Antonio fortifies a normative all-male musical imaginary from the festival's inception. The poster features what is recognizably the standard Tex-Mex conjunto band ensemble, including drums, bajo sexto, (electric) bass, and the button accordion. In fact, the instruments are prominently featured as an instructive chart. The band is encircled by distinguishable references to the "home" of Tex-Mex conjunto music, including San Antonio's skyline and the state of Texas that sits on top. The 1993 poster features a *cholo* masculinity.[75] *Cholo* has become less a clear marker of gang affiliation or as a synonym for "homeboy" than representative of a unique set of Mexican American cultural codes, including language, style, rhythmic gait, standing poses, and music, including oldies such as "Duke of Earl" and "Angle Baby." *Cholo* masculinity is identifiable in this poster by the staple brimmed hat, the white sleeveless undershirt often referred to as a "wife-beater," and the slightly slanted "cool pose."

It was not until 2002 that the first woman accordionist was featured on a Tejano Conjunto Music Festival poster. Notably, the 2002 Tejano Conjunto Music Festival was unveiled in May, eight months after September 11, 2001. The poster is chock-full of Chicano and American nationalist symbols that merge to form a spectacular illustration of what Caren Kaplan, Norma Alarcón, and Minoo Moallem refer to as the nationalist discourse of nation for woman.[76] A *vela* (candle) of the Virgen de Guadalupe—the utmost symbol of the Mexican nation—is positioned at the right bottom corner. The red and white stripes of the American flag are draped across the back of the image while the young woman accordionist, dressed in tight leather pants and a blouse with starry sequins, squeezes the accordion outward to signifying sound. The accordion itself is covered with the symbols of the multiple nationalist projects—Texan, American, and Chicano—that are ever linked to what we now recognize as the state of Texas and that have always been discursive components of *Tejas* identity formations. The lone star flag (originally the flag of the Republic of Texas), the Statue of Liberty, and the United Farm Workers eagle are grafted onto the accordion. In this poster, the woman accordionist sounds *Tejas* in the festival for the very first time. Yet, I argue that she can only do so, as symbolized by her body's assemblage of multiple nationalist projects, in a moment when the nation is in need of retuning and refastening itself through the reproductive promise of the female body. The female accordionist has rarely been the public performing body of Tex-Mex conjunto music. When she has been, she has had to labor through a century of masculinist discourses that have rendered her female playing body unfit for the discourse of musician, as dissonant in audible archives, and as *curiosa* in Tex-Mex conjunto music.

Just as the accordion has been worked by musicians to produce sound, so too have dominant ideologies of accordion musicianship worked to discipline masculine- and feminine-gendered bodies into their proper place in *Tejas*.

I turn now to Eva Ybarra, the artist who has sonically echoed throughout the soundscape of *Tejas* from the last decades of the twentieth century to the present. Very few Tejana accordionists have fronted their own conjunto or have appeared on recordings. Ybarra and her few contemporaries have labored under the constraints of gendered representational codes. That notwithstanding, Ybarra disrupts heteronormative discourses fixated on protecting women's bodies from the supposed danger that playing the accordion poses to the female body. For example, Ybarra's mother once told her that "women do not have strong-enough backs to play an accordion."[77] The queer coupling of Ybarra's female body coming into contact with the accordion—an instrument whose body is discursively female—looks *curiosa* and resounds as dissonance in *Tejas*.

Ybarra's Body as Queer Discord

In *Tejas*, the accordion produces a musical logic of Tex-Mex conjunto sound to set in motion a heteronormative temporal cadence of unified

Tejano Conjunto Music Festival official poster, 1982.

Tejano Conjunto Music Festival official poster, 1993.

Tejano Conjunto Music Festival official poster, 2002.

belonging. As such, the sounding of *Tejas* is produced by the accordion even as the sound is visually shaped in conjunction with the contours of the male body. Richard Leppert argues that "precisely because musical sound is abstract, intangible, and ethereal—lost as soon as it is gained—the visual experience of its production is crucial to both musicians and audience alike for locating and communicating the place of music and musical sound within society and culture."[78]

Similar to the ways in which we read certain fashion styles as unpleasant to the eye or, say, the color of a room as loud, Ybarra's accordion-playing female body sounds off, discordant, *curiosa,* or queer. Thus, I examine the musical life and accordion musicianship of Eva Ybarra in order to analyze how the musician's gendered body, visual narrations of heteronormative masculinity in posters and video documentaries, and the accordion instrument have co-constitutively produced a sounding of *Tejas.* Moreover, my analysis of Ybarra demonstrates that her feminine-presenting female body has been deemed to be discursively unfit and thereby sonically dissonant within *Tejas.* I argue that her queer discordant presence pierces through a *Tejas* that has been charted through visions, codes, and narrative structures to allow for the possibility of alternative *Tejas* imaginaries that make legible and audible the too loud, too odd, and too weird.

Whereas scholarship addressing audioscapes has effectively established the relationship between sound and racialized subjectivities and new configurations of place among minoritarian cultures, there persists a need to question the too often unexamined constructions of gender and sexuality in studies of musical sound.[79] Moreover, it is critical that such explorations move beyond additive diversity models concerned by and large with increasing the numbers of women musicians in the literature. In other words, merely the inclusion of Ybarra as rare female accordion-playing body does little on its own to disrupt Tex-Mex canonical narratives or the power of the accordion, even while the merging of her body with the accordion produces a visual disruption in the otherwise normative sounding of *Tejas.* The visual of Ybarra's accordion-playing body, set against examples such as Tejano conjunto festival posters, represents what I term a "sonic scene." In other words, a "sonic scene" (where "scene" captures what is "seen") follows the spirit of the expression "a sight to be seen" when describing an unusual phenomenon or object. A "sonic scene" captures this similar kind of rare and odd experience, but in sonic terms such as the color of one's outfit being "too loud." A sonic scene may occur during a live musical performance when your visual attention is drawn to the skills of an incredible guitarist that seem to suppress everything else from being heard, with the appearance of someone displaying working-class-of-color style that clashes with a middle- or upper-class venue, or with the communication mannerisms of someone who uses extreme hand or other bodily gestures when conversing that you seem to "hear" from across the room. With regard to women/queers of color, a sonic scene is a sight that sonically registers as exceeding the limits of normative class, race, and gender parameters of the acceptable, proper, and expected.

According to Martha Mockus, the accordion is both the "polyphonic emblem of cultural authenticity and the struggle for ethnic identity—lost, erased, reformed, and remembered"—as well as a "living organism often compared to parts of the (female) body, and crudely sexualized by those who play it."[80] It is conceivable, then, to imagine the Tex-Mex accordion not merely as a part of the female body, but as the female body

Eva Ybarra plays accordion in the family backyard at age four. Photograph courtesy of Eva Ybarra.

itself. Ybarra's femaleness melds with the feminine-gendered instrument to sound against the heteronormative *Tejas* imaginary. When Ybarra straps the accordion to her chest and squeezes out the first notes, she stages *una curiosidad* that churns out an inharmonious reverberation of Tex-Mex conjunto music.

The rarity of looking at and listening to a female accordionist has always brought me back to the impression its distinct sound leaves on the ear—its trainlike high-pitched bellowed vibrations piercing the air—and how its audible force sets in musical motion representations of gender and sexuality. More precisely, I am compelled to consider how the female body, historiographic discourses, and musical instruments work to produce a sound that is simultaneously audible *and* visual.

While the compatibility between a masculine-gendered body and the accordion solidifies traditional sonic demarcations of *Tejas,* some may argue that the mere vision of a female accordionist does little to disrupt a masculinist soundscape. I have found, through my ethnographic fieldwork and based on my own listening ears, that one cannot fully engage Tex-Mex women accordionists without seeing them. When it comes to Ybarra, she has often said that despite getting invited to music festivals and special events, she is rarely invited to play on recordings like other accordionists.[81] Her female accordion-bearing body demands that I engage the visual symbolics of the sound that she produces.

Throughout the twentieth century, the accordion became the foremost symbol of Texas Mexican cultural production. When the accordion cranks out that distinctive percussive sound, it enables what Sheila Whiteley, Andy Bennett, and Stan Hawkins refer to as the "mapping of the relationship between music, space and place."[82] In turn, the accordion lays sonic claim to a distinct subject formation of Texas Mexican subjects. Accordion sound becomes a sonic compass for movement marked by those bodies that recognize how to keep the beat in a spatial trajectory. The path orchestrated through the accordion sound indeed has a sense of logic—even as the dancing logic of counterclockwise motion is always counterhegemonic to normal clockwise forward progress.

The sounding of *Tejas* brings together dissonant narratives with incompatible bodies of women who play instruments codified as masculine. Queer discordance occurs when Tejanas' bodies come together with the accordion in *Tejas* because Tex-Mex conjunto sound has been overdetermined by constructions of class and race that assume heteronormative masculinity. Such dissonance can recalibrate our listening to inform our understanding of racial, gender, and sexual subjectivities within particular musical sonic imaginaries.[83] Certain instruments have come to represent etiologies of musical genres, cultures, and subjects: for instance, the brass trumpet emblematizes jazz, the electric guitar, rock.[84] The power of such musical instruments and the soundscapes they produce allow us to "hear with our eyes" and "see with our ears."[85]

Born in 1945 and raised in San Antonio in a musically inclined family, Ybarra recalls gravitating to the accordion at age five. In our interviews, she stressed that her accordion training resulted from listening to the radio and memorizing keys while watching others play: she was quick to point out that she did not learn the technique from her father or brothers but rather learned by ear. Ybarra's listening ear is what allows her to access what Roshanak Kheshti theorizes as the "aural imaginary" or contact zone located within the listener's ear.[86] Ybarra's self-apprenticeship represents a rupture to traditional accordion genealogies, a break from what Rosa Linda Fregoso, drawing from Lorena Oropeza, refers to as the heteronormative "metaphoric chain linking family to nation: la familia = la raza = the community = the Chicano nation."[87] Ybarra's apprenticeship often came directly through her engagement with radio: "I grew up pretty much a loner. I listened to the radio and learned music this way and sometimes by watching my brothers play."[88] Ybarra states:

> My brother Pedro played the accordion and I liked it very much. I was always tagging along after them, and sometimes they'd run me off, because there were a lot of men and there weren't any women. But I was there for the accordion atmosphere. That's why I'd follow them, and I'd feel sad because they'd run me off, and I wanted to be watching, listening to the music.[89]

Ybarra considers herself a self-taught accordionist, having learned keys and combinations by watching and listening and practicing on her own.[90] It is worth noting that both Alonzo and Ybarra learned to play by ear rather than through the musical patrilineal knowledge base of many of their contemporaries. Her preference was often to retreat to a space in her house where she could listen to the radio alone, imagining the instrument close to her body and imitating tunes with her fingers. Spanish-language radio was often her primary teacher of song and instrument. She recalled the house being filled with music all the time, even country western music, one of her favorite genres: "There was a radio in the living room and one in one of the bedrooms. If it wasn't the radio it was one of my siblings playing or tuning an instrument."[91] Over the radio Ybarra would hear the popular accordionists of the time, such as Flaco Jiménez, Tony De La Rosa, and others.

Ybarra taught herself by listening and imagining. For example, her brother Pedro would at times go over songs or melodies: "Well, to start with, just by watching, listening, playing. I learned by myself, and later, if I wanted my brother Pedro to help me, he would help me, teach me little runs or different polkas."[92] In describing how she developed her playing skills, Ybarra stresses the difference between learning runs or various parts of songs and learning the craft of playing the instrument:

Eva Ybarra, age five. Photograph courtesy of Eva Ybarra.

"I have to say this too. People, I hear them say a lot that my brother taught me to play. He never *taught* me to play, even though people say that. I watched him and learned, but he never taught me."[93] In fact, Ybarra recalled that her mother sent her to a neighbor down the street for piano lessons in hopes that she would prefer the piano, a more feminine-gender appropriate instrument.[94] Piano lessons did not dissuade Ybarra from going back to the accordion, but they did result, according to Ybarra, in her learning more music theory than most of the Tex-Mex accordionists she has come to know. Juan Tejeda asserts that Ybarra, Paulino Bernal, and Esteban Jordan are distinct accordionists because they have a vast knowledge of music theory and, in particular, when they play the diatonic button accordion, they use the complete chromatic scales available.

When I listen to Ybarra, I can hear sets of trills that remind me of a trumpet, especially in moments when she maintains the resuscitation of a high-pitched note. Although musicologists and scholars I have talked with disagree as to whether there is anything unique about Ybarra's accordion playing, I believe that the ways she merged her listening ear with her piano lessons—claiming that this is where she learned jazz and blues chords and how to play inverted chords—produce the unique echoes of bluesy, jazzy rock riffs in her music that fans often recognize.[95] Ybarra's listening ear taught her the knowledge of playing the accordion that was not passed on to her through a patrilineal genealogy and her few sets of early childhood piano lessons motivated her to stretch for those familiar jazzy and blues rhythms on her accordion. "I'll sometimes slide my hand across the keys very fast," she says, describing how she gets to where she wants to go with assembling rhythm in a song.[96] Small hands are perhaps the most persistent heteronormative discourse reproducing the idea that the female body is not capable of working the accordion:

> My hands are small, but once they're on the accordion, they stretch [Ybarra laughs as she motions with her fingers as if stretching to get to her key], and if I can't reach, I jump to get there.[97]

Recalling the stir created by Alonzo when she entered the music scene in Houston in the mid-twentieth century, there remains an oddness at the sight of Ybarra as a public playing accordionist. Ybarra recalls: "It was always fine for me to play the accordion at home. What was not supported was my interest in performing in public, to make a living playing and recording." During her childhood, Ybarra remembered "feeling funny" about playing the accordion, "like I was doing something wrong." She recalled her grandmother asking Ybarra's mother for permission to rear her granddaughter. Ybarra's grandmother felt she wasn't being raised well as a young girl because she played a man's instrument: "She didn't want me playing the accordion, and I begged my mother not to let me go with her because I knew she'd never let me play my instrument." Eventually, the pressure from such reaction was too much. The gender discourse that naturalized an incompatibility between Ybarra's body and the accordion led her away from the instrument when she was in her teens:

> Me complejé mucho porque [I would stress out because] I would hear people say a lot "That's a man's instrument," so I asked myself, "Should I stop playing the accordion?" This is not an instrument for a lady. So at about age fifteen I stopped playing. I remember my dad saying, "What's wrong with you, Eva, are you sick or something? Why aren't you playing?" And I didn't want to tell him. I was just like, "I don't know, Dad. I just don't want to play anymore." But I couldn't stay away. It's in my blood, and I had to start playing again. By then it was about a year, and I didn't even have an instrument anymore. I think my dad had sold it.

Ybarra recalled that as a youngster she was often picked on because children at her school knew she played the accordion. She is convinced that this teasing kept her from attending public school beyond the seventh grade:

> I remember this one time an older girl started a fight with me in the girl's bathroom. She was saying all kinds of things about me and about playing the accordion. I didn't understand. I told her, I told her, "I haven't done nothing to you." Even with all the instruments in school, I still loved playing the accordion.

It is likely that Ybarra's experience as a young girl who played a "man's instrument" was the impetus for her mother's discouraging her musical aspirations to be a public performer:

> I always wanted to be somebody, to do this for a living, but my mom, she didn't like the idea. She didn't want me to become a public, a famous person. It was OK for me to play, but not play publicly.

Perhaps the most persistent heteronormative discourse common to the histories and personal accounts of women accordionists is the idea that the female body is not fit to work the instrument. Unlike most musical instruments, the button accordion requires extensive upper-body strength. A bellows-driven instrument commonly referred to as a squeeze box, the button accordion requires simultaneous effort from the back, shoulders, arms, chest, and fingers. The chest compresses and expands as the upper body, instead of the lungs, breathes air into the instrument. As such, the operation of the instrument becomes, in effect, taboo for women because of its literal proximity to the breasts and concomitant symbolic impingement upon motherhood and reproduction. This kind of effort literally obscures the breasts in inappropriate ways; it bruises/redefines/bulks up, as it were, the musculature of the upper body in inappropriate ways. The specter of the accordion on Ybarra's female body is odd and ill fit because it disrupts larger sociocultural networks designed to keep female bodies safe and protected. Ybarra's willingness to play the accordion despite such taboos recalls Alonzo's unwillingness to cede to a jealous, threatening husband: both women ignored the taboos by challenging assumptions that women desire to be protected and saved.

Ybarra's accordion-playing body has pushed further my consideration of sound as more than merely its configurations through audibility. Simultaneously, I am hoping to avoid underestimating the body as mere representation, metaphor, or performing subject of sound. Rather, my aim is to be equally attentive to the fact that Ybarra's body literally works the accordion, an instrument that, in turn, works to produce a queerly sounded dissonance within the heteronormative borderlands imaginary. Ybarra introduces a different constitution of sound via the relationship of her body to the instrument. This is key when we acknowledge that listeners and dancers of Tex-Mex conjunto accordion sound represent public ears that hear what they hear but also hear what they see. When Ybarra straps the accordion to her shoulders and chest, she emits *una curiosidad* or a queerly odd sound that reverberates and sparks the audible senses as a "sonic scene."

Eva Ybarra playing at the Tejano Conjunto Music Festival in San Antonio.

Alonzo's and Ybarra's experiences demonstrate that the Tex-Mex accordion sound in borderlands music—the sounding of *Tejas* as a cultural imaginary—cannot be comprehended merely as audible soundings, especially when we consider Chicana/Tejana public performance within a highly masculinized musical sphere. Rather, their public cultural work requires a comprehension of *Tejas* through dissonance that is constituted by the visuals of seemingly incompatible female bodies working an instrument already overworked by reductive historical discourses, as well as the creative mechanisms Tejana accordionists use to outmaneuver normative gender constructions to become accordion musicians. When we consider the accordion as an instrumental medium that has propelled *la onda,* we must also acknowledge discordance within it; Tejana accordionists have fused their female bodies with the accordion that has produced a queerly gendered sonic reverberation in *Tejas, una curiosidad,* a discordant sound filled with untapped memories, labor histories, and pain. Ventura Alonzo has provided us with an analytic for giving legibility and audibility to women musicians who come across as *curiosa.* Eva Ybarra has taught us that the magnificent exertion to create Tex-Mex sound is a highly contested site of racialized gender politics where Tejanas have had to learn to stretch their ears for playing lessons and push their bodies up against discourses and ideologies that have discouraged them from conjoining with the accordion. Ybarra sounds an alternative *Tejas* where the counterclockwise circle is filled with gender-discursive change-ups, complex historical spins, and creatively empowered shuffles that yearn for nonnormative desires. Alonzo and Ybarra have played their accordions and so, now, we might imagine that on any given hot, humid summer night in the borderlands, the first riffs of an accordion sound.

FOUR

Sonido de Las Américas

Crossing South-South Borders with Eva Garza

IN 2007, I ARRIVED in Havana, Cuba, in search of Eva Garza. Following a fragmented archive that included family memories, scrapbooks, scattered discographies I compiled in U.S. and Mexican music registers, and various personal interviews, truth be told I was not very confident about what I might find. Garza's story is not unlike that of the other Chicana singers in this book whose sparse recollections and footnotes I have followed into more makeshift archives, Dairy Queen towns, and living rooms than I can remember. Unlike with Silva, for example, the more places I looked, the more I came across when it came to Eva Garza. I was continually amazed that her story had not circulated more.

I found Garza's elusiveness to be differently shaped, compared to other singers—with various beginnings and ends (including two different origins of birth), a subject in varied "official" music narratives, and partial discographies. As a researcher who prides myself in actively working against the positivist project of "data collection" as truth, I was nonetheless pleased to compile materials about Garza's recording and radio presence in Havana. Her musical career and life trajectory impressed on me that the presence of Tejana/Chicana singers lingers in seemingly contested spaces and temporalities:

> It's my second day in La Habana, staying at the Hotel Victoria in El Vedado. The woman in charge of cleaning my room, Gerlin, asks me what I'm up to and I respond by telling her that I'm doing research on a Mexican American singer named Eva Garza. ¡Ah!

> debes hablar con Carmen (another woman who works at the hotel) ella se acuerda de todos los cantantes de más antes [You should speak with Carmen, she knows all of those singers from the past]. The next day I catch up with Carmen and I ask her if she remembers a singer who may have sung in Cuba in the late 1940s, early 1950s, named Eva Garza. Without hesitation Carmen replies: "¡Ah! Sabor de Engaño" and begins to sing the song in perfect form . . . "sabor de engaño tienen tus ojos . . ."[1]
>
> It's been a few days since I first spoke with Flora Capote, Elba's mom. She's agreed to do an interview with me about popular Mexican singers who came through La Habana in the '40s and '50s and those she followed on the radio. After sharing an encyclopedia of wealth on singers she recalled since her childhood I ask her: "Bueno, el otra día me contaste sobre varios cantantes mexicanos de ese tiempo y quería preguntarte sobre una cantante que se llama Eva Garza . . ." [Well, the other day you mentioned various Mexican singers from that (early childhood) period and I want to follow up by asking about a singer named Eva Garza . . .] Before I could complete the sentence she begins: "Ay sí, cómo no, 'Sabor de Engaño'" [Of course, "Sabor de Engaño"]. I ask: ¿Qué te acuerdas de ella y de la canción? [What do you recall about her and the song?] Like on cue, Flora begins singing, "Sabor de engaño tienen tus ojos cuando me miras."[2]

The various Cubanos I encountered in Havana, including Flora[3] and Carmen, profoundly reminded me that a notion of locating Eva Garza according to points in space and time—about simply looking in the right places and asking the correlated questions—was incapable of deciphering the noncontinguous, nonlinear, temporal geographies of this dissonant diva; rather, hearing Flora and Carmen and countless other Cubanos sing "Sabor de Engaño" (Taste of betrayal) taught me a different methodology for locating Garza in Havana: listening to times past made present. In the spirit of Henri Lefebvre, I learned to listen to Havana "as an audience listens to a symphony."[4] Canonical music narratives work to uphold nationalist imaginaries in a nexus of music, nation, and "the" significant figures in a given genre. What is too often overlooked are inconsequential moments such as fan renditions of "Sabor de Engaño" that exemplify the ways a body recalls and how a song can locate someone like Garza that official or canonical discographies or biographies alone cannot.[5] This is an example of what Pierre Nora distinguishes between memory as "a perpetual actual phenomenon" and history as the always problematic and incomplete representation of the past.

Rather than locating the missing pieces of a unified history, my research in Havana revealed how Garza's cultural production and lived experience must be understood through a different analytic in order to articulate her dissonant Chicana subjectivity. I argue that Garza occupies a "dissonant scale" in borderlands music, as a Chicana singer who dwells in a mingling of variant times and places. As "La Voz de las Américas," for example, Garza cannot be located within a borderlands musical canon that relies on a U.S.–Mexico nationalist geography or a song repertoire that includes non-Mexican-origin music. Analysis of Garza's "subject-in-process," to employ Norma Alarcón's term, requires a nuanced or complexly configured multiple spatial-temporal compass that can register bodily flow and musical migration in other than a linear, unidirectional south-to-north migration of Mexican-descent peoples or one that marks place according to family genealogy.[6]

Music: Scales as Eva Garza: Las Américas

GARZA'S SUBJECTIVITY is everywhere, scattered in multiple places and times—sometimes discrete, sometimes overlapping—and yet she is "nowhere" in terms of Chicano and Tejano musical historiography. A dissonant diva scale locates direction in uneven and fragmented pieces, enabling me to comprehend Garza's gender and sexuality as composed of multiple and fragmented narratives: her familial genealogy that identifies her as a third-generation daughter of Texas; her self-constructed Mexican citizenship as participant in Mexican artistic labor unions; and her representation through the Mexican bolero, as a modern Mexican woman. Eva Garza is not legible within heteronormative/heteromasculinist spatiotemporalities of Chicano nationalist imaginaries. If, as Michael Lansing has asserted, "bodily identities remains tied up in social relations,"[7] then it is understood that any exploration of Garza requires us to consider bodies—her body, the bodies of Carmen and Flora who still sing her songs—as a critical scale to explore in the musical sonic imaginary of the borderlands. The body is, after all, as Neil Smith suggests, the most intimate scale or primary physical site where contestations over identity and difference occur.[8] Processes of spatial formation are relational; thus, Garza's Chicana subjectivity, as traced by a sonic compass along alternative spatiotemporalities, suggests critical interventions for reconfiguring constructions of regional musics and identities such as "Tejana" and their relationship to national geographies of race, gender, and sexuality, or what Gayatri Gopinath suggests as analyzing "the space of the region as a way of decentering and destablilizing dominant nationalist narratives and of foregrounding 'other' narratives that tell an entirely different story of gender, sexuality, and nationalist subjectivity."[9]

In music, a scale is a group of musical notes collected in ascending and descending order that provides material for, or is used to represent, part or all of a musical production, including melody and/or harmony. Various scales have come to represent unique formations such as blues scales and jazz scales. Scales are ordered in pitch or pitch class, with their ordering providing a measure of musical distance or, one could say, space. Gerhard Kubik has argued that some scales carry with them biologically reductive concepts such as "primitive" or as having an "evolutionary" sequence from simple to complex.[10] Despite the uniqueness of a musical scale, what is key—following this theory on musical scale—to my analytic framework are the discourses of coherence, linearity, and normative temporality. My feminist analysis of Eva Garza's gender and sexuality—in relation to the methodologies in canonical musicology that primarily have been concerned with who has been heard and who has created musical transformations in borderlands music—places in conversation the discourse of normative temporality according to musical scale with the discourse of spatiality in geographic scale posed forth by feminist geographers.

According to feminist geographers, scale is the social construction of space, "the embodiment of social relations of empowerment and disempowerment and the arena through which they operate.[11] In other words, scale is a social construction of place that aims to resolve contradiction and contestation. "It is geographic scale [body, home, community, region, nation, for example] that defines the boundaries and bounds the identities around which control is exerted and contested."[12] Scales allow for an analysis of Garza that works in tension with rigid notions of community or nation in dominant notions of Chicano music. Conventional Chicano music narratives are held together by similar discourses of musical and geographic scale such that representations of Chicana/o musical figures must fit the broader temporal logic of citizenship, south-to-north migration between the United States and Mexico, and Tex-Mex as "regional" music. For instance, Chicano musical figures have been easily mapped onto geographic landscapes that coherently fit the normative Chicano subject, within and in relation to the nation-state borders of the United States; thus, citizenship in this musical nation is clear in "Chicano rock and roll" or the "West Coast Eastside sound." By extension, there has been little room to capture the nuances of sexuality and gender as power pertaining to Chicana singers whose lives and work do not follow such normative temporality of musical and geographic scales.[13] Garza's music does not reflect or remain in the hegemonic geographic scale of *comunidad* or Tex-Mex "regional" Chicano music often narrated through patriarchal configurations of family and gender. Nor do her multiple citizenships—Mexican, Tejana, and of the Americas—cohesively fit a musical "home" located by normative Chicano spatial and temporal compasses. In analogous terms, we might say that music is to the geographic construction of scale as Eva Garza is to the Americas.

Listening through the dissonance for Eva Garza requires a conjoined sonic and sensory compass that allows for a methodological inroad to geotemporal processes of racial, national, and gender sexuality formation that are disavowed in dominant narratives of *la onda* as the sonic imaginary of the borderlands, what I refer to as a *transfrontera* musical compass. According to José David Saldívar and Sonia Saldívar-Hull, the notion of *transfrontera* pertains to geopolitical spaces in which Mexican-descent peoples manufacture new social relations, cultural productions, and border contact zones.[14] I extend the geopolitical spaces defined by *transfrontera* to argue for an analytic compass that locates the dissonance of Eva Garza. In my analysis, I have found that musical genre, migration pattern, and ambiguous citizenship narratives represent what Mary Pat Brady refers to as those spatial-temporal moments that disrupt national borders and national imaginaries as fixed in time. Eva Garza sounds a Chicana dissonant diva scale—in musical and geographic discourse—in Chicano borderlands music, that is, a scale that foregrounds mobility and contestation of normative gender boundaries.

In this chapter, the *transfrontera* musical compass is a listening instrument that does not trace histories and citizenship by normative temporal and spatial dimensions.

Garza cultivated a career through nonnormative temporal and spatial musical landscapes—represented by, for example, "good neighbor" radio, *cabaretera* cinematic representations, and passionate boleros—not easily traceable along normative Chicano migration patterns of settlement or geographically bounded notions of Chicano musical citizenship, but rather multisituated sonic circuits and the sensual song forms of bodily and emotional transport. In fact, a *transfrontera* musical compass may locate Garza's musical subjectivity in what Licia Fiol-Matta has referred to as "diva-scapes" or those places of desire, passion, and erotics where we imagine Latina divas to reside.[15]

Garza's singing voice was heartfelt and cavernous; when she sang she transferred emotions and tales from her core, grasping for deep exhalations of sentiment. Especially in rancheras and boleros, one can note her tendency to weep impassioned feelings into a song. Her voice tapped into an inner core filled with experiences, memories, departures, and returns. To be sure, Garza's voice was not exceptional or supreme, in the manner required of musicians and singers who become the epicenters of music canons. Rather than a voice or musical career that assures us by solidifying place and time, Garza's Chicana musical figure requires the listener, the historian, the witness, to be led and to trust in alternative notions of *comunidad* and "home" as imagined in flight and through transport across spatial temporalities. A *transfrontera* musical compass is a Chicana feminist methodology that requires us to trust in the magnetic force of singers like Garza who lead us through a borderlands imaginary where place is sonic and where sensualities mark time.

Sonic Compass

Garza was born on the west side of San Antonio in 1917, to parents from Roma and Austin, Texas, during a significant economic shift for Mexicans in Texas. According to David Montejano, the agrarian development of the early decades of the twentieth century marked the end of the class structure of Mexican ranch settlements.[16] "By 1920, the Texas Mexican people had generally been reduced, except in a few border counties, to the status of landless and dependent wage laborers."[17] San Antonio was also a central site for migration by Mexicans in the postrevolutionary era. It was a hub of economic and cultural activity ranging from train transportation of cattle to the North to a key cultural stop for Spanish-language entertainment. Thus, public venues including theaters and radio produced an active public cultural scene for both Spanish- and non-Spanish-speaking populations. The sonic compass, then, does not merely review Garza's participation in the significant era of early radio and recording as a way to confirm that she was "historically present." Rather, her early days in radio and recording exemplify the ways that "local" radio is simultaneously international and that early "local" recordings were not completely de-linked from nationalist recording companies' production of race and nation, nor their potential circulation beyond the local places where they were recorded. The sonic compass leading us through Garza's early life exemplifies the fact that spatial constructions are not givens but rather are always in process.

Garza's introduction to music occurred by her entering popular singing contests sponsored by local radio stations. She graduated from Lanier High School in 1934 and, despite excelling in sports—especially basketball and softball—she became interested in music. While working at a local theater in San Antonio, she would have opportunities to see popular female singers such as Rosita Fernández, who was often accompanied by her sister Berta ("Las Dinámicas Estrellas").[18] Singing contests for radio stations sponsored by local companies, including beer companies such as Montalvo and Pearl, were extremely popular in the 1930s and 1940s. Singing contests for radio exposure were almost always the launching pad for the careers of early artists such as Rosita Fernández, Rita Vidaurri, and others. In fact, these contests led to wide exposure and thus often radio and performance contracts.

At nearly eighteen, Garza had her first taste of what her talents might earn her when she won five hundred dollars for her rendition of "I'm in the Mood for Love," earning second place at a singing contest held at the Texas Theatre. Garza's desire to enter singing contests required a bit of strategy on her part because her father didn't approve. "My father worked at a barbershop nearby and so he told my mama that it was okay because he would keep an eye on her from there . . . still my mama didn't like it because she was very young."[19] Eva's sister Tina

Eva Garza, senior basketball photograph from Lanier High School, San Antonio. Courtesy of Tina Moore.

recalled that although she performed since her late teens in places like the Teatro Nacional located downtown, her parents were quite strict because there were very few public places seen as "acceptable" for young women to perform in.

As a result of this exposure, she was invited to work a few shows a week at KABC, operated by Manuel Lozano, one of the few brokered Spanish-language radio broadcasts in San Antonio, located on top of the Texas Theatre. Garza worked for KABC radio between 1932 and 1934 and also appeared on one of the most popular San Antonio radio shows, *La hora Anáhuac*. Although radio was a "local" broadcast, Garza's voice produced a Chicana representation through rhythms and lyrics irreducible to a geographic notion of local scale, including popular boleros and Cuban sons made popular through XEW radio broadcasts from Mexico City. It was not long after her initial appearances on San Antonio radio that nineteen-year-old Garza recorded her first songs, including rumbas, sons, and boleros, for Bluebird Records at the Texas Hotel in San Antonio. Songs such as "La Jaibera" (The crab catcher), "Caliente" (Hot), "Cachita," and "Cosquillas" (Tickling) were her first recordings at the Texas Hotel on October 23, 1936.

Early radio appearances and recording experiences of Chicanas/os raise interesting issues regarding the intersection of sound, technology, and what was considered "ethnic" music in early decades of the twentieth century. During the 1930s and 1940s, radio stations situated just across the U.S.–Mexico border, as well as radio XEW in Mexico City, formed a Spanish-language musical soundscape before the emergence of full-time Spanish-language radio. Moreover, "the Southwest was a favorite destination for major record labels in the 1920s and 1930s as they sought to fill the growing national demand for Spanish-language recordings; this interest in marketing Southwest regional ethnic music produced some of the earliest recordings by Mexican Americans in Texas."[20] In fact, according to Manuel Peña, there was a solid buyer–seller relationship between American recording companies and Spanish-language "ethnic" song recordings during the 1920s and 1930s that were favorite acquisitions by *mexicanos:* "Mexican immigrant communities in South Texas had an average of 118 records for every 100 people in the 1930s," as well as approximately twenty phonographs per every hundred immigrants.[21]

The emergence of increased Spanish-language broadcasting and sales of radios and phonographs among *mexicanos* in the region produced a musical sonic imaginary that Garza and other singers of this era were actively creating. By the 1920s, Spanish-language recordings became economically lucrative for record labels such as Victor, Columbia, Okeh, Brunswick, Vocalion, and American Record Company, which would send sound engineers around the Southwest to record. Recording sessions were impromptu spaces, mostly in hotel rooms, churches, banquet halls, and radio stations.[22] Makeshift recording spaces often presented logistical predicaments owing to the bulkiness of hauling sound equipment as well as negotiating racial segregation in Texas that prohibited *mexicanos* and African Americans from entering hotels and other commercial venues.[23] Churches were not hospitable when it came to certain musical themes and lyrics.[24]

According to Colin Bray and Jack Litchfield, Bluebird Records labeled B-2200 to B-4999 referenced an international series that existed between 1934 and 1942.[25] The Bluebird recording label was a sublabel of the RCA Victor Records company that was established in 1932 to address the economic impact of the Depression on record sales that hit an all-time low in 1933. Bluebird Records was considered one of the best-selling "cheap" or "budget" labels during the 1930s and 1940s that was introduced in order to compete with records labels under the American Record Corporation. "Bluebird recorded in Dallas and San Antonio almost once a year from 1929 to 1941."[26] Another record label that Garza recorded with was Decca, which also in 1932 began selling records for thirty-five cents, compared to the standard seventy-five cents sales price. Decca purchased Brunswick Records in 1932 and by 1934 launched recording deals in the U.S. record market.

The genres and composers of these early recordings—Luis Arcaráz, Rafael Hernández, and others—illuminate the "Latin" musical sphere of the time.[27] The acquisition of Spanish-language recordings throughout the Southwest by East Coast record companies such as Bluebird and Vocalion, among others, included South Texas regional music such corridos as well as Mexican and Caribbean music such as boleros, sons, and rumbas. Thus, such early Spanish-language recordings by "Tejano" singers prompt a consideration of the ways in which multiple spatial scales coexist to produce varied configurations of Chicana gender and sexuality. Take, for example, Garza's recording of "Cachita" in San Antonio:

Cachita
(Rafael Hernández)

O-ye-me Ca-chi-ta
Ten-go u-na rum-bi-ta
Pa' que tú la bailes co-mo bai-lo yo,
Mu-cha-cha bo-ni-ta
Mi lin-da Ca-chi-ta
La rum-ba ca-lien-te es me-jor que el fox

Listen to me my Cachita
I have a little rumba
So that you can dance to it like I do,

Pretty girl
My beautiful Cachita
The hot rumba is better (to dance to) than the fox (trot)

Garza's subjectivity in singing the lyrics to "Cachita" in San Antonio cannot be reduced to a regional Tejana borderlands scale. Garza's musical product is constituted by varied racial discourses, including those that subordinated *mexicanas,* as well as exoticized "Latin" rumba-moving bodies. My sonic compass locates her subjectivity as composed through multiple scales: a locally situated body and voice, a music-product recording distributed and heard in both private and public spaces, a music whose Afro-Caribbean beat is located outside a borderlands often imagined along a south-to-north U.S.–Mexico axis.

By the 1940s, the sonic compass draws our attention to the initial stages of the Second World War when radio technology would come together with the nationalist project of the "good neighbor" programs to engender a sonic production of "woman as nation," and Eva Garza became "la voz de las Américas" (the voice of the Americas).[28]

By mid-1940, military advances of Nazi Germany triggered deep concerns about security for the United States. Advances in military strength by opposing countries and a looming economic downturn for Latin American countries also generated anxiety about the potential fertile ground for a political, economic, and cultural invasion by Germany and its allies. On August 16, 1940, the Office for Coordination of Commercial and Cultural Relations (renamed the Office of the Coordinator of Inter-American Affairs [OCIAA] in 1941) was created by order of the Council of National Defense.[29]

A separate entity established by order of the Council of National Defense, the OCIAA's operation was funded by a combined force of nonpaid volunteer labor and private business. Its mission was to assist in coordination and implementation of policies and programs that carried out the ideological framework of Roosevelt's Good Neighbor Policy. Its objective was to stabilize Latin America by curtailing any tide of Nazi economic and ideological incursions by both deepening U.S. influence in Latin American countries and cultivating the flow of cultural and economic trade along a north–south axis.[30] "The US Office of Inter-American Affairs, under Forney A. Rankin, sponsored the diffusion of NBC and

CBS's training and programming activities in the Americas." Together with the vision of William S. Paley, "La Cadena de las Américas" (Network of the Americas) was born in 1941 and would stretch voices and programs across the Latin American continent.[31]

The objective of Columbia radio's "good neighbor show"[32] was to "reflect faithfully the cultures of both North and South America [by assembling] special staff and talent in its New York studios who were recognized throughout the other Americas as authentic and friendly voices."[33] CBS reaped a publicity bonanza from La Cadena de las Américas, including features in *Fortune* magazine, that at once solidified the imperialist project of Roosevelt's "good neighbor" policies while reifying the power relations between the United States and Latin America. To be sure, the "hemisphere network was profitable patriotism that launched hope for development of commercial advertising and exchange of goods."[34] Initially, the network was composed of sixty-four stations in eighteen countries.[35]

Broadcasting on La Cadena stations was a multimedia operation consisting of rebroadcast shortwave transmissions of CBS programs as well as brief fifteen-minute newscasts sent via radiotelephone.[36] The program featured notables ranging from Edward G. Robinson to Rita Hayworth.[37] According to *Time* magazine,

> The main importance of the new network is that it opens a vast field of listeners to US broadcasts. From Mexicali to Cape Horn there are roughly about three and half million receiving sets, only half of which can pick up short wave. In the past, listeners to the short-wave sets received all the attention of Axis and US broadcasts. Now CBS programs reach South American listeners regularly over their own stations (La Cadena has 46 long-wave, 30 short-wave outlets in Latin America).[38]

During its initial period, La Cadena sent seven hours of Latin-tailored programs south on a daily basis. By the end of 1945 it was composed of 114 affiliated stations in twenty Latin American nations featuring "a growing parade of the best entertainment in the hemisphere."[39] Director Edmund Chester stated that he wanted to "send news programs that present an accurate picture of the day's developments, cultural shows that present the people of the US as romantics with souls, not as cogs in the national industrial machine."[40]

Every nationalist project needs a "sweetheart." The term is a common reference of endearment for women, young and old, most often within a community or familial unit. It is rarely used in reference to a man, the exception being young boys. Thus, "sweetheart" is gendered feminine. The term is commonly used to give special designation to the "woman" or "girl" counterparts of a male community, such as the sweetheart of a sports team, fraternity, or even a musical genre as in "the international sweethearts of rhythm," the first racially integrated all-women's jazz band.[41]The term has also been used as a cultural reference to endearing female figures of "nation." Thomas Edison is said to have dedicated his signature in actress Mary Pickford's autograph book to "America's sweetheart." Famed Argentinian-born actress Libertad Lamarque, who starred in numerous Mexican films, is often referred to with the nickname "sweetheart of the Americas." Whatever the historical context of war, "sweetheart" signifies hegemonic heteronormative discourses of "nation," including family, patriarchy, and home. Through the audio broadcast of music and voice on one of the most pivotal media strategies of Roosevelt's "good neighbor" program, Garza would become a "sweetheart of the Americas," a reference that became popular by American GIs who sent her fan mail. Tina Moore recalled her sister Eva Garza appearing in a New York newspaper feature where Garza is seen surrounded by her fan mail.[42]

In early 1942, Garza was spotted by a CBS radio talent scout singing at a local New York show. Similar to her experience with the Sally Rand dance revue, Garza was chosen because she sang "Latin" songs and because of her local following on New York radio and in nightclubs. Garza was fair-skinned and English-speaking and thus represented a nonthreatening race representation that was easily transportable in public marketing of the radio program.[43] As another example of the multiple scales Garza's subjectivity occupied—within this nationalist sonic project—she was racially staged to the broadcasting public as a "Mexican señorita" while she was to be the earliest, and, according to my records, the only U.S. Latina ever to appear on CBS radio's *Viva America* program (on La Cadena de las Américas).[44] *Viva America* aired Thursdays at 11:30 p.m. on WABC-Columbia.

In 1943, Garza was featured in a *New York Times* article titled "Among Those at the Microphone." The caption beneath her photo reads:

"This will introduce you to Eva Garza, Mexican songstress and one of the featured performers on WABC-Columbia's new Latin-American musical, 'Viva America' (Thursdays at 11:30 P.M.)."[45] As such, the transport of Garza's voice and U.S. mass media representation established *Viva America* as a powerful racial-spatial-gender project for listening ears across the Americas. During 1944 through 1946, *Viva America* aired weekly during evening time slots. Days and times varied from Thursdays at 11:30 p.m. to Saturdays at 8:30 p.m.[46] Moreover, programs were recorded for rebroadcast by the Office of War Information and the Armed Forces Radio Service.

RADIO THE NEW YORK TIMES, SUNDAY, JANUARY 23, 1944.

Among Those at the Microphone:

This will introduce you to Eva Garza, Mexican songstress and one of the featured performers on WABC-Columbia's new Latin-American musical, "Viva America" (Thursdays at 11:30 P. M.).

Tomorrow, at 7 P. M. on WJZ-Blue, brings Horace Heidt, the master, and his orchestra in a new thirty-minute program of music. No pot of gold this time.

Eva Garza featured in the *New York Times* with other performers on *Viva America,* January 23, 1944.

Garza on CBS radio, New York City. Photograph courtesy of Tina Moore.

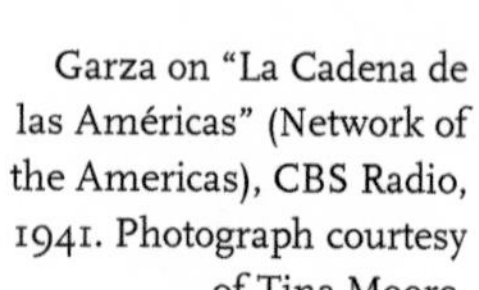

Garza on "La Cadena de las Américas" (Network of the Americas), CBS Radio, 1941. Photograph courtesy of Tina Moore.

During these critical years of U.S. "good neighbor" policy, Garza's voice would cross nation-state boundaries, militarized boundaries of short-wave radio channels for soldiers, and enter the radio boxes of local listeners in San Antonio. From roughly 1942 to 1945, her voice was launched across the Americas by a broadcasting force that was at once powerful in its magnificent broadcasting reach and problematic as a vast cultural-imperialist force. With a combined broadcast force through long-wave and short-wave stations as well as rebroadcasts of voices and music, entertainers such as Garza were assured a "tremendous audience, especially true because in almost every case the station connected with this new network is the most popular in the territory it covers."[47]

Technologies of sound recording and radio broadcast Eva Garza's voice across multiple musical scales, and therefore both reflected and inflected local, regional, and national constructions of race, gender, and sexuality. In canonical narratives of Tejano/Chicano borderlands music, notions of "home" and "locality" are key. These geopolitical constructs mark the origins of singers and follow their musical contributions along a heteronormative temporality—for example, versions of the musical icon

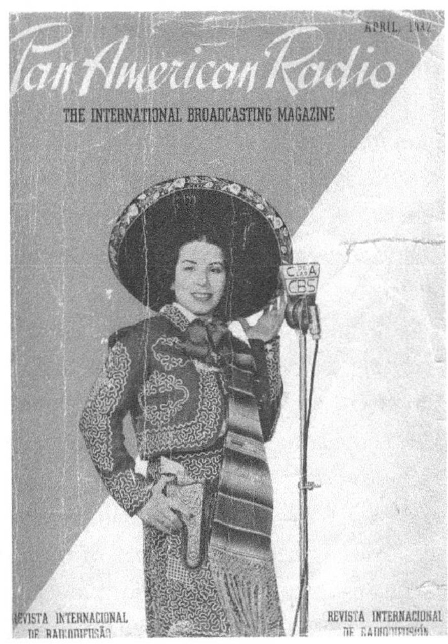

Garza on the cover of *Pan American Radio: The International Broadcasting Magazine,* April 1942. Photograph courtesy of Tina Moore.

figure's "success story" that often play out in music exhibits that feature a local singer who becomes a national icon: along the way, there is an origins community of family and home that marks their ultimately musical legacy. This type of heteronormative temporality is inadequate in accounting for Garza, whose gender and sexuality are constructed by simultaneous temporal and spatial scales—audio broadcasts that locate her as far away as Brazil and recordings that give songs multiple beginnings—each representing racial and nationalist registers.

Sensuality Compass

A *TRANSFRONTERA* MUSICAL COMPASS locates Garza's subjectivity as dissonant to heteronormative borderlands music constructed as "home" and denoted by belonging, identity, and security.[48] Garza's body is a moving body, literally through travel, and figuratively through the passion and emotions in songs. Her body, as discursively inscribed by social-structural systems of sexuality, gender, race, and citizenship, is not distinguished within the imagined "home" of borderlands music. Garza's nonnormative temporal and spatial musical movements require attention to places, in flight and in sight, where she is imagined. Sensuality offers such a compass for reimagining and assessing Garza in a way that does not compel her representation back into a bounded sonic imaginary of the borderlands. Garza's bodily movements—from the early days of performing with Sally Rand's erotic dance troupe to song repertoire such as rumba, guaracha, and bolero—construct Chicana/Tejana gender and sexuality along nonnormative temporal and spatial structures of "home."

Garza's earliest opportunity for remunerative labor came when she was selected as a dancer to join Sally Rand's dance troupe. Although Garza's sister Tina could not recall which show's name among several Rand sponsored during those years, Garza most likely danced with the "Star-Studded Review." Sally Rand and her "fan dance" fame are worthy of review in this chapter because she was Garza's earliest public performing "role model" and because of the early impressions Rand possibly made on Garza's gender performativity, especially her body's connection to the stage.[49] Garza's mobility beyond the region of South Texas literally and figuratively occurs through the libidinous dance space produced by the Sally Rand dance troupe.

Sally Rand was born Harriet Helen Beck in the Ozark Mountains of Missouri. She is associated with placing sexuality on the public stage. Interested in dance from an early age, she ran away to join a carnival as a teenager.[50] In the mid-1930s, she took advantage of the "world stage," performing at various World's fairs and expositions. Rand introduced the "fan dance" at the 1933 Chicago World's Fair after a successful Chicago run in 1932 with the "Sweethearts on Parade." After performing at the 1936 San Diego Exposition, she continued on to Texas, where she was credited with having "brought nudity to Dallas."[51] Rand performed a nude show at the Frontier Centennial in Ft. Worth in 1935, part of the Texas Centennial State Fair celebrations that occurred in 1936, the one hundredth anniversary of Texas independence. Such appearances and her staple "fan dance" would garner Rand a lifelong iconic status crediting her with bringing public sensuality to the mainstream stage.

Although Mexican Americans, like other racial-ethnic groups, existed in racially segregated communities in Texas, Spanish-language media covered a variety of "American" or mainstream English-language cultural events. Thus, Garza's sister Tina Moore recalled that Rand was a very popular and fascinating performer to the Spanish-speaking public of South Texas. She was so popular that, for example, in 1937 she appeared in the regional coverage section of *La Prensa (Diario Popular Independiente),* San Antonio's daily Spanish-language newspaper. The feature, titled "La Bella Artista Sally Rand Cambia Sus Globos y Abanicos," was a six-image spread detailing the numerous outfits and costumes Rand wore for various social events.[52]

It was big news in San Antonio when Garza was selected to go on tour with the dance troupe during the summer months of 1937. Moore recalled that Rand and a male producer friend of hers came to their family home in order to seek permission from Garza's parents to allow her to travel with the dance group. According to Moore, Garza's parents agreed because Rand emphasized that there were always mothers of some of the young women who traveled as chaperones. Garza toured with Sally Rand's dance company for about a year:

> She [Sally Rand] just hired her, just contracted her to go on tour with her . . . so that is how she started or actually that's what made her career . . . she was singing here [San Antonio], people used to see her, I mean she used to sing on the radio and they used to see her at the [Teatro] Nacional . . . she was very young.[53]

Garza was very well known locally by 1937, having recorded and appeared in numerous radio shows. According to Moore, Rand was searching for someone to join her dance troupe who had "Latin looks." Notable local singers such as Rosita Fernández and Coquita Wilson tried out but Garza's strong voice won her the "Latin" spot in the show. Fernández and Wilson were local notables as well, but much more aligned with Mexican musical tunes. Garza's racialized gender was not represented musically through standard Mexican songs that were common among other *mexicano* singers such as *canción ranchera*. For the audition, Garza sang "La Jaibera," a rumba that she had previously recorded, composed by Mario Suárez, and "El Manisero" (The peanut vendor), another popular rumba that first gained notoriety when recorded by Rita Montaner in 1927–28 for Columbia Records.[54] Rand's choice for a "Latin" singer arguably distinguished Mexican tunes from "Latin" tunes. I contend that part of this distinction on Rand's part—given her background and interest in erotic dance—was the way certain "Latin" music such as rumbas and guarachas propelled sensuality and eroticism. Alicia Arrizón asserts that "while sexuality is characterized by sex, sexual activity and sexual orientation, to be sensual is to be aware of and to explore feelings and sensations of beauty, luxury, joy, and pleasure."[55] Following Arrizón's assertion, I contend that some of Garza's musical repertoire, especially boleros, rumbas, and guarachas, produced public performance of sensuality. A sensual compass locates Garza's bodily moves as a Chicana subject-in-process,[56] through song as well as her bodily gestures, across multiple spaces and times.

After her performance and travel experience with the Sally Rand troupe, Garza began her own touring ensemble that included herself and friends Rolando Morales, María Luisa Álvarez, and Dolores Martínez. As a soloist and with the group, Garza toured some of the most famous nightspots along the Southwest and the West Coast, enjoying the freedom to travel as well as to earn her own wages. It was on one of these tours, while doing a radio show in Juárez, that she met Felipe "El

Charro" Gil (of the famed Charro Gil y Sus Corporales). Felipe was the brother of Alfredo Gil, who would later form the famous Mexican Trío Los Panchos. Felipe and brother Alfredo, "el güero"(the blond), formed the group Dueto Bojalil Gil and later the Hermanos Martínez Gil. These groups were the first seeds of what was to become the legendary Trío Los Panchos composed of Alfredo, Chucho Navarro, and Puerto Rican singer Hernando Avilés. The Gil family and Garza would forever be merged in music and cinema when Trío Los Panchos arrived on the Mexican public stage in 1948.[57]

Garza and Gil married in 1939. Much to Gil's dissatisfaction, Garza would keep her last name. Neither Gil nor many of the promoters Garza came across thought it was appropriate that she travel solo as a married woman, and so eventually Gil would reduce his time a musician and devote most of his efforts to managing her career.[58] After they married,

Eva Garza (out front on left at arrow penned by sister Tina Moore) performing with Sally Rand at Majestic Theatre in San Antonio, circa 1937. Photograph courtesy of Tina Moore.

Early publicity photo of Charro Gil and Eva Garza, early 1940s. Photograph courtesy of Tina Moore.

Gil and Garza settled in New York, where she recorded her first songs for Columbia Records. It was around this time that sister Tina Moore recalls that Garza "went international," physically departing from the local and regional contexts of South Texas and the East Coast.

During the 1940s, Eva performed consistently throughout the major bolero music markets, sometimes singing with Alfredo Gil and sometimes as a soloist with a varied music ensemble. Eva joined some of the biggest lineups for XEW radio. It was quite common to be in radio show lineups with the likes of Pedro Infante and Pedro Vargas. Garza would go from radio to singing at nightclubs. Garza's sister Tina recalled: "I lived with her on and off for about twelve years in Mexico City . . . she was one of the most popular singing stars in 1950 to 1953."[59] Garza's voice churned out some of the most popular songs of the era composed by Agustín Lara, Gonzalo Curiel, and Joaquín Pardavé, among others.[60]

Garza's performance circuit took her from New York to Mexico City to Havana, Cuba, and eventually to numerous other cities including Buenos Aires, Argentina, and Bogotá, Colombia.

According to Gilles Deleuze and Félix Guattari, rhizomes offer an alternative to the vertical root/tree structure of dichotomous arborescent thinking.[61] By extension, a notion of musical "rhyzome" (rhythmic rhizome) acknowledges horizontal connections within social relationships—in this case, of music and varied citizenships that exist along a nonvertical migratory pattern. Eva Garza's musical practices represent a rhythmic rhizome that recognizes migration flows of Chicana and Chicano cultural production against the standard sociological south-to-north vertical flow from Mexico to the United States, but follows her Chicana/Tejana bolero singing "body" along horizontal bodily and musical moves across Mexico and the Caribbean.[62] Following the work of feminist geographers such as Doreen Massey, Katherine McKittrick, and Linda Peake, such movements often perform important political labors.[63] First, they trouble the seemingly stable boundaries of dominant raced and gendered spatial orderings such as "nation" or "region"—material and metaphoric strategies of masculinist, heteropatriarchal management that function to constrain physical and cultural mobility of women of color. Second, they reimagine and thus "respatialize" relations of gender, race, and place in ways that open up new ways of knowing, imagining, and being.

As I mentioned in my chapter on Chelo Silva, the bolero is a product of numerous cultural contact zones between the United States, Cuba, Mexico, and other parts of Latin America; one of the bolero's most significant sites was Mexico City, where it was transformed and urbanized by composers such as Agustín Lara. Critical to this transformation was the explicitness of sexuality, especially evident given the venues in which Lara found allegories for songs—the bordellos and brothels of Mexico City. In turn, Garza's travels would take her from San Antonio to the metaphoric city of sin, capturing the spirit of Adela Pineda Franco's descriptions of themes in Lara's Mexican boleros.[64] And yet, even the city of sin required proper legal documentation. According to her son Felipe and her sister Tina, in order for Garza to work in some of the most established clubs in Mexico City and to broker the most lucrative contract deals for recording and appearances on radio, she had to join a labor union representing Mexican singers and performers.[65] Motivated to join a labor union as well as by advice from her husband, Alfred "El Charro" Gil—that being a U.S. citizen would not give her as much singing credibility as identifying as Mexican—Garza would become identified as having been born in Villa Frontera in Coahuila, Mexico. Garza cultivated an illegitimate citizenship of the Mexican nation.[66]

Around 1946, she made her initial visit to Cuba, living in Havana for months at a time while performing in various capacities for a span of six to seven years.[67] Manuel Villar similarly recalls the strength of the Cuban peso—equivalent to the U.S. dollar—during the 1940s and the motivation many singers had for traveling to perform and record in Havana: "En el caso de las mexicanas, por ejemplo, si venían, cuando regresaban a su país el cambio les favorecía ostensiblemente" (In the case of Mexican performers, for example, if they came, when they returned to their country the exchange rate would favor their earnings greatly).[68] According to Helio Orovio,

> Amado Trinidad que tenía mucho dinero, la llevó a RHC Cadena Azul, que fue inaugurada en 1940. Después, Laureano Suárez tenía la costumbre de que cuando los artistas pegaban en la RHC Cadena Azul él les ofrecía más dinero y se los llevaba para su emisora Radio Cadena Suaritos. Así hizo con Eva Garza y en 1947 ella era una de las grandes figuras, una de las más grandes cancioneros de esta emisora radial.[69]

> Amado Trinidad, who had a lot of money, took her to radio station RHC Cadena Azul, which was inaugurated in 1940. Laureano Suárez then took her over to his station Radio Cadena Suaritos because he had this habit of noting artists who were popular and then influencing them to come over to his station because he could offer them more money. That's what he did with Eva Garza and in 1947 she was one of the big figures, biggest singers on this radio station.

Garza's initial arrival in Cuba was framed by the great popularity of Mexican trios and boleros that, between 1948 and 1959, were among the most acclaimed musical styles to circulate in Cuba.[70] Orovio stated further that Garza continued traveling to Cuba during the early 1950s because during that time Mexican artists, and those from other places including Puerto Rico and Argentina, traveled back and forth constantly, thereby creating a great economic exchange that offered many possibilities to earn money as a singer.[71] Although Garza performed there for many years, she never lived permanently in Cuba. She was among the many artists who traveled and performed in Cuba from the mid-1940s to the mid-1950s, as is evident from the list of notables mentioned in Rita Montaner's biography: "En nuestra capital se presentan Esperanza Iris, Mercedes Caraza, las hermanas Águila, Pedro Vargas, Eva Garza y Felipe Gil, de México: Bobby Capó, Mapy y Fernando Cortés, de Puerto Rico; Olinda Bozán, Amanda Ledesma y las compañías de Paulina Singerman y de Gloria Guzmán-Juan Carlos Thorny, de Argentina."[72] The following passage, with regard to the relationship between sensuality, spatiality, and temporality in guaracha and bolero music, is informative; the passage captures assertions by Neil Smith that the body is a geography that allows us to understand the visceral materiality of broader scales of spatiotemporal formations:[73]

> Opposites that harmonize their differences are the bolero and the guaracha . . . Curved pronouncement of the baroque, theory and practice of the baroque—that is the guaracha. Restless by definition, elusive when persecuted like the will-of-the-wisp, incisions quick to turn around, erotic accumulations that disappear while they take on a form, that is the guaracha. Lineal combination that contains its own classicism and puts it into practice, that is the bolero. Still, by definition, it can be danced within the eternity of a floor tile, with a synchronic tension that beautifies it, erotic, accumulations concretized by suspended fragilities: that is the bolero. The guaracha is the vibrating hunt. The bolero is the feast of the hunter and hunted. The guaracha opens our bodies, it authorizes displacement; through diligent wiggling, it exhibits the most desirable parts, the sections to be wet, the straits to be pulped. The bolero encloses the body, prohibits displacement, reduces rotations to the intent of a life-giving death. In the guaracha, joys are extroverted, passions fly from one side to another, pleasure and love become alelujas. In the bolero, joys are confined, the bodies are smoothed yet aroused, pleasure and love become aleluyas.[74]

Orovio recalled that Garza sang a variety of popular songs of the time, including boleros and guarachas, and that she is closely connected to Cuban nationalist narratives of guaracha music and one of the most notable Cuban composers of guaracha, Humberto Jauma:

> La entrada de Humberto en el mundo musical fue a través de Agustín Lara, el poeta-músico y la cantante Eva Garza. Yo jugaba a la pelota e iba a México de vez en cuando. Cuando estaba en Cuidad México, pues yo tocaba bastante bien el bajo, me recuerdo que tuvimos que acompañar a Eva Garza. Ella era muy linda, pero muy desentonada. Y siempre teníamos que estarle haciendo señas para que "entrara." Juama recuerda cómo Eva quería cantar una guaracha y le pidió que hiciera un número. ¡Imagínese! a mí que jamás en mi vida me había dado por ser compositor. Día tras día, Eva me preguntaba: ¿Ya hiciste el número? Se volvió una sanguijuela y no me quedó más remedio que hacer la guaracha. La composición la vio Agustín Lara, que dirigía la orquesta y le dijo a Humberto: Tú eres compositor, y deberías dedicarte más a hacer canciones.[75]

> Humberto came into the music business by way of the musician/ poet Agustín Lara and the singer Eva Garza. I played baseball and traveled to Mexico every so often. When I was in Mexico City—well, I played the bass pretty well—I remember we had to accompany Eva Garza. She was very pretty but sang way out of tune, and we always had to signal her to come in on cue. Juama remembers how Eva wanted to sing a guaracha and asked him to come up with a number. Imagine that! Me! Being a composer had never once occurred to me. Day after day, Eva would ask, Did you write that number? She nagged and bugged me until I finally had to write the guaracha. Agustín Lara, the bandleader, saw the finished piece and told Humberto: You are a composer, and you should dedícate more time to writing music.

Eventually, Jauma would compose numerous hit songs—sung by artists including Vicentico Valdés and Monna Bell, among others—including "Sólo por rencor," "Hay algo en ti," "Estás como mango," and "No te quedes mirando." Cuban musicology of guaracha music thus represents Garza's body as a centripetal site for Cuban guarachas.

According to scholars, the Afro-Cuban rhythmic form of guarachas is generally characterized by lyrics of popular diction, masculine and phallocentric perspectives, burlesque, satirical and parodic tones "from marginalized positions" that I argue represent a platform for those explorations and negotiations over joy, beauty, and pleasure that can be registered as sensual.[76] Moreover, Aparicio reminds us that key constructions of gender are produced in such music. She notes that a naturalized gender distinction is often referenced between guarachas and bolero musical texts, "a naturalized dichotomy between the genre of the guaracha as a nonfemale text and the bolero as the quintessential expression of sentimentality and thus femaleness."[77] As such, Garza's guarachas literally and discursively move Chicana subjectivity along a temporal-spatial path that does not follow the common vertical south–north, Mexico–U.S., immigrant–citizen discourse that has worked to solidify a Chicano borderlands sonic imaginary. In 1948, Garza recorded one of her biggest guaracha hits, "Saquito al bate" (Saquito at the bat) for Columbia Records. The song's protagonist was one of Cuba's most famed guitarists, Nico Saquito (given name Antonio Fernández), who composed many popular guarachas.[78]

Garza appeared on various Cuban media. According to José Reyes Fortín, Garza made numerous recordings including for Panart Cubano, which was founded in 1944 and during the 1940s was considered to be one of the most powerful recording companies in Latin America.[79] Fortín explained that radio and television stations in Cuba would take advantage of contracting famous singers recognized throughout Latin America to appear on Cuban media. Garza appeared on programs such as *La fiesta con Bacardí* sponsored by Radio CMQ, a daily program from 10 to 10:30 p.m., during the first years of 1950s. Cuban actor Rolando Ochoa hosted the program, which was aired live and was taped. According to Fortín, the common practice was to contract singers for the entire week, so it is understandable that singers who appeared weeks at a time became familiar to their listening public. Accompanying orchestras included those of Gonzalo Roig, Adolfo Guzmán, and Enrique González Mantici, who was also director of the orchestra for CMQ radio, founded in March 1948 by Goar Mestre.

Garza's popularity soared in Mexico and Cuba after she recorded "Celosa" (Jealous) and "Sabor de Engaño" (Taste of betrayal). In fact, they were on the record that launched Columbia Records's recording activities in Mexico. "Sabor de Engaño," written by noted Cuban composer Mario Álvarez, was among Garza's earliest gold records and it is the song, guided by a *transfrontera* musical compass, that still locates her in the prerevolutionary Cuban imaginary. Garza's other gold record songs during this time included "Celosa," "Sin Motivo" (Without motive), "Frío en el alma" (Cold in the soul), and "La Última Noche" (The last night), written by songwriters including Lara, Gonzalo Curiel, and Joaquín Pardavé. During the mid-1940s through the 1950s, Garza's voice circulated in Cuba and other parts of Latin America via the Seeco record label, considered the premier label in Cuba at the time. Helio Orovio and Manuel Villar stressed that Garza's recordings on Seeco are key because Seeco songs conferred a prestigious reputation on the singer and were among the songs in highest demand by the public. According to Josh Kun, Sidney Siegel began the Seeco record label in East Harlem, "a label he dedicated to 'the finest in Latin-American recordings.' Seeco built consumer bases in New York and in Cuba and Puerto Rico (at times boasting that seventy-five percent of its sales were on the islands)."[80]

Garza also appeared regularly on television and performed in clubs such as the famed Tropicana and the Teatro Americano. Garza mainly performed in Havana, but a flyer indicates that she did perform on the north coast of Oriente Province in the town of Puerto Padre, for Unión Radio, a Havana station that had a national reach. Most likely, Unión

UNION RADIO Y CMKY
Presentan todas las noches a las 7.30
El Concierto "COMPETIDORA GADITANA" con los destacados artistas internacionales de fama mundial:
EVA GARZA
"LA NOVIA DE LA CANCION"
El Charro GIL: "La Voz Jarocha del Cancionero Mejicano"
LOS CANCIONEROS DEL NORTE Y LA ORQUESTA COSMOPOLITA
EXTRA..! SENSACIONAL..! EL JUEVES 26
PRESENTACION PERSONAL DE EVA GARZA Y EL CHARRO GIL
en los estudios de la CMKY y en el Teatro Rívoli, en DOS Tandas.
No pierda la oportunidad de ver y admirar, por primera vez en esta ciudad, a tan destacados artistas, ídolos del Continente.
Y muy pronto en el Programa Competidora Gaditana EL TRIO MORENO

Flyer announcing CMKY radio show with Eva Garza.

Radio and CMKY collaborated for this nightly showcase held at the Teatro Rívoli.[81]

Garza also sang on one of the more popular television musical programs in Havana, *Duelo de Pianos,* with notable singers and composers such as Agustín Lara and Consuelo Velázquez. In fact, Garza recorded an entire album composed of Lara's compositions, *Eva Garza Intrepreta a Agustín Lara.* The back cover reads:

> MUSART Records is honored to present this soloist internationally known as "La voz más bella de América" [The most beautiful voice in America]. There is something about Eva Garza that allows us to evoke yesteryear; her interpretations are smooth and are desired by many of the vocalists following behind her. Eva Garza has made history for Latin American song today with her profound heartfelt impact. This album of her interpretations represents the best testimony to Agustín Lara's songs.[82]

Garza appeared on Havana's Radio Cadena Suaritos and on RHC Cadena Azul, where she was often accompanied by famed Cuban pianist and composer Isolina Carillo. Even today in Havana, Garza's music is featured on shows like *Discoteca de Ayer* (Yesterday's music) on Radio Progresso every Sunday from 8 to 10 a.m. and on *Memorias* (Memories) on Radio Rebelde, also on Sundays. Radio producer and Cuban musicologist Manuel Villar described the show as featuring a variety of artists and their most famous renditions in the spirit of "best of" that (re)introduces key details about the singer's life and the song featured. Such radio programs represent a configuration of temporality and spatiality where Garza is situated. Not only is Garza—as are other featured artists—recalled through the yesterday of her recorded songs. Seventy-eight rpm recordings are rare soundings of Garza's past because much archived material of taped television and radio programs has been lost or destroyed since the postrevolutionary period in Cuba. I asked Villar: "Los programas de la radio esos como [Radio programs such as] *Jueves de Partagás, Cabaret Cabaret, Regalia,* ¿esos se guardan [are those saved somewhere]?" Villar: "No hay nada de eso" (There is nothing left of this). As Flora and Carmen reminded me early on, what does in fact locate Garza's presence today is not institutional archives but registers of *sabor* and sensuality in the singing of her boleros, such as "Sabor de Engaño."[83]

On the day before I departed Havana I came across Manuel Villar, now in his late eighties, sitting in the lobby waiting for me. I had not expected to see him again and was pleasantly surprised; he said that he had returned to bring me a gift to take with me. He handed me an old reel of audiotape wrapped in a makeshift cardboard cover that had some of Garza's songs listed, written in ink by hand. Villar had transferred copies of the 78 rpm records he had of Garza, the ones he plays on his radio show. He wanted to make sure I had them, just in case I was missing any of her music. I looked at his list and did indeed have other versions of these recordings, yet those included on the reel could not be considered the same songs I had. The recordings that Villar took such care to record for me were the actual records that he and other radio programs have been playing of Garza in Havana for more than half a century. The audio reel contains so much time. I kept it near me the entire trip back to the West Coast. I could only imagine the sounds on that audio reel, filled with skips and scratches, and the grooves carved through, play after play. When I returned home I anxiously tried to find someone with equipment and expertise to transfer the songs into a digital music file or any manner that would allow me to listen to them even once. The audio reel, I was told countless times, was of a type of audio technology that cannot be played or copied by any of the contemporary audio equipment those I sought assistance from had. The reel is incapable of crossing temporalities of technology. Garza's voice remains suspended in Havana's reel time; the recordings played over and over on Sunday mornings in Havana remain dissonant to ears on borderlands time, a sensuality that resides in a unique Cuban spatial temporality.

The bolero soundscape was arguably conceived as one of the most transnational musics in Latin America during the first half of the twentieth century and was constituted by cabaret clubs, radio broadcasts from border stations in the U.S. Southwest, XEW in Mexico City, and CMQ, RHC Cadena Azul and Radio Cadena Suaritos in Havana, along with recordings, jukeboxes, and the *cabaretera* genre of Mexican cinema.

In 1953, the union between Garza and Felipe "El Charro" Gil came to an end. The divorce left her with two young children to raise on her own and with the help of her sister Tina. According to Tina, Gil became increasingly controlling and domineering as Garza became more successful and Garza could no longer negotiate both career and marriage.

Durante la serie *Duelo de pianos.*
Arriba izquierda: Vicente acompaña a José Antonio Méndez y a Amparo Montes.
Arriba derecha: Alejandro Algara, Eva Garza, Agustín Lara, Vicente Garrido y Consuelo Velázquez
Abajo: Carmela Rey y Los Cuatro Soles, con Garrido al piano.

Newspaper clipping of the popular television musical program *Duelo de Pianos* in Havana. Eva Garza is pictured in upper right corner between Algara and Lara. Photograph courtesy of author.

Tina filled in as manager and sometimes as caregiver for the children when Garza traveled: "Well, I was her manager and she not only had the movies, but she had the nightclub too at that time, El Patio . . . the movies, theater, and radio station was three things . . . that's the nightlife . . . it was always rush rush rush."[84] Garza established a level of independence that was less common for Chicanas. This economic stability was something she was not willing to give up.

From 1949 to 1958, Garza appeared in more than a dozen Mexican motion pictures, including *Amor Vendido* (1950), *Arrabalera* (1950), *Cárcel de mujeres* (1951), *Mujeres sin mañana* (1951), *Paco el elegante* (1951), *Acapulco* (1951), *Mujeres que trabajan* (1952), and *Pistolas de Oro* (1957). In *Si fuera una cualquiera* (If I were just anyone, 1949), she is cast to play the character Eva in a film playing the role of a two-woman drug-dealing team. In *Amor Vendido* (Love for sale), Garza sings during one of the musical intermissions with artists such as Toña La Negra.[85] In *Arrabalera* (1950), she performs with El Trío Martino along with other singers who make an appearance, including José Alfredo Jiménez, Chucho Navarro, and Fernando Fernández. Garza also appeared in *Cárcel de mujeres* (Women's prison), starring Katy Jurado, where she again appeared singing in a club. In *Mujeres sin mañana* (Women without tomorrow, 1951), starring Leticia Palma and Carmen Montejo, Garza appeared with Los Churumbeles.

In 1951, in *Paco el elegante* (Paco, the elegant one), Garza is the featured singer during three musical interludes. That same year, she appeared singing with Luis Arcaráz and his orquesta in *Acapulco,* directed by Emilio Fernández and marketed as "la primer comedia moderna" (the first modern comedy). In 1952, Garza would draw on her dancing experience with Sally Rand when she appeared as a dancer in *Mujeres que trabajan* (Women who work). In 1957, she appears with the trio Hermanos Reyes in *Pistolas de Oro.* In one of her last movies, she appears in the 1958 *Bolero Inmortal.* Garza plays Lucha Medina, a "washed-up" bolero singer whose sexual appeal has passed and who is replaced by a younger singer. Divorced and alone, Lucha sees no dignified way to end her career, so, in dramatic bolero style, she decides to take her own life.

The 1940s and 1950s were the decades of the *cabaretera* in Mexican cinema, described as a genre that incorporates aspects of Mexico's urban melodrama with popular music such as the Cuban danzón, rumba, and bolero. The cabaret club scene was a major social milieu of the bolero. Lament, sadness, and betrayal would be the new keywords for both musical and cultural life in these narratives. Movies brought the bolero to life by signifying the gender and sexuality ambivalence of emerging subjects in the modern Mexican nation.[86] Gender and sexuality were constructed through extended temporalities of emotions and sensuality. According to Sergio de la Mora, *cabaretera* melodramas of the 1940s and

1950s—narratives that centered on "fallen women," protagonists who ranged from jail inmate, to prostitute, to divorcée, to extramarital lover, and tragic club dancer—were almost always plagued by love gone bad.[87]

Ana López refers to these performances by singers, in *cabaretera* movies, such as Garza as "narrative stoppages" that do not stand outside of the film narrative but are an extension of the narrative itself, via the song lyrics or gestures of the singers that reflected the emotional tone.[88] Moreover, the movie audience was not merely a movie viewer but, because these narrative stoppages collapsed spatial distance, the audience could be transplanted to the movie's social framework in which the film performance was happening. The club audience in the film became one with the audience watching the movie in the theater. Music performances thus relocated movie watchers into the spatial-temporal zone of the film narrative. Tina Moore reminded me that it was through the magic of cinema that Garza could return across *la frontera* to their hometown of San Antonio through her appearance as a Mexican actress in Mexican movies that would screen in Spanish-language movie theaters throughout the Southwest, including San Antonio's Teatro Alameda.[89] If, as Ana López argues, that "social fantasy" was produced by such roles, representations, and musical performances filled with sultry gestures, bodily breakdowns of tragic love gone bad, and unconventional notions of romance, then by extension a *transfrontera* musical compass locates yet another spatial-temporal sonic-sensual zone in which Garza's sexuality and gender are represented.

Sabor: Reimagining the Borderlands

Feminist queer scholarship by Frances Aparicio, José Quiroga, and Vanessa Knights has convincingly argued that the bolero song tradition represents a powerful music stage for the public performance of the ugly sides of love.[90] It is arguably the most influential style of song that informs a discourse of excessive desire and explicit sexual politics in Latino music. I contend that this is partly owing to the ways the bolero facilitates the production of "space" and "time" at the scale of the body. In bolero song, time can be endless, represented by the notion of pain and loss and through the performative extensions of vocals. Therefore, Mexican women composers and singers of the bolero have emphasized the incredibly powerful space that the bolero represented, especially during the early decades of the twentieth century.[91] Writing and interpreting boleros fostered transgressive modes of social and sexual agency. According to Knights, the bolero still creates, through listening to recordings or singing aloud, "a fluid space for diverse subjectivities to be expressed, thus 'queering' the normative heteropatriarchal constructions of gender and sexuality." The manipulation of time and space in bolero song lyrics and performance make possible the remapping of boundaries between bodies and discourses of identities and communities.

Sabor de Engaño (Taste of Betrayal)
Columbia Records, 1948 (bolero)

Sabor de engaño
tienen tus ojos
cuando me miras

Sabor de engaño
siento en tus labios
cuando me besas

no eres sincero
cuando me dices
que aún me quieres
si en tus palabras
se nota el filo
de la traición

Es imposible
seguir finjiendo
de esta manera

yo te agradezco
con todo el alma
tu noble empeño

y te prometo
sentirme fuerte
cuando me digas
que no me amas
que es para otra, tu corazón

A taste of betrayal
I sense in your eyes
when you look at me

A taste of betrayal
I feel on your lips
when you kiss me

you're not sincere
when you tell me
that you still love me
if in your words
I sense the edge
of your betrayal

It's impossible
to continue pretending
this way

I thank you
with all of my soul
for your noble effort

and I promise
I'll stay strong
when you tell me
that you don't love me
that your heart belongs to another

In "Sabor de Engaño," the woman character has keen sensory perception for being able to taste a lover's betrayal, marking a common characteristic of boleros, where, as Knights has argued, there is an inversion of power, in which women are the subjects who initiate confrontation to expose the lover's wrongdoing rather than maintaining a normative passive femininity and merely turning a blind eye. The woman in this narrative is straightforward in engaging the betraying lover and does not offer forgiveness, but rather insists on separation and termination of their union. By extension, boleros offered women listeners narratives in which women are the subjects initiating breakups, divorces, and terminations of relationships. Likewise here, the woman character seems so capable of adjusting to ridding herself of her betraying lover that she sarcastically thanks him for his "noble efforts" at pretending to love her and promises to stay strong, yet requires that, in the end, her lover have the nerve to speak what her own perceptive senses know to be true. This end to the song exemplifies well what Knights points to as ways boleros centralized the motif of separation for women to voice their desire for an alternative, "independent path in life in which the emphasis is on mobility and freedom of movement clearly subverting the gendered binary divisions of masculine activity and feminine passivity."[92]

For Garza, bolero music and its circuits of travel made possible a literal self-displacement from her familial geographic origins. The most striking example of Garza's self-displacement of her birth and musical "home" is her death in 1966. Having traveled from a residence in Buenos Aires to Arizona, where she was to begin a series of singing engagements, she unexpectedly passed away in Phoenix. Rather than returning her body to be buried in her birthplace of San Antonio, she had given her son Felipe specific instructions that her final "home" was to be in Mexico City, among the star-studded cast of the Panteón Jardín, the Mexican cemetery of musical and cinema stars.[93] In the end, Garza was still not locatable, having exceeded the normative spatial scale of the "local" or "home" of *la onda*. Following the trajectory of her multi-spatial-temporal career, she had profoundly configured her own end in time in her own self-proclaimed spatial representation of "home."

As I traveled throughout Havana, my mentioning of Eva Garza jolted people's recollections of her, almost always prompting them to sing "Sabor de Engaño." The material archives could not locate what the sonic sensations of bodies did. Hearing Cubans sing "Sabor de Engaño" urged me to listen and validate the bodily senses as another spatial-temporal modality where Garza is located, for her subjectivity is scattered across various scales, ranging from the imaginary to the embodied. If we can comprehend that music has the capacity to tap the various senses of our bodily being, then we should consider the bolero song form as a *sabor* (taste) of Garza's representation that lingers inharmoniously within Chicano canonical music narratives the privilege "great man" music tales or region and locality as tropes of authenticity. Music moved Garza's body even as her body moved music across the Americas, and still moves the bodies of *cubanas* and *cubanos* whose mobility is marked by unique spatial temporalities.

In the multiple research sites I have visited, Garza is ever-present, yet too out of place to fit a normative temporality of Mexican wife or of the Chicano homeland of *el norte*. Iris Zavala suggests that the bolero foregrounds a dramatic narrative in which "desire is never fulfilled, always remaining as absence, never actualized into sexual or erotic pleasure."[94] Like desire, Garza's gendered subjectivity has been an absence, never actualized among the heteronormative musical narratives of Chicano borderlands imaginaries.

The breaks in linearity—Garza's travels across geopolitical borders, cinematic images that carry her presence in another time and place—establish a dissonance with heteronormative constructions of certain nationalist imaginaries. Garza is what I refer to as a *mejicana*—produced in relationship to competing nationalist constructions of Tejano, Chicano, and Mexican—having birth origins in Tejano South Texas, rearticulated through the imperialist subjectivity of American "good neighbor" radio, and dissonant within the normative spatial-temporal limits of *la onda*.

As Mary Pat Brady observes: "If the production of space is a highly social process, then it is a process that has an effect on the formation of subjectivity, identity, sociality, and physicality in myriad ways. Taking the performativity of space seriously also means understanding that categories such as gender, race, and sexuality are not only discursively constructed but spatially enacted and created as well."[95] Brady goes on to argue that gender, sexuality, and race are spatially enacted and created, emerging "through the production and sedimentation of space."[96]

A *transfrontera* musical compass finds direction in uneven and fragmented pieces enabling me to comprehend Garza's musical figure as composed of multiple and fragmented narratives: her familial genealogy that identifies her as a third-generation daughter of Texas; her self-constructed Mexican citizenship fabricated through a false tale; and her representation as a *bolerista,* as a modern Mexican woman. Her musical map is produced through a disjointed temporal flow of geography, song, and media. Garza's representation is at once compliant with Mexican nationalist music narratives as it is dissonant to normative Chicano constructions of family, locality-as-authenticity, and citizenship. Garza is most legible in the sexual imaginary of the bolero, a subjectivity-in-process, discursively and literally produced through bolero song, cinematic character roles, and the musical venues that afforded her access to independent wage earnings rather than a reliance on marriage.[97] Metaphorically, Garza registers as a Chicana who is too loud, too late, and too out of place for normative legibility.

Eva Garza's Chicana representation is composed of spatial-temporal movements constituted by class and race/ethnic epistemologies that enabled a self-cultivated career and a life always interconnected with the cultural labor she learned from a very young age. Tracing Garza's musical trajectory has meant trusting a *transfrontera* musical compass to lead me through multiply situated soundscapes and disconnected narratives across the Americas. As such, Garza's music and lived experiences represent a resounding Chicana musical force that requires us to taste lingering deceit and to move our bodies to recalibrated sonic limits of alternative borderlands imaginaries.

FIVE

Giving Us That Brown Soul

Selena's Departures and Arrivals

IN THE LATE 1960S TO EARLY 1970S, the term "brown power" came to designate a Chicano slogan that represented assertive claims ranging from empowerment, to ethnic pride, to calls for addressing economic, political, and social inequality of Chicanos/Mexican Americans in the United States.[1] Some uses of "brown power" also represented a prideful claim to being brown-skinned people.[2] This claim to brownness was also making an appearance in Chicano/Tejano music. In his 1972 hit song "Las Nubes" (The clouds), Little Joe Hernández calls out, "¡Órale raza! Gimme some of that bro-o-wn soooul!"[3] More than just a hugely popular Tex-Mex polka, "Las Nubes," a typical dancing polka tune with the Tejano orquesta style, was part of Little Joe y La Familia's album *Para La Gente* and became the anthem for the United Farm Workers of America struggle for labor and civil rights.[4] Born in 1940 in Temple, Texas, a small town between Austin and Dallas, Hernández's subjectivity was shaped within the social and cultural contexts of the African American section of Temple. He learned blues and jazz from his black neighbors and *música mejicana* and country western through the radio playing at home.[5] Consistently influenced by the African American music of his youth, Little Joe would eventually be nicknamed the "king of brown sound."[6]

Las Nubes
(Wally Almendarez)

[instrumental lead horns]
¡Ay!
Oooooh ay ya ya ya
¡Órale raza! Gimme some of that brown soul!
Ya todo se me acabó, no me puedo resistir
si voy a seguir sufriendo, mejor quisiera morir,
yo voy vagando en el mundo, sin saber adónde ir
Los años que van pasando, no me canso de esperar
y a veces que estoy cantando mejor quisiera llorar
¿para qué seguir sufriendo? si nada puedo lograr

Las nubes que van pasando, se paran a lloviznar
parece que se sostienen cuando a mí me oyen cantar
cuando a mí me oyen cantar, se paran a lloviznar
parece que alegran mi alma con su agua que traen del mar.

[musical interlude]
Ay, yeah!
[clapping to the beat]

¡Arrímense! ¡Arrímense! (Little Joe)
Ahh ahh ahh ahh ahh
[clap]
¡Ay! [Grito]
Give it to me now! ¡Ayyyy!

The city surrounds him closely
The crowd seems to pass him by
His heart is still back home in Texas
Beneath his beloved sky
And life treats him so unkindly
He wishes that he would die
His life has become so empty
It's now just a broken sigh
The one filled with pride and courage
But all that has now subsided
It's now just a hallow storm drop
A drift in an endless sky

A drift in an endless sky
So lost to the world is he
A man who has been forgotten
Alone with his misery

Alone with his misery
He dreams of his childhood days
Though god made his children different
We're different in so many ways

Ugh! Give it to me give it to me give it to me now. Ugh!
[musical instrumentation completes song]

Portia K. Maultsby argues that "the call for Black Power evolved into a political movement to which Black people assigned cultural meanings labeled 'soul.' The term 'soul' became a signifier for 'blackness.'"[7] I argue that Little Joe's call for Chicanos to extend their "brown soul" is a similar signification for brownness that emerged within the Chicano cultural-nationalist discourses of the late 1960s and early 1970s. Moreover, Little Joe's Chicano "brown soul" reflected the musical merging of African American soul that had crystallized in the late 1960s, R & B, and funk with Tex-Mex orquesta music.[8] Little Joe's "brown soul"—as a Tex-Mex musical sounding of African American soul music and the cultural discourse of "brown power"—produced a musical *movimiento* masculinity.[9] Although musical influences from African American–derived R & B, soul, and funk had been central to various music within "la onda Chicana"—or Tex-Mex orquesta style of the 1960s–70s—Little Joe's "brown soul" became the icon of Chicano/Tejano musical sounding of "brown soul."[10] The merging of rock, soul, and funk is not unique to the musical soundscape of what the music industry refers to as "Latin soul"—although, generally speaking, "Latin soul" has been more a reflection of West Coast Chicano and East Coast Latino (mainly Caribbean) artists of this period. Contextualized within historical cross-cultural influences, "Latin soul" encompasses the integration of boogaloo and/or funk and R & B within Latin music. Unlike scholarship that has analyzed the African-derived underpinnings of (mostly) Caribbean-based music like salsa, the African diasporic sound has remained highly underacknowledged in Chicano music scholarship. What has evolved, I contend, is a musical configuration always already racialized in relationship to Anglo/

white-dominant masculinity and constricted by relations of resistance and subordination to Anglo racism.

"Las Nubes" would become the musical anthem of the United Farm Workers of America and, more broadly, a Tex-Mex musical sounding of Chicano nationalism. In "Las Nubes," the clouds represent a vision of freedom and escape—the dream of a better day. The song's first section is in Spanish: it begins with the pain, suffering, and endless misery of a life of never-ending subordination and exploitation. In the original 1972 version of "Las Nubes" quoted above, the second section switches to English, a linguistic code prevalent among Chicanos who reside in the United States. In Texas, in particular, the use by *mexicanos* of Spanish and English recalls the racism as experienced by those elders who were violently punished for speaking Spanish in public, especially as youth in schools, as well as the school segregation they experienced.

In the English-language lyrics, "Las Nubes" moves away from the first-person recounting of a nameless, albeit miserable, Spanish-speaking subject to a third-person English narration of a masculine Tejano subject who has suffered an equally miserable existence. The lyrics follow a heteronormative temporality of childhood memories and adult misery. As a normative iconic masculine *movimiento* figure, this lost Tejano subject fulfills the characteristics of dominant Chicano masculinity constituted by working-class (migrant) labor, race, gender, and assumed heterosexuality.

There are a number of theorizations of what can be referred to as "brown studies." José Esteban Muñoz's analysis of "feeling brown" considers the ways "minoritarian affect is always, no matter what its register, partially illegible in relations to the normative affect performed by normative citizen subjects."[11] Ralph Rodriguez's study of Chicana/o detective fiction references "brownness" to describe Chicana/o detectives in his book *Brown Gumshoes: Detective Fiction and the Search for Chican/o Identity*.[12] Curtis Marez has theorized "brown style" to describe a Chicano working-class sensibility as a "critical discourse that simultaneously counters Anglo repressions, opposes the white-supremacist assumptions of highbrow taste, and affirms the qualities of Chicano difference."[13] My analysis of Selena's music and performance intends to contribute to such studies of "brownness" by thinking critically about Chicano music's "brown soul." I began with Little Joe's call for Chicanos' "brown soul" because this Tex-Mex orquesta moment and Little Joe himself have come to represent the historical, political, and gender parameters of "brown soul" in Chicano music. It is my assertion that Little Joe's 1972 "Las Nubes" articulated a "brown soul" that emerged within the Chicano or brown power discourses of race, nation, and culture; thus, Little Joe's "brown soul" registers brownness as marked by cultural-nationalist constructions of gender, masculinity, and class. I argue that at the end of the twentieth century there would be another configuration of Chicano/Tejano "brown soul," the dissonant strands of brown soul echoed in the African diasporic rhythms of cumbia and moved by the brown body of Selena.

Making Face, Making Brown Soul

On March 31, 1995, Latinos around the United States and abroad mourned the death of Selena Quintanilla Pérez, one of the most significant Mexican American singers of the end of the twentieth century. Without a doubt, Selena was a significant presence within Tejano music, an industry that boomed in the early 1980s. Her success, however, did not prefigure the extent to which she had moved Tejano music, nor the degree to which her fans would keep moving to her music well after her death. While Tejano music is debatably defined along a range of musical, symbolic, and stylistic characteristics, it is most commonly recognized as yet another transformation of Tex-Mex conjunto and orquesta music and more easily identified by singers and bands associated with it.[14] What is unique about Selena's era of Tejano music is that it became commercially institutionalized as a recording genre, through music awards and a boom in radio stations that were specifically named "Tejano." In the 1980s and 1990s, groups like Selena, Emilio Navaira, Grupo Mazz, and La Mafia came to define Tejano music—despite their unique sounds—to Tex-Mex music fans as well as to broader music publics.

English-language mainstream media in the United States, even in heavily Latino cities, were especially caught off guard trying to make sense of Selena and her death. On the fifth anniversary of *People en Español,* editor Angelo Figueroa recalled that the impact of Selena's death, in effect, launched the periodical by bringing to the fore the very public grief of a largely untapped Spanish-speaking readership:

> Marzo de 1995. Un editor de *People* en Nueva York recibe una llamada telefónica desde Texas avisándole que han asesinado a Selena. "¿Quién es Selena?", pregunta el editor. Cuando cuelga, una latina, empleada de limpieza, le dice quién era y, además, le explica que su muerte es un evento noticioso muy, pero muy grande. Las estrellas se alinean y por primera vez en la historia de la revista se decide imprimar el número de esa semana con dos portadas: una para distribuirla en Texas, en la cual se destaca a Selena; y otra para el resto del país, con el elenco de la popular serie televisiva *Friends*. El número con Selena se agota inmediatamente. Le sigue rápidamente un número especial como tributo que vende casi un millón de ejemplares. De repente, todo el mundo en Time Inc., la empresa dueña de *People* y otras 32 revistas, supo quién era Selena. Un año después nace *People en Español,* un descendiente directo de una joven cantante texana, cuyo legado superará por mucho el tiempo que vivió entre nosotros.[15]

> March 1995. An editor of *People* in New York receives a phone call from Texas informing him that Selena has been murdered. "Who is Selena?" asks the editor. When he hangs up a Latina cleaning employee informs him who Selena is, and also explains that her death is a newsworthy event that is very, very significant. The stars are aligned, and for the first time in the history of the publication a decision is made to create two different issues for the same week: one for distribution in Texas has Selena on its front cover, the other to be distributed throughout the rest of the country has a front cover of the cast of the television series *Friends*. The issue with Selena on it sells out immediately. This is followed by a special tribute issue that sells nearly a million copies. All of a sudden the entire Time Inc. company, owners of *People* and 32 other publications, knew who Selena was. One year later, *People en Español* is born, a direct descendant of this young singer from Texas, whose legacy will exist long past her short time among us.

The mainstream press introduced Selena to the American public via coverage of her tragic death. The large outpouring of grief in Chicago, Los Angeles, Miami, New York, and all across Texas represented a voice calling forth the attention of the American public to the loss felt within the Latina/o community, yet the mainstream media were challenged from the outset to define "Tejano music" to a mass audience.

From Univision's *Primer Impacto* to VH-1's *Behind the Music,* media coverage of Selena's life and music was channeled through the hegemonic narrative of a Latina "crossover" artist's American "success story." The mass media's labeling of Selena as a "crossover" singer transformed her from an accomplished figure within Latina/o and especially Mexican American communities to a marginalized young woman on the brink of success who did not live to see the release of her all-important English-language album.

When Selena's life came to a tragic end in 1995, she was arguably the most visible public face of Mexican-descent peoples in the United States. Throughout her musical career, Selena "gave good face," in the queer sense to project confidence, sensuality, and sexual agency. This allowed her to carve out a powerful place and notoriety not many Tejana singers before her had attained—despite the entrenched institutional sexism of the Tejano music industry. Sexist discourse pertaining to Selena's music persists, even after her passing, with claims of her continued presence in popular culture often reduced to her sexual attractiveness or to capitalist ventures. Lost in such debates has been a careful consideration of the cultural and racial contexts of Selena's music and performative aesthetic—in particular her meaningfulness to those subjects whose "face(s)" upset hegemonic notions of racialized femininity and sexuality. For immigrant *mexicanas,* brown-skinned Chicanas, working-class Latinas, and queers, Selena offered specific performative and sonic instructions for "making face."

In the introduction to her 1990 feminist of color anthology, *Making Face, Making Soul/Haciendo Caras: Creative and Critical Perspectives by Women of Color,* Gloria Anzaldúa defines the act of *haciendo caras*—piercing looks and facial distortions—as a politically subversive gesture: "'Face' is the surface of the body that is the most noticeably inscribed by social structures, marked with instructions on how to be *mujer, macho,* working-class, Chicana."[16] In Anzaldúa's rendering, women and queers of color are experts at "making face." Ever aware of the structural inscriptions "carved and tattooed with the sharper needles of experience" that publicly display their bodies as counter to racial, sexual, and gender normativity, women and queers of color have learned to devise material and sensorial techniques to "make face." "Making face" is a literal and figurative "telling off"—that may range from a subtle eye gesture to adorning the body with an excessive material aesthetic—directed at social structures that continually attempt to relegate nonnormative subjects to varying degrees of disenfranchisement.

Below, I analyze the making of Selena's "face"—the structural inscriptions of racialized sexuality she represented within Chicano/Tejano public cultures—and the making of Selena's brown soul. I maintain that the various ways in which Selena "makes face" illuminate race, class, gender, and sexuality as structural systems of power; Selena's negotiations with these systems of power enabled a unique configuration of her brown soul as cultivated through African diasporic sound and a queer-of-color sensibility. Selena's brown soul prompts an alternative borderlands imaginary remapping Chicana/o musical subjectivity through African diasporic sounds of cumbia. Hearing Selena's brown soul demands reckoning with a larger network of racialization; as listeners, we must tweak our ears to listen through the dissonance, to the ways in which blackness is too often subsumed or additive within the borderlands imaginary of hegemonic Chicano music. Selana's brown soul represents a sonic imaginary that highlights a differently configured and racialized Chicano musical topography. My analysis of Selena's brown soul not only brings to the fore the black echoes in her music and performance but also illuminates how Selena's dissonant brown soul destabilizes heteronormative masculinity in Chicano music.

My rendering of brown soul acknowledges the effacing of African diaporic musical sound in Selena's signature cumbias and English-language ballads that were dismissed merely as "crossover." While there are numerous examples of Chicano music and dance studies that analyze Chicano musics' melding and fusion with, for example, jazz, hip-hop, and rhythm and blues, there has not been a similar commitment to analyzing Selena's cumbias; her African diasporic sound has remained dissonant.[17] Selena's musical sound, I contend, is centered on African diasporic sonic production in a range of ways that propose a broader challenge to the relationship between Chicano music, Tejano music, and transnational African diasporic musical sound. Moreover, this musical dissonance is also part of what I describe as Selena's brown soul, a queer sonic formation, counterhegemonic to white, middle-class feminine aesthetics, U.S.-based assimilationist language trajectories, and south-to-north migration patterns of Mexican-descent peoples.

Feminist analyses of Selena by Frances Aparicio and Deborah Paredez are examples of much needed discussion of Selena's music that prioritizes the influence of African American music and dance.[18] I extend this analysis here and assert that Selena's iconic representation of Chicano music, best exemplified by her nickname "la reina Tejana" (Tex-Mex queen), or sometimes "la reina de la música Tejana" (the queen of Tejano music), has been narrativized to fit a heteronormative narrative of Chicana gender and sexuality that is devoid of blackness and queerness.[19] Thus, I analyze Selena's brown soul through a "queer-of-color" model that is concerned with "challenging ideologies of discreteness [and] attempts to disturb the idea that racial and national [and sexual] formations are obviously disconnected."[20]

My queer-of-color analysis considers Selena's musical sound of brown soul—mostly recognized through cumbias and heartfelt English-language ballads—as part of the circulation of African diasporic sound. Selena's Tex-Mex cumbias as connected to African diasporic sound prompt us to reconsider a north-to-south movement of Mexican music that troubles hegemonic discourses of Chicano/*mexicano* "crossover." Moroever, this reconsideration of Selena's cumbias is never disconnected from queer gender and sexuality influences that complicate nationalist notions of "Chicana" subjectivity.

Selena's unique sound moved through the influences of African American– and Latino-derived disco, rhythm and blues, soul, hip-hop, and freestyle. Much of this influence is evidenced in her now signature renderings of the cumbia, an Afro-Colombian genre popularized within Mexican music. Selena's brown soul counters the ominous assimilationist narratives of her representation and music as "crossover." If we can entertain any notion of crossover in Selena's music, surely it should not be one charted along an unproblematized south-to-north axis that emblematizes, among other assimilationist processes, the moment when Spanish speakers become English speakers; migration patterns from *el sur* (south/Mexico) to *el norte* (north/United States); and recordings that employ U.S. pop in order to obliterate racialized genres. Selena's brown soul counters this trend; she complicates how Chicano music has reflected and produced Chicana/o identities and subjectivities through departures and arrivals that move against assimilationist code terms such as "crossover."

Selena began singing before a live audience at the age of nine. By the time she died at nearly twenty-four, she had lived more than half of her life as a cultural worker. Her sister, Suzette Quintanilla, says that their band actually started off singing old-school country tunes as a group named Seven Pearl.[21] After performing for supper clubs in and around Lake Jackson, Texas, Seven Pearl eventually became Selena y Los Dinos. Suzette and her brother A. B. Quintanilla have often indicated how difficult it was to be taken seriously by the Tejano music industry: "We were told by all these macho men that Selena would never make it, but she kept pushing, pushing, pushing."[22] As a result of her efforts, the timing and pitch of Selena's voice would not go unrecognized for long. As a teenager, in 1983, she won her very first award, "New Female Vocalist," from the Texas Association of Spanish Announcers.

After the release of her 1984 debut album *Mis Primeras Grabaciones* on Corpus Christi–based label Freddie Records, Selena would go on to record at least one album a year during the next ten years. In 1985, just shy of her fifteenth birthday, she was beginning to be recognized by the larger Tejano music industry, and was nominated for "Female Vocalist of the Year" and "Female Entertainer of the Year" at the annual Tejano Music Awards.[23] When Los Dinos joined Selena onstage during the acceptance of her first Tejano Music Award in 1993 for "Female Vocalist of the Year," she turned the microphone over to her band and brother and said, "I'm gonna let the guys say something because I always get to talk and they never get to talk and so I'm gonna let them." A. B. exclaimed: "To all the people that said 'a female could never make it in this business,' this goes out to all of y'all."[24] Both Suzette and A. B. acknowledge the gendered labor Selena (and her band) exerted in confronting sexism within an industry that time and again disregarded the possibility that a young woman had anything to offer. Not without irony, then, was Selena's 1987 album titled *And the Winner Is. . . .* From the time she received her first award until her death, Selena would become a dominant fixture at annual awards shows in Texas.

Baila esta cumbia

SELENA reconstructed regional Tejano music as she redefined the cumbia in ways that made explicit its sounding as part of a musical legacy of black diaspora. The race and class foundations of cumbia reveal the complex ways in which music both reflects and produces transnational Latino popular culture. Deborah Pacini Hernandez reminds us that Colombian cumbia has African musical origins and also draws from tri-ethnic populations of African, European, and Native ancestries.[25] "While cumbia stands independently as a genre, it belongs to the greater body of music known as 'tropical music,' which emerged from the dance band arrangements of Afro-Columbian *[sic]* music styles on the Atlantic coast in the mid 1930s and 1940s."[26]

> In Colombia, cumbia began as a form linked to Afro-Caribbean cultures on the northern coast and became a national genre only through its reification as folk music, or through processes of cultural whitening and mestizaje. In other places, such as Argentina, Peru, Mexico, and the U.S.–Mexico border, cumbia became associated, in different ways, with the racialized urban poor.[27]

Pacini argues that blackness in relationship to cumbia has shifted in meaning as varied musical renditons of cumbia have made their way across the Americas. In particular, a racialized tropicalization of cumbia has occurred in Mexico. Of particular relevance to this chapter is both cumbia music's export from Colombia beginning in the 1950s and its diasporic forms in the 1980s and 1990s. In fact, L'Hoeste argues that it is precisely cumbia's lack of musical complexity that forged its musical pliability across the Americas.[28] One example is Mexican cumbia styles that are argued to be a direct influence of rock and roll's arrival from *el norte* in the 1950s. Interestingly, 1950s rock and roll, cumbia, and Mexico would converge in one of Selena's earliest musical performances.

In 1987, Chicano rock-and-roll legend Ritchie Valens obtained long overdue accolades when the movie *La Bamba* placed Chicano cinema on the Hollywood map and spotlighted East LA's rock-and-roll history via Los Lobos' subsequent greatest hit, honoring Valens's hit song "La Bamba." Late that same year, a sixteen-year-old Selena, along with her band Los Dinos, would take the stage at a cultural festival in Matamoros, Tamaulipas, Mexico, as part of a caravan of artists composing the *Johnny Canales Show*.[29] On this stage, Selena y Los Dinos brought together seemingly different worlds in music, cumbia and freestyle, in her group's rendition of "La Bamba" or, as Canales himself referred to it, "La Bamba al estilo de Los Dinos" (La Bamba in the style of Los Dinos).[30]

Selena y Los Dinos could have chosen to play a more traditional rendition of "La Bamba" that would have allowed them more resonance with a Mexican nationalist imaginary that holds the tradition of Son Jarocho music among the nation's most exemplary cultural traditions. Not so ironically, the Mexican nationalist narrative of Son Jarocho music and dance has also elided blackness in Mexico, especially its African-Mexican presence in Veracruz, where the song tradition emerged. If nothing else, staging a version of "La Bamba" more musically aligned with a Mexican nationalist rendition may have endeared the band to the local audience. Selena y Los Dinos chose not to reproduce the popular Los Lobos rock-and-roll version; in choosing not to do so, they effectively rejected a facile alignment with Hollywood's Hispanic citizen-subject as constructed through Ritchie Valens's filmic characterization. Instead, Selena's performance blasted the synthesized sound of freestyle with her own mix-and-match sampling of dance steps from cumbia, to the snake, throughout the wide geographic expanse of the *Johnny Canales Show*'s reach. As Mary Pat Brady argues, it is this performative visuality of Selena's body where race and citizenship function.[31] The live televised performance captures the staging of a racialized gender performance that obviously did not register with her audience or with the nationalist gender-normative discourse of *mexicanidad*.[32] This is exemplified further by Selena's English-language responses to Canales's questions posed in Spanish.

During this performance of "La Bamba," Selena works the dance floor just as she had worked the music industry. Even at sixteen, she grasps for a way to stay alive in front of an audience that cannot make sense of the subject on display. Employing some of the most significant features of freestyle, Selena samples dance moves and vocal styles—grafting cumbia moves more likely recognizable by her audience to freestyle moves that marked her nonnormative musical subjectivity. Even in this early performance, we can note the vocal style and inflections she would continue to draw from in her later years, albeit with a much stronger and more polished voice.

Freestyle is often described as a fusion of vocal styles from disco with the syncopated synthetic instrumentation of electro. Fans and music journalists argue that freestyle emerged as a way to circumvent the backlash against the elimination of dance music from the radio airwaves. A significant connection that bridges disco and freestyle is the dance floor. Certainly, the dance steps, beats, and aesthetics change between the two genres, but the dance floor remained central in the staging of freestyle's visibility—a creative, physical working of space that for queer folks, working-class women of color, and youth of color remained a critical site of display within the crumbling structural realities around them, including economic downturns, displacement trends in urban areas, and, most significant, the increasing deaths owing to HIV/AIDS. We cannot, therefore, underestimate the connection between bodies and dance in certain historical contexts or, to paraphrase Shannon, the power of "bodies displayed through the dance."[33]

Selena's self-fashioned sartorial style drew from the freestyle clothing, hair, makeup, and accoutrement registers of the time even as they set the performative tone of what was to come. Selena would continue to highlight her self-fashioning through such excessive cultural codes of disco and freestyle. An often-dismissed element of her cultural work is her design and tailoring: not only did she choose the costumes she wore, but, with the exception of a few others, she designed and sewed them herself. Feminists of color have theorized this attentiveness to aesthetics as a self-cultivating process through which racialized and working-class women establish a public armor against the debilitating realms of either hyperexploitation or invisibility.[34] This is the type of armor that disco and freestyle music afforded young women of color. The excessive style markers that have now come to represent Selena—the rhinestone bustier, the silver spandex, the bright colors, and multiple accessories—were not about selling herself to heterosexual men's desire, but rather, allowed her to claim her groove, publicly registering a self-pleasure that drew on disco and freestyle diva currency. The moves and style Selena found in freestyle would empower her enough to ask her visibly shocked Spanish-speaking Matamoros audience, in English, "Am I bothering you?"

Selena's initial trip to Mexico, her self-fashioning, her musical performance, and her working of the stage as a dance floor do not reflect a desire to comfortably accommodate to normative standards of gender within a masculinized conjunto- or orquesta-driven Tex-Mex genre or a drive to impart a safe public sexuality that would have been more legible with her Mexican audience. Selena's performance of freestyle- and disco-infused cumbias was of music she had grown up with; it was a young Tejana's performance through music that was discursively responding to U.S. social politics of the time: social welfare and health policies during the 1980s consistently placed nonheterosexual, nongender-conforming, and queer subjects under attack. This early performance exemplifies why Selena resonated with those who desired to claim their racialized sexuality within structural systems that aim to fix their bodies to a disempowered status. During this Matamoros performance, Selena utilized the stage as a dance floor in ways the queens, disenfranchised racialized women, fags, and Latina/o youth had "worked it" during the days of disco and freestyle.

The 1987 Matamoros performance was not an anomaly. Selena regularly deployed freestyle elements in brown soul. A 1991 performance of "Where Did All the Love Go?" at the Tejano Music Awards reflects the pain of love lost, the dramatic sensibility that could only be found in the voices of tortured hearts. Again, instead of predictably drawing from traditional Tex-Mex music, Selena performs a song from the tradition of freestyle love ballads best exemplified by Lisa Lisa and Cult Jam's 1987 hit "All Cried Out." In this performance, Selena's vocal style and performative aesthetics recall the tropes of freestyle ballads.[35] Interestingly, these ballads are often characterized by themes similar to bolero music, with their desperate, passionate, and excessively dramatic elements. "Freestyle songs," explained freestyle singer Judy Torres, "are like really dramatic Spanish soap operas—being in love, breaking up, catching someone cheating on you—intense and passionate, slightly overdramatic."[36] This excessiveness that Selena drew from, in her self-fashioning as well as in the performance of her music, is located not along an assimilationist continuum but along a sonic circuit derived from the queer sensibilities of disco and freestyle.

The disco and freestyle sensibility Selena embodied through performance, style, and dance moves was distinct from other Latina singers, who, I argue, may have drawn from the music but not necessarily from its queer essence. The most obvious example is that of Latina musical icon Gloria Estefan, who released her highly disco-influenced album *Gloria!* into the popular music sphere in 1988. Estefan, who debuted the album at the famed Studio 54 in New York City, may have sounded disco, but Selena sounded queer. [37] As a queer musical icon, Selena was not merely "la reina Tejana" (the queen of Tejano music) but one that arguably evoked a "snap queen" sensibility in Latino music.[38] Generally a mode of articulation ranging from approval to speaking back to established authority, the snapping of fingers before the term "queen" aligns Selena's femininity more readily to nonnormative sexualities, including those of effeminate gay men of color, than to an uncomplicated femininity working in the service of heteronormativity.

From the moment Selena stepped onstage in the Houston Astrodome in 1995, she became—in terms of public representation, income, record sales, and sought-after record contracts—one of the most powerful Mexican American women singers in the United States. Upsetting typical notions of a fixed and unitary south-to-north trajectory for the crossover artist, Selena instead redirected her moves in the United States toward Latin American markets. She became, by then, recognizable in cities beyond the typical Tex-Mex music fan base of northern Mexico, garnering a following in Puerto Rico, El Salvador, and Honduras.

Selena began her 1995 Astrodome concert with disco diva Gloria Gaynor's "I Will Survive."[39] She was dressed in her self-designed, handmade, tight-fitted, sparkly silver and purple pantsuit, silver rhinestone-studded accessories, and high-heeled silver boots.[40] The video footage of this concert often leads me to muse that this self-fashioning of Selena would have made African American gay disco diva Sylvester proud, for silver high-heeled pumps were his fashion trademark.[41]

What is manifest in Selena's disco and freestyle infused cumbias is not only a transnational Latina/o queer imaginary but one that is transgenerational as well. Selena discursively summons prior generations of dancing bodies that lived in the disco and freestyle eras along with generations of Latinas/os who have migrated to the United States over the decades. Selena's music creates a queer transnational dance floor that keeps nonnormative gender and sexuality subjects moving, bumping, and gliding. She literally and figuratively channeled the labor of queer/women of color singers who came before her. Over the course of nearly a dozen years of live performance, endless bus rides, and numerous handmade costumes, Selena (full-lipped, big-hipped, and brown-skinned) embodied a powerful sense of self that continues to resonate with queer Latina/o publics. To outside audiences, especially Latinos south of the U.S.–Mexico border, Selena embodied a uniquely gendered working-class racialized aesthetic for Tejano music, a cultural sensibility that came to stand for Mexican American experience in Texas to audiences unfamiliar with Tex-Mex negotiations of racialized identity.

In 1989, Selena y Los Dinos hit number 8 on Billboard's Hot Latin tracks with their "Contigo quiero estar." This accomplishment led Selena to sign a recording contract with the then newly established recording label EMI Latin, a move that officially marked the beginning of her international trajectory.[42] In the years to come, Selena y Los Dinos were a constant presence on Billboard's Latin charts with songs such as "Baila esta cumbia," "La Carcacha," and "Como la flor," among others. These songs would lead to the 1992 concert recording of *Selena Live!* that would garner the artist a 1993 Grammy for "Best Mexican American Performance." Selena's 1994 release of *Amor Prohibido* would result in several number 1 hits on the Latin music charts, including "No Me Queda Más," "Bidi Bidi Bom Bom," "Amor Prohibido," and "Fotos y Recuerdos." *Amor Prohibido,* which brought Selena her second Grammy Award nomination, would supplant Gloria Estefan's *Mi Tierra,* which had held the number 1 spot on the Billboard Latin Tracks for fifty-eight weeks.[43] *Amor Prohibido* remained at the number one spot for seventy-eight weeks, the most consecutive weeks.

In arguably the most notable concert performance of her career, Selena performed before a record crowd of sixty-one thousand at the 1995 Houston Livestock Show and Rodeo—outselling Vince Gill and Trisha Yearwood, some of country western's biggest performers. Selena's heavily Texas-Mexican and *mexicano* fan base displaced the Anglo Texan population of East Texas usually drawn to the Houston rodeo. Selena's opening set of songs exemplifies another transformation of Tejano music. Instead of beginning the show with her biggest Tejano hits, a country western tune appropriate to the rodeo setting, or the debut of one of her English-language pop songs, Selena began with a disco medley, harking back to childhood musical influences—not unlike those of Little Joe Hernández—that drew from a legacy of African-derived music production, including R & B, soul, freestyle, disco, and funk music. In this concert performance, she draws from African American disco icons Gloria Gaynor and Donna Summer. Metaphorically, her medley of disco hits brings together Tejano and African American histories within a highly Anglicized public site, the Houston Rodeo.[44] Throughout the opening medley, Selena addresses the audience in Spanish and English, at one point calling out—"Let me hear you, Houston, Tejas, México"—to publics whose subjectivities represent the residual legacies of territorial shifts and contested citizenships. The Latin percussion beats interject transitions between the various disco songs, discursively linking queer dancing bodies of disco with the broader Latino musical public sphere.

"Techno Cumbia," one of Selena's signature hits, is another auditory locator of African diasporic musical sound in Selena's repertoire. To be sure, cumbias were Selena's bread and butter. However, to view Selena's cumbias as merely accented or fused with hip-hop and funk marginalizes blackness and dismisses cumbia's musicality. Listening through Selena's dissonance means centering African diasporic sound in her Tex-Mex cumbias. In brief, Selena's brown soul prompts us to comprehend Chicana/o Tejana/o musical subject formation differently, as never seamlessly de-linked from blackness in the Americas. As such, Selena's brown soul has remained dissonant within hegemonic and heteronormative sonic imaginaries of the borderlands. Selena's brown soul contests the nationalist limits that have stabilized what we come to regard as Tejano or Mexican cumbia. Frances Aparicio provides an insightful assessment of nationalist parameters stabilized by notions such as Tejano cumbia or Mexican cumbia when she states that "the common African elements of cumbias, Afro-Caribbean dance styles, and hip hop could be foregrounded as a common racial genealogy that has been partially silenced by the national values associated with these dance forms."[45]

A closer reading of "Techno Cumbia" reveals the fusion of rap lyrics with the satirical perspectives on stereotypical representations of lazy, working-class, overweight *mexicanos*. The first part draws the listener in with an aggressive challenge to get onto the dance floor. Backed by electric synthesizer and guitar, the song includes second-line drumming from New Orleans and horn charts inspired by Caribbean soca.[46]

Techno Cumbia
(A. B. Quintanilla and Pete Astudillo)

Si vienen a bailar,
Pues vamos a gozar
Si vienen a dormir,
salgan fuera de aquí

If you come to dance,
Well, we're going to enjoy ourselves
If you come to sleep,
Get out of here

The (now) recognizable digitized vocals characteristic of techno and house music emerging in the late 1980s subsequently follow several sets of lyrics:

[digitized voice]
Esto es el ritmo de mi cumbia
Que te va a mover
La techno-cumbia que te traigo
Te dará el placer
Para que muevas tu cuerpo,
De la cabeza a los pies
Y ahora que estamos de fiesta,
Repitan todos después

This is the rhythm of my cumbia
It's going to move you
The techno-*cumbia* that I bring you
Will give you the pleasure
So that you move your body
From head to foot
And
Everyone
now that we're in a party mood
Repeat after me

At this point Selena draws on the classic hip-hop anthem "hip-hop hooray . . . ho . . . hey . . . ho" created by Naughty by Nature that has become the musical interpellation of those in the hip hop nation. Selena sings "hey," and Los Dinos respond "ho," as the song segues into one—if not the earliest—rap to appear in a Tex-Mex cumbia in the 1990s:

Hey (hey), ho (ho), hey (hey)
No me dejen sola
Este reventón sí es para toda
La bola

Hey (hey), ho (ho), hey (hey)
Don't leave me alone
This blowout is for all the masses

In an interesting move, the rap segment pokes fun at a stereotypical Mexican family (especially noted by names such as Juan, María, José, and Rosa) who all eat and drink too much during socializing. The rap lyrics work to make explicit racialized stereotypes to which Selena herself, like many Chicanos, could relate:

Rap:

¡Mira Juan! no se puede ni mover
Pues le pesan los zapatos
Mucho lodo ha de traer (hey)
Mira a María no se mueve de su silla
Es lo que te pasa siempre sí
Si comes muchas tortillas (hey)
Mira José pues no más está sentado
Se tomó muchas cervezas y
Ahora camina de lado (hey)
Mira Rosa no se quiere levantar
Porque trae rotas las medias,
No la vayan a mirar

Look at Juan he can't even move
Because his shoes are heavy
They must be full of mud (hey)
Look at María she doesn't budge from her chair
That's what always happens to you, if
If you eat too many tortillas (hey)
Look at José he's just sitting down
He had too many beers and
Now he walks sideways (hey)
Look at Rosa she doesn't want to get up
Because her stockings are torn
She doesn't want you to notice

In the last segment of the song we can note the hip-hop DJ influence of scratching vinyl records on the turntable:

Muévele, muévele y alto *[scratch]*
[repeats three times]
No le muevas tanto, alto
Ah all right, ah oh yeah
[repeats three times]

Move it, move it, and stop *[scratch]*
[repeats three times]
Don't move it so much, stop
Ah all right, ah oh yeah
[repeats three times]

The cumbias "Techno Cumbia," "Bidi Bidi Bom Bom," and "La Carcacha" all exemplify the race and economic codes—self-references to racial stereotypes, carving out space through sound, creating material goods pieced together from leftovers—that appear in musical genres like hip-hop. Whether they reference reclaiming a barely functioning old car (referred to in Spanish as "una carcacha") in the barrios or the high-tech crude sounds of urbanscapes, such sounds represent auditory sites that could resonate with economically downtrodden folks. This musical repertoire would be reflected in the music A. B. Quintanilla continued with his new band the Kumbia Kings. A .B. explains that he wanted the Kumbia Kings to aspire to an urban sound that seemed to easily transition from Selena's cumbias: "I had a year [after Selena's death] to rethink the music. The sound of the Kumbia Kings is the sound Selena would have evolved to. I had to find a fine line where the cumbias ended and the urban stuff began."[47] The fine line between the two is actually where I maintain that Selena's aesthetics and musical performance resided. Music critics—and Selena's sister Suzette herself—described the Kumbia Kings' style as somewhere within the Colombian dance rhythms of cumbia, urban R & B rap, and reggae dance-hall style.[48]

Suzette Quintanilla continued by explaining that Selena y Los Dinos never used the formulas of regional Tejano music as their guide. Rather, they scrapped together a reflection of what they experienced musically.[49] Particularly as a female-headed band, Selena y los Dinos already went against the norm, so "why try to follow what others are doing?" Suzette explained that their strategy was quite simple: "One thing that you do. Don't worry about what the neighbors are doing. You worry about what you're doing. And if you're able to do what you're doing and people like it, that's all you gotta worry about."[50]

Feminists of color have theorized how women in racialized communities utilize collaborative conversations and cultural exchanges across various racial-ethnic and queer communities in order to address patriarchy and homophobia within communities of color. As a woman in the industry, Selena was not afforded the usual mechanisms of support enjoyed by men. Furthermore, the distinction between the notions of success and survival is key to understanding how Selena y Los Dinos utilized difference while making music differently. Responding to my questions about what challenges the band faced with a woman lead singer, Quintanilla concurred that it was the most difficult barrier to break in the Tejano music industry:

> There was always going to be some form of negativity and you have to fight that. I mean, there were times when we wanted to quit. What you have to do is not so much succeed but survive. At the time, it was about survival. It wasn't about succeeding: it was about survival. I don't know if sweet revenge is the word to use but it's kind of, you know, what I mean, it's kind of good you can go back and say, "Ahhh!" [gestures with her fist].[51]

Brown Soul

Selena's entrepreneurial goals and deep commitment to self-fashioning also represented a key working-class element to her music and performance. Selena uniquely merged fashion and style with the production of her music, reinserting and reconfiguring a working-class Chicana/women-of-color aesthetic. Selena created most of her costumes by hand and combined material, accessories, and color in order to establish a racialized representation performed on her own terms. The self-crafted costumes were as integral to her music as lyrics and sound.[52] Selena's aesthetic was grounded in a style of working-class self-fashioning, a "funky, irreverent stance that debunks convention and spoofs protocol."[53] Selena's style would not register within the realm of haute couture, but it did connect with working-class Latinas and queer/femme men and women who recognize the skill of "making face" through fabric and accessories. I argue that Selena is often not credited with being the first pop singer to initiate her own clothing line, in what is referred to today as the "branding" of popular music singers. She was ahead of her time in bridging arenas of music and fashion, a marketing teleology now almost expected of any successful music icon.

Selena's investments in self-designed style are best exemplified by her purple flared bell-bottom pantsuit, the outfit most associated with her. In her manipulation of material culture, Selena demonstrated her agency, just as other working-class women of color negotiate texture, color, and accessories in order to (re)configure their own bodies, sexuality, and racialized representations.[54]

Selena's success in new Latin American music markets was not without obvious challenges posed by rigid systems of racialization that remain entrenched in racist hierarchies of color. Larry Rohter of the *New York Times* reminds us that Selena was not an automatic sensation in Mexico, despite what proponents of a simplistic notion of Selena-as-crossover artist would have us believe, especially as her music began to make inroads into non-Tejano regional class markets: "South of the border, too, there was resistance at first to what Selena represented. In the upper-class neighborhoods of Mexico City, she was at first derided as *naco,* a racial and class slur meaning coarse or vulgar, because of her mestizo or mixed European and Indian features, which were a marked contrast to those of the typically fair-skinned and light-haired soap opera stars."[55] Suzette proclaimed: "There's a lot of Latinos that are very popular, and I'm not dissing anybody here but are fair-skinned, blonde hair and blue eyes, and that's great, but really, in reality she's one of the few that I can honestly say has dark skin, had the black hair, and she lived in the barrio."[56]

Bell hooks has argued that race, gender, color, and sexuality combine to produce a unique manifestation of subordination for darker-skinned women: "[j]ust as whites now privilege lighter skin in movies and fashion magazines, particularly with female characters, folks with darker skin face a media that subordinates their image. Dark skin is stereotypically coded in the racist, sexist, or colonized imagination as masculine. Hence, a male's power is enhanced by darker looks while a female's dark looks diminish her femininity."[57] Suzette observed: "I always felt like the biggest crossover—more than the English, which is a huge thing for a Mexican American growing up in Texas and a huge accomplishment—

was a crossover south, to probably be the first person to be really accepted in Mexico."[58] Selena became the foremost representative of a booming Tejano music genre in the twentieth century, but acknowledgments of her achievements are often highlighted by her performances or dancing, thereby creating a gendered hierarchy of distinction between dancer and musicians. Selena's brown soul included not only musical compositions, instrumental arrangements, and singing, but style and dance performance as central to the making of her music. The manifestation of this unique brown soul translated urban hip-hop cumbia-driven sound to a contemporary generation of Tejanas/os who grooved to cumbias differently than they did to Tex-Mex conjunto or orquesta. Furthermore, Selena's brown soul moved Tex-Mex cumbias not simply in a unidirectional move of Tex-Mex cumbias south to Mexico and other parts of Latino America but also in a circuit of African diasporic sound. One might call this a queer misdirection instead of a simple musical migration: Selena's cumbias track the Afro-Colombian cumbia that became popular upon its arrival to Mexico in the 1940s and 1950s—tinged by a racist association with tropical blackness[59]—then moved through an accordion-fused transition in South Texas, later fused with African American– and Latino-derived echoes of hip-hop, rap, and freestyle, and then turned back around to circulate among the African diasporic sounds of Latino music:

> We went to South America and Guatemala; we played there and that was on. It was awesome. Guatemala City. I'll never forget that. We were all cool, and we land, and we look out the window, and there was like a crowd of people. We were, like, "Is Ricky Martin here?" [Laughter] It doesn't usually get all crazy with people until you get to the hotel or actual concert venue, so you're all cool looking out the window and you see signs. It was like something out of the movies, and we all looked at each other, like, "That's for us?" It was our first time playing there, and we sold out the venue and there were like thirteen thousand people. It was awesome.[60]

At the time of her death, Selena was making inroads into Central America. She played Guatemala in mid-1994, and there were plans for a tour of South America later in 1995.[61] The history and culture that mark Selena's subjectivity as "la reina de la música Tejana" discursively engaged the histories and cultures of African diasporic musical sound, an engagement that was evident in the musical duets and group material Selena was recording with well-known artists such as the Nuyorican hip-hop group the Barrio Boyzz and Honduran pop singer Álvaro Torres.

In 1992, Selena recorded "Buenos Amigos" with Torres on his Capital EMI album *Nada se Compara Contigo.* The song was later released as a single and garnered Selena her first number 1 record on the Latin Billboard singles chart. "Dondequiera que estés," with the Barrio Boyzz, was released on EMI Latin in 1993. Music videos of each song were produced and circulated widely throughout the Latin American market. In fact, Selena inserted these Latin music collaborative projects into *Tejas,* as well. Unlike the few other Tejano bands such as La Mafia and Mazz that carved out a space for their music in Mexico and Central America, Selena engaged in a remapping based on collaboration with artists from other musical, regional, and cultural traditions. Suzette Quintanilla maintained that the band's travels to Latin America hinged on the enthusiastic audience reception they received after appearing on the *El Show de Cristina* in Miami in 1994.[62] *El Show de Cristina* gave her visual exposure that followed closely behind the voice that accompanied Torres and the Barrio Boyzz. To be sure, it was rare to see a U.S.-born, brown-skinned, dark-haired young Latina singer sitting center stage on *Cristina.* In this interview, Selena introduced a differently racialized Chicana subject to Spanish-speaking audiences across Latino America, fielding questions quite well in Spanish, but relying just enough on her Tex-Mex *pocha* Spanglish to make explicit her social location as a third-generation Mexican American.

Selena's musical and bodily circulation across such places like Guatemala, Puerto Rico, and, at the time of her passing, Chile, Venezuela, and Brazil, throw for a loop the normative geographic as well as gender registers that uphold the dominant construction of Chicano music. An excellent example is the popularity she had among Caribbean fans and singers. The 1996 compact disc titled *Recordando a Selena (Remembering Selena)* was recorded by Familia RMM, a collaboration among Latino *salseros,* Celia Cruz, Manny Manuel, Yolanda Dukes, Celines, and others. *Recordando a Selena* rerecords Selena's biggest hits as salsa and merengue tunes. The compact disc's title track makes clear the significance of Selena's music in the broader Latino public, and the liner notes call to Selena through verses of some of her biggest hits:

Y de aquel *amor prohibido*
Que murmuran en las calles
Hoy se siente tan callado
Del vacío que dejaste

And of that *forbidden love*
That is murmured in the streets
Today feels so silent
From the void you left behind

The remixed salsa and merengue songs in *Recordando a Selena* are tagged by some of the most highly respected Caribbean *salseros.* As each singer sings his or her own name within each song, the compilation builds on an intersection of musical genres that discursively re-members or reembodies Selena within the broader Latino American public sphere. "Recordando Selena," the only new song written especially for the CD, features the combined singing of all the participating artists, each of whom takes on a separate segment of the song comprised of lyrics from Selena's hits.

Dondequiera que estés
Tu público te recordará
Tu canto, tu modo de ser
Siempre vivirás
[repeat chorus]
Es para ti nuestro canto

Wherever you are
Your public will remember you
Your song, your way of being
You will live forever
[repeat chorus]
Our song is for you

Each singer then sings different sets of lyrics that are meant to pay a more personal tribute to Selena. For example, Celia Cruz's lyrical tribute ends with her personal signature *¡Azúcar!*.[63]

En este gran homenaje
No me podía quedar

Por eso mi linda Selena
Hoy vienes a inspirar
¡Azúcar!

In this great homage
I couldn't stay behind
That's why my beautiful Selena
Today you come to inspire
¡Azúcar!

Angie Chabram-Dernersesian has asserted that in addressing transnational travel within the arena of cultural productions, Chicano scholars need to stop celebrating transnationalism just because it crosses borders.[64] She challenges us to be critical of transnational frameworks that merely celebrate mobility without accounting for the manner in which race, class, gender, and sexuality intersect within global capitalism. Selena's music excursions south were anything but a flawless musical movement free of contradictions or of the ways racialized women's bodies are exploited. Certainly, contemporary economic policies favoring a major recording company's interventions into Latin American markets offer a significant context for making sense of Selena's Chicana subjectivity. In addition, we cannot underestimate the fact that Selena's participation in Latino music occurred within the context of the North American Free Trade Agreement (NAFTA), legislation passed in 1994 with a significant policy impact on cultural production on both sides of the U.S. border. That said, I argue that Selena's brown soul does not underestimate the complicated relationship between power and pleasure in music. Musical icons like Selena have much to offer the dynamic productions of nonnormative gender subjectivities.

Selena y Los Dinos' music often cut against regional geography delimited by the accordion-driven sound of South Texas as well as renderings of language and racial authenticity (of a *pocho* sensibility) that have long been considered the foundation of Chicano music.[65] Selena's racialization as Latina, when specifically linked to a discourse of crossover artist, erased an often underacknowledged crossover into Latin American markets because there was no explicitly racialized leap. A singer of cumbias and rancheras, Selena made sense in the racial register of mainstream America; in contrast, the hip-hop, freestyle, and disco-infused sound at the core of her singing style, performance, and recordings did not. The musical term "crossover" that has been used consistently in reference to Selena's cultural significance elides the contextual complexity of her social location and racialized representation within a broader Latina/o cultural sphere. Moreover, it dismisses what I term the topography of Selena's transformations and remappings of Chicano music.

Clearly, the term "crossover" refers to the movement of music from "'specialized,' 'peripheral' markets into those of mainstream pop"; thus, it makes sense to describe Selena's last project of producing an English-language pop album as a crossover.[66] The term as used to capture Selena's music and icon status also made racialized sense because her representation as Latina was "naturally" that of a Spanish-speaking subject. As Reebee Garofalo suggests, the crossing over of artists and audiences in different music genres is extremely political because the industry is organized by the racialization of music genres.[67] Because crossover tends to assume homogeneous musical forms and cultures, it fails to convey the complexity of multisituated, nonnormative Chicana subjects. I maintain that Selena's brown soul highlights the contextual signposts of race, sexuality, gender, nationality, class, color, language, and generation that conventional deployments of genre crossover elide. Selena's crossover was north to south, tracing over the U.S. nation-state border with Mexico where her *naco* subjectivity illuminated the obstinacy of Mexican nationalist racism.

George Lipsitz asserts that crossover reifies "the subject of Western popular music" and marks a linear pattern of success in terms of dominant codes of race and language.[68] Thus, crossover also fails to capture shifts and transformations in contemporary American popular culture, particularly as increased transnational movements of capital and culture impact Mexican-based music and cultural practices that have their origins in Texas. Conventional dialogues of music crossover stifle the sociological complexity of such occurrences.

For Chicanos who reside in the United States, the notion of crossing (almost always conceptually linked with a fixed, unitary border) consistently resides in the psyche as a metaphoric term for racialized difference, no matter how many generations they have resided in the United States. Inquiry: "when did your family cross over?" Newspaper headline: "Woman and her children die while crossing the border." Conversation:

"Vamos a cruzar al otro lado" (We're going to cross over to the other side). Chicano humor: "Better have your papers in order or they might not let you cross back over." Chicano politics: "We didn't cross the border, the border crossed us."

The notion of crossing remains imbued with the historical telling of a population. Each troubled history of the interstices of the U.S.–Mexico border—colonization and the subsequent mappings of nations and states; labor migrations rife with violence inflicted upon young, brown, female bodies; the violent operations of Immigration and Naturalization Service (INS) surveillance; and the racist legacy of segregation imposed on *mexicanas/os* in Texas—adds to the palimpsest of "crossing (over)."

Even so, the ideological ramifications of crossing in a south-to-north direction still presage moving toward something better—country, language, job opportunities—all perpetuated by American ideologies of success, democracy, and progress:[69]

> Some see the idea of "crossover" as utopian, a metaphor for integration, upward mobility, and ever-greater acceptance of marginalized groups by the larger society. Others see it as an inevitable result of dividing and hierarchizing musical styles and audiences: a "mainstream," after all, can only define itself in relation to the "margins." Put another way, the term "crossover" implies that there must be discrete boundaries, for recording can only "crossover" when one field is clearly demarcated from another.[70]

A more fully contextual analysis of the social location of Selena's music breaks through just such a demarcation between mainstream and margin. The discursive operation of music crossover that frames Selena's career is linked to a racialized notion of success embedded within a U.S. assimilationist narrative: working-class Mexican American girl lives out the American dream by breaking in to U.S. pop music. In this vein, director Gregory Nava opens the film *Selena: The Movie* with Selena's most significant performance at the Houston Astrodome. Nava's movie reproduces a Hollywood feel-good plot in which the minority girl obtains the American dream. Thus, he employs the opening disco medley set in order to represent Selena as having made it, having crossed over as an English-language music pop singer. This model of assimilation epitomizes precisely the ways in which the presupposition of "a discrete, homogeneous, and thoroughly unified center in any society fails to describe the dynamism and complexity of contemporary culture."[71] Omitted in the equating of the disco medley as merely English-language "crossover" music is disco's queer-of-color musical legacy, especially through disco icons such as Donna Summer and Gloria Gaynor, whose songs Selena performed that day.[72]

Selena's musical success in Mexico, Puerto Rico, and other Latin American markets represents a metaphoric U-turn: she travels along a north-to-south axis, effectively reconfiguring the notion of professional success for English-speaking Mexican Americans born and raised in the United States. As Suzette Quintanilla explains:

> It was very satisfying. [Tejano music artists] say that one of the hardest things is to be able to cross over into Mexico. A lot of people, people here in the states or *mexicanos aquí en los Estados Unidas [sic],* to accept a band from Mexico, no problem. We ain't got no problem with it, but to be able to get the people from Mexico to accept because they have this thing that you're from over here. "You think you're white. You think you're Anglo, so we can't accept you over here," and especially if you don't know how to speak Spanish they look down on you. They look down on you because they think that you're putting the race down. Like you're not proud of your culture. So, to be able to cross from the United States that way is a huge accomplishment, I mean huge.[73]

With reference to their first trip to Mexico City, during which Selena held her first Mexican press conference, Quintanilla adds:

> People were like, "They're gonna eat you up over there. They're just gonna shred you," cuz the newspapers over there, they're not nice about it. They'll straight out tell you, you know, that you stink cuz you don't know how to speak Spanish, and they have no problem printing that. And I thought, "Oh, my god, Selena doesn't know Spanish," and me. I would never say anything. I was like, "Uuhh sí, no," you know?

During 2005, Latino gay bars in cities across the United States honored the tenth year of Selena's passing with Selena look-alike pageants and drag musical performances of her greatest hits. Such is the extent of Selena's continued popularity that she is now among the drag performances featured in gay Latino/a clubs, along with, for example, Paquita La Del Barrio, Paulina Rubio, and Ana Gabriel. On a humid Friday night in August 2005, I entered one of the more popular gay clubs in Mexico City, El VIP, for a spectacular tenth-anniversary event. To the right of the entryway stood a huge cardboard cutout of "La reina del Tex-Mex" welcoming all who entered. Inside, the scene was reminiscent of many gay bars in the United States: loud house music and roaming lights surrounded a plethora of well-dressed gay men and a smattering of women.[74]

The VIP Selena anniversary event was thematized by a reenactment of Univision's anniversary special "¡Selena Vive!" (Selena lives!), originally telecast live from Reliant Stadium in Houston on April 7, 2005. El VIP's salute included drag performances of Ana Gabriel, Paulina Rubio,

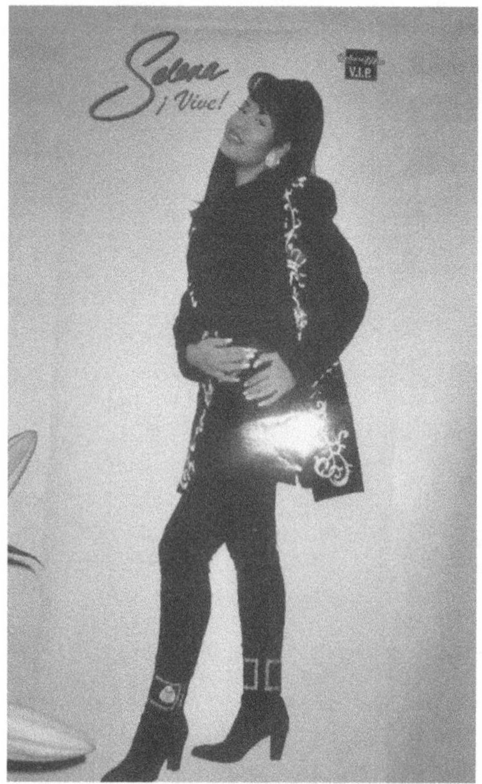

A life-size poster of Selena in El Club VIP, Mexico City. Photograph by author.

and others who performed Selena songs on the television special. More than just a drag reenactment of the television special, El VIP's event shifted the transnational circuit of contemporary Latino music through the queer femininities of Latino gay drag, enacting and validating non-heteronormative constructions of desire, affect, and memory.

The most popular performance that night was by "María," whom I came to learn was one of the most recognized Selena drag performers in Mexico City. María appeared that evening as classic Selena, dressed in the purple pantsuit and high-heeled silver boots and performing a medley of cumbias. During my backstage interview with María before she jetted off to do another anniversary performance at club El Ansia, she stated:

> Interpretar el rol de Selena es una experiencia que me hace sentir humilde. Es un honor sentir el espíritu de Selena cada vez que me presento en el escenario porque ella significó mucho para la comunidad gay. Además, lo sabes, yo interpreto a Selena porque me parezco a ella: soy morenita, tengo los labios llenos, tengo todos los pasos y movimientos de Selena.[75]

> Performing Selena is a humbling experience. It's an honor every time I step onstage and feel Selena's spirit because she meant so much to the gay community. Plus, you know, I perform Selena because I look just like her: I'm brown, I have full lips, I've got all the Selena moves.

María said that she performed Selena at some of the more popular gay clubs in various Mexican cities and even planned to travel to Los Angeles that December. As Selena, María, in her travels throughout Mexico and across the U.S.–Mexico border, personifies more than a traveling drag show. María-as-Selena symbolizes an alternative borderlands imaginary set in motion by Selena through brown soul. Selena's cumbia moves charted her literal movement across nation-state borders and pushed against normative limits of gender and sexuality. To paraphrase Angie Chabram-Dernersesian, it is crucial that Chicana/o Latina/o studies chart transnational movements that reclaim social identities that have been linked to the narrowing of social, political, and economic spheres.[76] Most significantly, Selena traversed the normative boundaries of gender by publicly staging a representation that exceeded the color lines of hegemonic femininity in the United States and, I would argue, in parts of Latino America as well. The genesis of María's Selena cannot be reduced to a mere drag interpretation of yet another Latin singing icon: more precisely, María is the sonic reverberation of Selena's brown soul enabled through disco and the counterhegemonic femininities performed within freestyle. Selena's brown soul constitutes a queer sonic circuit that continually crosses back and forth across geographic, gender, and genre borders.

Scholars, popular media biographers, and music critics have attempted to make sense of Selena's rise to fame and continued fandom beyond a U.S. context, especially across Mexico, Central America, and

María, a popular drag performer, as Selena at El Club VIP, Mexico City, 2005. Photograph by author.

Puerto Rico. Feminist analyses have contributed complex assessments of Selena that move beyond the shortsightedness of Chicano/Tejano ethnomusicology and Latin music journalism—heteronormative realms that consistently reduce Selena's continued record sales, dedicated fan-club base, and musical rotation on radio and dance clubs to a sexy body or the globalized economy of Latin music.[77] Critical attention to early Selena demonstrates her transformative musical performance, which draws from disco and freestyle. This musical base provided her with a bold sensibility that would increase in proportion to fan base and public power. A recontextualization of her musical inflections within disco and freestyle provides us with a very different articulation for staging racialized gender and sexuality. Moreover, genre constructions of Chicano and Latino music are not reduced to the Spanish language. As Alexandra Vázquez asserts, the striking unwillingness to use Spanish in the majority of freestyle music being produced and sung by Latinas requires a more complicated analysis of Latina subjectivities and representations than reductive models of assimilation allow.[78]

In the last decades of the twentieth century, Selena was not just a hugely popular performer or an increasingly powerful Latina presence in popular culture. She was all of these and brown. Amazingly, still today there are few brown-skinned Chicanas/Latinas—La India is one striking example—who stage such a powerful public presence. To be young, brown, and female in the increasingly globalized Spanish-language media means being a subject always within the gaze of heterosexual hypersexuality. The nonnormative publics—the drag queens, the browner-skinned, the *nacos,* the nonheterosexuals, and the informal economy clientele—locate a meaningful validation of nonnormative sexualities, desires, and representations in Selena. Selena's brown soul is a queer diasporic sound for "those who stand on the outside of the dominant constructed norm of state-sanctioned white middle-and upper-class heterosexuality."[79]

My assertion of Selena's dissonant brown soul within *la onda* is guided by queer studies scholarship that forges recognition and analysis of queer as more than merely that which is stabilized by lesbian and gay subjects.[80] Instead, queer studies encourages us to make central "not only the socially construed nature of sexuality and sexual categories, but also the varying degrees and multiple sites of power distributed within all categories of sexuality, including the normative category of heterosexuality."[81] Queer subjects are not necessarily those who neatly fall within fixed references of gay or lesbian. Extending these articulations of the term "queer" to my analysis of Selena's subjectivity and fandom recognizes the nonheteronormative racialized and sexualized subjects who locate an empowered sexual agency and a gendered class aesthetic precisely by "making face."

Selena's brown soul takes account of racialized sexuality as power as more than those bodies reducible to gay or lesbian subjects, but also of racialized femininities too often hypersexualized that generate sexual agency through their own terms of self-pleasure and movement through music. I reflect, for instance, on the summer when I walked into an

Selena in the 1980s on the front cover of the compilation album *Mis primeros éxitos*. Produced by A. B. Quintanilla.

ice-cream shop in the central plaza in Guanajuato, Mexico. While waiting in line, I heard Selena's "Baila esta cumbia," "El apartamento 512," and "Bidi bidi bom bom" blaring from a boom box behind the counter. I asked the young *mexicana* working at the register where the songs were coming from. She explained that she was a lifelong fan and had made the cassette herself with her cassette player and her friend's compact disc player. I asked her where the friend purchased Selena's CD, and she told me that it was purchased from a street vendor. The class and race realities of such informal economies of exchange and circulation are characteristic of the racialized bodies who move (to) cumbias; let us recall that the *norteño* cumbias that were pushed to *el norte* into South Texas and further into the United States were considered "the preeminent voice of working-class Mexicans."

Selena's self-cultivated performance transcended the normative gender boundaries of Mexican-descent genres in the United States such as Tex-Mex music or cumbias, where heterosexual femininity solidifies around Chicano/Tejano masculinity. Selena's sound enables nonheteronormative bodies to move symbolically and, quite literally, traverse gender and geographic boundaries through a queer diasporic sound. Certainly, capitalist ventures in the continued releases of recording compilations have perpetuated Selena's presence in Latino America's musical world. But, at the same time, if one listens closely to her music and is especially attentive to who has remained a persistent fan base since her passing, it is not difficult to ascertain who keeps Selena moving and who is still moved by her.

Although many mainstream music critics came to dismiss disco music as nothing more than danceable pop, feminist and queer studies scholars have reclaimed early disco histories as the spaces of "outcasts" and marginal subjects—namely, economically disenfranchised blacks, Latinas/os, and gay men and lesbians.[82] According to John-Manuel Andriote, "from this ethnic, sexual, and socioeconomic mélange would arise the extraordinary musical, social, and cultural phenomenon that became disco."[83]

Reclaimed from mainstream dismissals of disco are the dancing bodies of the racially and sexually deviant. One cannot underestimate the power of sexual agency and resistant aesthetics that came to be located on disco dance floors throughout global cities like New York and

Los Angeles, marked unequivocally by people of color who utilized this musical site for gender and sexuality subversion. As Kobena Mercer reminds us, "it is through the medium of music—always associated with dance and the erotic potentialities of the dance floor—that black men and women have articulated sexual politics."[84] I would extend the spirit of this assertion to argue that disco and freestyle manifest a significant musical medium for racialized queer publics.[85]

In the 1980s, the fused sounds of African American and Puerto Rican hip-hop would come together with the vocal styles of 1970s disco, music sampling, and dance improvisation to form freestyle, a musical formation Alexandra Vázquez posits as an artistic arena for the "liberation from culturally stifling parameters of conformity" pertaining to *latinidad*.[86] The musical formations of disco and freestyle arguably represent a significant cohort of women of color singers and music producers within contemporary U.S. history. Shannon (given name, Shannon Greene) is often credited as a founding force in freestyle. Her 1983 song "Let the Music Play" can be considered the first major freestyle hit. Although there are numerous perspectives on the origins of freestyle, most fans and music critics agree on several points: New York is its birthplace; there are variations among East Coast, West Coast, and Miami sounds and artists; and freestyle peaked roughly between 1985 and 1992, with major record labels providing mass audience appeal by 1987. Besides the New York–Miami–Los Angeles milieu, the genre of freestyle also had strong bases in Chicago, Houston, and Philadelphia.[87]

Of significance here is that freestyle, like disco, opened a great deal of public space for African American women, Filipinas, and Latinas. Disco is associated most often with Donna Summer and Gloria Gaynor, and freestyle with artists such as Lisa Velez and Shannon.[88] In 1985, Lisa Lisa and Cult Jam's "I Wonder If I Take You Home" became the first freestyle record to crack the American Top 40. Toward the end of 1986, Exposé (consisting of Jeanette Jurado, Gioia Bruno, and Ann Curless) released their debut album *Exposure,* with smash hits including "Come Go with Me," "Let Me Be the One," "Seasons Change," and "Point of No Return." The success of Exposé's album solidified the power of freestyle music in the broader musical arena. By 1987, freestyle was at its peak. Lisa Lisa and Cult Jam's hits "Head to Toe" and "Lost in Emotion" were among the chart busters that moved young people to take back the dance floor with moves like the snake. The fashion accoutrements of freestyle became central to the sonic register of the music itself: young women of color came to the clubs equipped with fanned bangs, Z. Cavaricci pants, big shimmery earrings, bold colors, and black liquid eyeliner. Young people of color found visibility and validation through freestyle, and it is within this context that many like a young Selena located their voice.

Selena's cumbias propel a queer imaginary of the borderlands through the embracing of disco divas, hip-hop-infused cumbias, and the performative aesthetics of freestyle that must be comprehended simultaneously as a sounding of and through African diasporic sound. Disco and freestyle moved Selena and Selena moved cumbias and English-language love ballads across nation-state borders and across the linguistic assumptions that too often reduce *latinidad* to Spanish-language or Tex-Mex cumbias to the "blue-collar country cousins with limited dance moves."[89]

To young women, *jotas/os* (queer Latinas/os), and brown working-class communities, Selena was an icon way before her death.[90] Selena's representation still resounds meaningfully within *Tejas* and Latino American musical imaginaries that push against the limits represented by heteronormative boundaries of gender, hierarchies of racialized femininity, and the marginalization of blackness. Selena remains a powerful presence within Latin/o public culture; her queer sonic circuit still flows back and forth across timescapes and nation-state borders; and her music still spins a borderlands imaginary that continually loops the groove of transformative hope and desire for queer subjectivities. Selena's brown, queer fan base comprises bodies that continually reverberate to Selena's cumbia moves; when these bodies move, they symbolize the perilously high stakes of publicly negotiating pleasure, desire, and sexual agency through configurations of power based on class, race, sexuality, and gender. As a dissonant diva, Selena negotiated such high stakes. As a cultural worker, she utilized cross-cultural influences of African diasporic sound, working-class Chicano aesthetics, Tex-Mex cumbia, and self-fashioning skills that sound a borderlands imaginary through brown soul.

EPILOGUE

The Borderlands Rock Reverb of Gloria Ríos and Girl in a Coma

In the geomusical locality of San Antonio, Tex-Mex music has reigned as a preeminent musical force that has cultivated *mexicana/o* social identities and charted the contours of histories. Although what one considers Tex-Mex music can more often be defined by what it is not than by what it is, the sounds of Tex-Mex orquesta and accordion-driven conjunto—with their associated dances the cumbia and the polka—along with their more contemporary transformations of Tejano (since the 1980s), represent the broader parameters. Tex-Mex music has persistently sounded responses to calls to remember the Alamo; it has affirmed cultural politics and unabashedly expressed contradictions that bring joy and pleasure.

I began this musical journey with Rosita Fernández in order to critically engage the notion of dissonance as a feminist-of-color analytic for listening to and for Chicana singers who represent strident, inharmonious, or cacophonous musical subjects, performances, and narratives that have been unheard, misheard, or too simplistically heard within the canonical Chicano musical sonic imaginary I call *la onda*. Rosita's call for us to remember her offers us different ways to imagine the borderlands through a musical career that has sounded through arguably one of the most infamous calls that has shaped Tejana/o subjectivity, the call to remember the Alamo. Dissonant sounds and distorted representations are often too messy to engage; they take too much energy to move through and make sense of, and they make us vulnerable for what we might hear. Shouts—from calls to remember the Alamo to "el grito de Dolores" (the cry representative of Mexican independence)—have produced sonic imaginaries of home, identity, and belonging for Chicanas/os; it is, then, fitting to close the journey that began with Rosita Fernández by contemplating different shouts that call forth new imaginaries.

The post-Selena era of Tex-Mex music, 1995 to the present, has been rather quiet since the loss of that young brown Tejana from Corpus Christi whose big voice, cumbias, and captivating stage presence gave Texas a different public face. If we understand Selena's representation as the magnificent arrival and equally grand departure as the hush of Tex-Mex in the twentieth century, then we must consider the shouts, clamorous vibrations, and stunning musical chaos of Girl in a Coma as further Tejana commotion. Girl in a Coma is a musical commotion that not only represents gender and sexuality dissonance within *la onda* but bursts through the dominant parameters of geographic place, gendered politics of instrumentation, and the embodiment of resistance. Moreover, Girl in a Coma's musical sound represents a sonic circuit that moves through the place of San Antonio, the bodies of *mexicanas* in rock, and across borders of nation and gender. There has been a rocking reverb in Tex-Mex music; it echoes between the presence of Gloria Ríos's "primer grito del rock-and-roll en México" and the pasts in Girl in a Coma's music.

Born and raised in San Antonio, Girl in a Coma is composed of Phanie Díaz on drums, Jenn Alva on bass, and Nina Díaz on vocals. Having played music together since they were in high school, they were greatly influenced by groups like the Smiths, who they honor with their band's name, based on the Smiths' song "Girlfriend in a Coma." While the band sees itself as musically connected with the work of Nirvana, the Ramones, Morrissey, and others, it maintains a persistent connection to San Antonio and Tex-Mex music. The ways in which Girl in a Coma engages with Tex-Mex music are not direct or fastened to the musical sounds that have lingered around them, yet their music moves through those sounds. As Jenn Alva observed about the band's connection to Tex-Mex, "It's not intentional, it just is because that musical sound has always surrounded us."[1] Girl in a Coma's reminders of the prominence of Tex-Mex music in the background of their lives, along with how critical the

Ramones and the Smiths have been, correspond to how their music is less a production *of* Tex-Mex than, more precisely, a production *through* it. Girl in a Coma's music wails *through* Tex-Mex sound, exemplifying what Stuart Hall describes as identities and cultural productions as constituted with and through difference, not despite it.[2] Girl in a Coma's music moves within and through Tex-Mex sound—literally and symbolically surrounding the band's cultural milieu—but is not necessarily of it, thereby enabling an alternative racialized gendered sensibility of what constitutes Tex-Mex music.

Girl in a Coma's moving through the musical sounds that have shaped their subjectivities as Tejanas is exemplified in their 2010 album *Adventures in Coverland,* which featured covers such as "While My Guitar Gently Weeps" (The Beatles), "Transmission" (Joy Division), "As the World Falls Down" (David Bowie), "Come On, Let's Go" (Ritchie Valens), "Walkin' after Midnight" (Patsy Cline), and "Femme Fatale" (Velvet Underground). Most notable on this album is the band's version of "Si una Vez" by Selena. They first considered a cover of "Techno Cumbia" because, as Jenn Alva explained, "*cumbia* music we grew up on is just everywhere in San Antonio."[3] They chose "Si una Vez" because it was one of their favorite songs. Jenn Alva explained: "Her music was on constantly in our household. She was doing something very important for our culture and something new."[4] Phanie Díaz further stated that they "felt the original version [of the] song already had a hidden punk quality.[5] Alva noted that "Si una Vez" is sung by Selena with "such an angry passion, kinda like punk";[6] it exemplifies both a sonic claim to Tex-Mex music as place, as represented through Selena's music, but also a listening through dissonance to hear residues of punk sound.

Girl in a Coma's second album, *Trio B.C.,* released in 2009, was described as a unique amalgamation of eclectic influences: oldies, rockabilly, 90s alternative, and contemporary indie rock. Phanie Díaz explains: "We chose *Trio B.C.* as the album title because it was the name of our grandfather's Tejano band way back in the '50s, he was our first musical influence. He would play us guitar and sing and we would love to watch him in the garage with a cold beer in his hand, playing his records and singing along like he meant it. His passion is our inspiration. We hope to make people feel that way about our music."[7] Identifying their music as indie rock, band members have stated that what is important for them is not falling within a certain kind of rock genre, but rather creating music for their listeners that, as Nina Díaz explains, gives them "the ability to sing, and scream, and break from personal inhibitions."[8]

The one song that stands out as unique on *Trio B.C.* and from other earlier recordings is Girl in a Coma's first Spanish-language song, "Ven Cerca" (Come closer), described in an online music review as "a noisy dissonant cover of the 1960s original by Los Spitfires."[9] Sung by lead vocalist Nina Díaz, "Ven Cerca" is a deep, sultry, and sensual interpretation of the lyrics. The barely audible enunciation of the lyrics operates in conjunction with Alva's thunderous guitar and Díaz's drums, evoking the mid-1950s to mid-1960s bustling Mexican rock-and-roll scene that included bands such as Chikos del Rock, Los Rockets, Las Moskas, and others.[10] In fact, in 1963 Julia Elisa Del Llano Macedo, or Julissa, was one of the earliest women to be a lead singer in a Mexican rock band, Los Spitfires. Los Spitfires recorded three albums for CBS Records and their biggest hit was "Ven Cerca."[11] Girl in a Coma's "Ven Cerca" is a rock reverb that discursively connects the band to a critical female vocal intervention in Mexican rock; Julissa is said to have sung the song in such a provocative tone that it was banned from radio.[12] Furthermore, I contend that we should also recall that Julissa's Mexican rock vocals are part of a unique iconography of woman in Mexican rock, a cohort whose beginnings bring us back to Gloria Ríos and San Antonio.

Born in Sweetwater, Texas, on September 17, 1928, Gloria Ramíres Gómez, whose stage name became Gloria Ríos, grew up in San Antonio from the age of three. When she was only thirteen years old, she dropped out of school to join the now-famed performance group La Chata Compañía Mexicana, whom Alicia Arrizón calls the embodiment of an emerging Mexican American aesthetics.[13] Ríos's experience with La Chata's performance troupe cannot be underestimated as this was one of the earliest Mexican American female-headed performance troupes, whose shows ranged from comedic skits to burlesque comedy. The Companía Mexicana traveled throughout the East Coast, Southwest, and Midwest. Ríos's travels with the group garnered her considerable experience and independence.

In 1945, at the age of seventeen, with permission from her mother, Ríos took the train to Mexico City, where she thought she might have an opportunity to earn money as a dancer. The San Antonio of Rios's youth was a cultural milieu of significant transformation, including media and public performance. For example, the Teatro Nacional was the premier Mexican theater during the 1930s and part of the commercial landscape chiefly operated by Mexicans for a Spanish-speaking Mexican public. In 1949, the Teatro Alameda was the largest movie palace dedicated to Spanish-language films and the performing arts. English- and Spanish-language radio also circulated the sounds of local singers and bands, as well as those broadcasts originating from Mexico City's XEW.

Ríos was especially drawn to jazz and swing music. According to her daughter, Regina Martínez, Ríos garnered quite a bit of local acclaim from her dancing to swing music.[14] Her major passion as a performer was dance, and her dance skills eventually opened up doors to perform at some of Mexico City's most popular cabarets and theatrical venues. Eventually, her dance skills would lead to numerous movie appearances.

From 1947 to 1952, Ríos appeared as a dancer in several movies, including *Voces de Primavera* (Voices in springtime), *Buenas Noches mi Amor* (Goodnight, my love), and *Te Sigo Esperando* (I'm still waiting for you). Ríos's dancing and improvised musical moves on screen and on stage would become popular among young Mexican women, according to Mario Sanabria of the rock-and-roll band Los Locos del Ritmo.[15] Ríos was a popular Mexican vedette before she burst onto the music scene. In fact, it was vedette performances in cabarets, nightclubs, and burlesque halls that early on incorporated rock and roll as part of their repertoire.[16]

In 1954, Ríos sang "El Relojito" live on XEW radio, followed in 1955 with the formation of one of the first Mexican rock-and-roll bands, Gloria Ríos y sus Estrellas del Ritmo (composed of Mario Patrón, Tomás Rodríguez, Cuco Valtierra, Leo Acosta, and Enrique Almanza). In fact, band member Enrique Almanza recalled in an interview that it was Ríos who approached him with her desire to form the best musical group of jazz and rock in Mexico. Asked by Arturo Lara how he and the other band members came to know the musical repertoire of rock and roll, Almanza says, "It was Gloria who arrived to Mexico having had those ideas."[17] Ríos's rock music not only thrust rock and roll into Mexican public culture but created a space for women to thrust their bodies as well. As Lara stated, Gloria Ríos "fue una bomba muy sensual y hermosa que despertó a la mujer mexicana para bailar y cantar el rock-and-roll" (was a very sensual and beautiful bombshell who awoke the Mexican woman to dance and sing rock and roll).[18]

In 1955, Bill Haley and the Comets' "Rock around the Clock" was featured various times throughout the movie *Blackboard Jungle* starring Glen Ford and Sydney Poitier, eventually soaring to the top of the Billboard charts and into homes and sock hops across America. Halley would also become a popular performer in Mexico after *Blackboard Jungle* circulated in Mexico with the title *Semilla de maldad* (Wicked seed).[19] According to Eric Zolov, *Blackboard Jungle* "established the association between the new youth culture and delinquency worldwide" as "the first film to include a rock 'n' roll song as part of its soundtrack."[20] *Blackboard Jungle* further cemented the association of rock and roll with juvenile delinquency.[21]

In 1956—a year before Freddy Fender's entry into Mexican rock and roll with "No Seas Cruel" and two years before Ritchie Valens burst onto the American rock-and-roll scene—Gloria Ríos literally and figuratively shouted rock and roll into the Mexican music scene. In 1956, Rios would become arguably the earliest rock-and-roll performer in Mexican media when she appeared in the movie *La locura del rock 'n roll* directed by Fernando Mendéz. Rios's version of "Rock around the Clock," titled "El Relojito," would soon thereafter become a huge hit single when it was released on RCA Victor.

Initially, rock and roll's entry into Mexico was less propelled by youth culture than by its popularization from orchestral jazz bands performing mostly for working-class and middle-class adults. In Ríos's singing of "El Relojito" in the movie *Las Locuras,* one can see an example of that jazz and swing influence in the construction of Ríos's band. Two key things set Ríos apart from the norm of rock and roll's entry into Mexico: she was young and she was Chicana.

The scene of Rios performing in *La locura del rock 'n roll* begins with a wide shot of the audience followed by the first sounds of the band, and then the camera cuts to Ríos, stage center, while her band is positioned to her rear left. The camera closes in on Ríos's face as she sings directly to the audience, inviting us to "vengan a bailar el rock 'n roll" (come and dance rock and roll). Almost immediately one notices the influences of Ríos's fondness for swing, bebop, and jazz. For example, throughout the song, she seems to be cultivating a dance that may be recognized as part twist and part jitterbug.[22] In addition, at about the midpoint of the song, Ríos launches into a classic jazz scat, most associated with Ella Fitzgerald. In fact, Ríos's daughter Regina Martínez told me that Ríos was a fan of Fitzgerald's music, having listened to her on the radio.[23]

During the last third of the performance, it's all hip action as Ríos sways her hips with fast feet action while we witness her body and the music become one.[24] The camera pans back and we see Ríos dressed in a full-length gown typically worn by cabaret performers. It is tightly fitted, but that does not prevent Ríos from flinging her body to the beat. Finally, the camera closes in again on Ríos. As the song reaches its peak, she sings "si te emocionas, pagas un grito" (if you're feeling it, let me hear you scream). Ríos screams wildly and crazily jumps in the air. Her body launches into faster motion, almost as if she is physically propelling rock and roll to take off. It is this moment in the film that is symbolized by Mexican rock historian Arturo Lara's assertion that "Fue una mujer, Gloria Ríos, la que pegó el primer grito del rock-n-roll en México" (The first defiant cry of rock and roll in Mexico came from a woman, Gloria Ríos).[25]

In addition to her recording and film performance of "El Relojito," Ríos also recorded other Spanish-language rock-and-roll hits for the RCA label, including "La Mecedora" (The rocking chair), "Hotel de Corazones Rotos" (Heartbreak Hotel), and "Ahí Nos Vemos Cocodrilo" (Bill Halley and the Comets' "See You Later Alligator"). From 1956 to 1958, she appeared in some of the earliest rock-and-roll movies, including *El Compás del Rock-n-Roll* (Rock-and-roll beat), *La Rebelión de los Adolescentes* (Youth uprising), and *Juventud Desenfrenada* (Unbridled youth). In *Juventud Desenfrenada,* Rios sings the soundtrack of Bill Halley's "Rock around the Clock" in its original English form.[26] Ríos's *grito,* launching rock and roll into Mexico, created room for future Mexican women singers in rock such as Julissa of Los Spitfires. The rock reverb of Julissa's "Ven Cerca" fittingly has an end in the sonic landscape of Gloria Ríos's beginning, San Antonio, a city persistently imagined by calls and shouts to remember. These echoes of Ríos's rock, crossing borders of nation, gender, and language, allow for new imaginaries of the borderlands, being pushed further to the limits of Girl in a Coma's sonic moves through Tex-Mex.

Girl in a Coma's first recording contract in 2006—signed by Joan Jett's label Blackheart Records—resulted in the release of their debut album *Both Before I'm Gone.* The album reached number 23 on Billboard's Heatseekers Chart and number 21 on iTunes. The song "Clumsy Sky" won a 2007 Independent Music Award in the best song-punk category. "Clumsy Sky" became Girl in a Coma's first music video, directed by independent filmmaker Jim Mendiola.

Band members and Mendiola could think of no more appropriate site for the band's first video than Lerma's Nite Club. Lerma's Nite Club is located in San Antonio's Westside. It is inarguably a cantina institution;[27] it is one of San Antonio's most historic spaces for Tex-Mex conjunto music, and arguably the longest-running live conjunto music venue in South Texas. It is a prototypical Tex-Mex conjunto cantina—generally speaking, a family-owned working-class bar nestled within a neighborhood area surrounded by homes as well as places of daily activity like grocery and liquor stores. Built in 1942, the partitioned building has operated as various locally owned businesses, including a dry-cleaning business, a grocery store, and a tire shop. The space that is now Lerma's was once El Sombrero, another popular conjunto music venue, before it was purchased in 1951 by Pablo Lerma. Lerma's is a working-class dive where music bounces off mismatched furniture, across a worn-out dance floor and stage, and through bad acoustics and wiring. The cantina is the kind of place that serves only two kinds of canned beer, where the bar's background mirror is filled with taped pictures of relatives, and whose smell lingers from the generations of dancers, hook-ups, and *peleas* (or barroom brawls). It's a space that, because of a poorly constructed foundation, usually allows the surrounding neighborhood to hear and imagine the bodily movements and physical transactions taking place on the dance floor. The cantina is a sonic-spatial reference for Tex-Mex music.

Dominant narratives of the cantina space have often worked to contain gender and sexuality through class-inflected notions of respectability and decency. In institutional memory, the cantina is where heteronormative masculinity is reduced to registers of rigidly normative gender and sexuality constructions commonly represented through the clientele of single men and heterosexual coupling. Moreover, another figure that has persisted in cantina space—too often inaudible and illegible in *la onda*—is the *cantinera,* that female figure of questionable sexuality. The *cantinera* is the one who sits alone at the edge of the bar but doesn't leave alone, the one who can occupy an entire table by herself without question, the one who operates through a system of nonverbal codes and hushed gestures, waiting for the right moment to come along.[28]

> Picture me away. Are we alright now? Are we alright now? Something's gonna happen. You are waiting. Are you waiting for my sign? Slip away now. Bite our lips now. Deep in the crowd. Are you waiting for my sign? In the back row. We will be alone. As they walk by. As they walk by.[29]

The introductory lyrics to "Clumsy Sky" could characterize a space of clandestine relations, of secrets, of shadow figures waiting for a sign, in the back row, deep in the crowd. The song was written by lead singer Nina Díaz, who composed the lyrics based on a coded language she and a partner created to communicate with each other.[30] The opening of the video for "Clumsy Sky" includes panning shots of Lerma's bar and elderly men playing dominos who are representative of the cantina's clientele. The close-up shot of a wall splashed with photos of Tex-Mex conjunto accordionists such as Narciso Martínez, Valerio Longoria, and Flaco Jiménez suggests the sound that has emanated from Lerma's for decades. Girl in a Coma's performance of "Clumsy Sky," situated with this iconic Tex-Mex musical venue, I argue, is less a gender reappropriation of the cantina space and more precisely a piercing echo of the working-class femininities and sexualities that have long populated the soundscape of cantina culture.[31]

After panning the opening shots of the bar, the music transitions to the main raucous beat and the camera focuses on the stage as the band plays. The video was shot in very do-it-yourself fashion that included friends and filmmaker/director Mendiola's father. Even Nina and Phanie Díaz's own stepfather (who plays the bartender) was invited to be part of the video.[32] Lerma's, as the site of their first video, is representative of the band's career trajectory, consistently connecting their representation to San Antonio. As Jenn Alva states, "Austin is cool, but San Antonio is almost like secret cool. We have amazing bands, we have great art, and all of it is influenced by Tex-Mex and Mexican culture."[33] Equally significant was that they would be singing on the very stage that is shown in Gregory Nava's 1997 Warner Brothers biopic *Selena*.[34] The stage is recognizable by the large painting of Jesús Helguera's 1950 painting *Grandeza Azteca* depicting the now-staple image that appears on most Mexican bakery calendars of the tragic love between Aztec princess Ixtacihuátl and her lover Popocatépetl.[35]

> Are you ready? are you ready for my sign? and we are the stars that light up the night. we are the stars that light up the night. ("Clumsy Sky")

Nina Díaz's thunderous vocals, the raucous electric guitar, the dancing bodies, burst through heteronormative parameters of what sounds Tex-Mex in the space of Lerma's cantina. The *vato loco* (crazy guy), the lesbians clasping each other's hands, the uncoupled dancing bodies—all represent an iconography of nonconforming genders and sexualities in "Clumsy Sky." The strident punk sounds, the moshing bodies, the racialized classed genders all create a sonic imaginary of alternative memories, of alternative subjectivities, and perhaps even a place to reside for those *cantineras* left sitting in the margins of Tex-Mex music.

This borderlands rock reverb represents yet another critical intervention this book intends, a reference to what I refer to in the title as Chicana music, not as a marker of female-based or feminine music but the naming of a commitment to push our senses to listen to and for Chicana musics and performances that seem inharmonious to our ears, or, as in this case, that seem unfit in a hegemonic Chicano borderlands imaginary; if we listen to what is dissonant in Chicano rock, including the music of Gloria Ríos, the hidden punk in Selena's "Si una Vez" by Girl in a Coma, then we must seriously consider and take risks to name the politics of gender and sexuality as listening to Chicana music.

The dissonance representative of such divas in this book encourages complex analytic and methodological tools of analysis. As a feminist methodology, diva dissonance illuminates musical productions and representations that reveal the ways nonnormative gender and sexuality have been foreclosed around *la onda*'s sonic imaginary of the borderlands. Moreover, dissonant divas also represent a methodology for articulating musical sound as more than audible through vocals and tunes, but also audible and visible in the female body. Divascapes filled with class, race, and sexuality tensions and alliances are differently gendered musical configurations of sound that cannot be overdetermined by geographic nation-state borders or canonical musical genres.

In the closing of Girl in a Coma's "Clumsy Sky" music video, a hand places a picture of the band among the collage of elder Tex-Mex iconic musicians posted on Lerma's Nite Club wall. The spirit of this motion symbolizes the ways diva dissonance, as exemplified by the Chicanas/Tejanas in this project, is not merely a move to cover up past music histories of *la onda* in order to make Chicanas in music audible and legible. The gesture of the picture remaining within a collage of past musical artists is the similar gesture of this project: to listen through, within, and against structural limits of power; rather than clearing up the structural noise or static that has left Chicanas in music unheard and misheard, we should instead listen to their stories, related gossip, musical interpretations, performances, and narratives among the commotion. Listening to Chicana music recalibrates the musical compasses of geography, the masculinist representation of instrumental sound, and claims the striving for passion that sonically reimagines the borderlands.

Acknowledgments

This book owes any contribution it will make to the voices of the women in these pages. I thank Rosita Fernández, Eva Ybarra, Ventura Alonzo, Phanie Díaz, Nina Díaz, and Jenn Alva for opening their hearts to trust in me and this work. I also appreciate the trust of family members who took time and care to retrieve memories and share ephemera of Chelo Silva, Eva Garza, Selena, and Gloria Ríos: Tina Moore, Regina Martínez, Angélica Silva, Alfredo Gil Jr., Américo Paredes Jr., and Suzette Quintanilla. I am grateful to the numerous other singers and musicians who shared their stories with me who do not appear in these pages but whose spirits are nonetheless woven throughout; I especially thank Rita Vidaurri, Laura Canales, Carmen Marroquín, and Nellie Cantú. I will remain forever humbled by these experiences of listening.

The seeds of this project emerged from both tragedy and fortune. When Selena was tragically killed in 1995, her loss prompted me to ask and excavate the stories of Chicana/Tejana singers who came before her. I was fortunate to be surrounded by faculty at the University of California, Santa Cruz who helped me develop the first seeds of what would culminate in this book. I am especially appreciative of my dissertation committee members: Herman S. Gray always engaged with the roughest inklings of ideas, modeled what it meant to mentor, and reminded me that my role in the academy is to think radically; Patricia Zavella guided me along every step of this book and I am especially thankful for the ways she always brought me back to Chicana feminist ethnography as a political practice. I am indebted to the critical race feminist training of

Dana Takagi, Olga Nájera-Ramírez, and Rosa Linda Fregoso. Although she was not on my committee, I thank Angela Y. Davis for independent studies coursework that challenged and transformed my critical race feminist analysis of women of color in music. The Chicano Studies Research Center (CSRC) and the Department of Latin American and Latino Studies (LALS) at UC Santa Cruz were the first funding support for the earliest research conducted and the first settings for presenting it. My thanks to the faculty and (then) graduate student colleagues associated with CSRC and LALS: Aida Hurtado, Norma Klahn, Gabriela Arrendondo, Russell Rodríguez, and Sarita Gaytan. In 2004, our community lost the brilliant light of Lionel Cantú, whom I miss and whose hummingbird spirit guided me toward completing what he saw as a beginning.

The research for this book required a tremendous amount of fellowship and funding support. I thank UC MEXUS: the University of California Institute for Mexico and the United States and the University of California Postdoctoral Fellowship Program. A postdoctoral fellowship from the Ford Foundation hosted by the UCLA Chicano Studies Research Center supported the time to think, participate in collaborative exchanges, and write. I give huge thanks to Chon Noriega, director of the UCLA CSRC for his unwavering mentorship and for research funding supported through the UCLA Strachwitz Frontera Collection of Mexican and Mexican American Recordings.

Thank you to my colleagues in the Department of Chicano/Latino Studies at the University of California, Irvine: Louis DeSipio, Ana Rosas, Gilberto Gonzales, Belinda Campos, Michael Montoya, Alejandro Morales, and Cynthia Feliciano. Viki Ruiz was a significant force of support and mentoring, and I am especially grateful for her feedback on the Chicana oral histories I conducted and analyzed. I cannot say enough good things about Raúl Fernández, who has blessed the pages of this book with his musical insight, his skill for storytelling, and his passion for listening to musical sound. Thank you for introducing me to La Habana. My research in Havana could not have been conducted without the support of Elba Capote, who assisted in helping me "locate" Eva Garza by inaugurating my experience of Havana with generosity, humor, and a wealth of knowledge. Special thanks to Ana Casanova for sharing her Cuban music expertise.

The following colleagues gave me feedback on ideas, conference papers, chapter drafts, and publications related to this book: Maribel Alvarez, Alicia Arrizón, Sergio de la Mora, Arlene Dávila, Gayatri Gopinath, Felicity Schaeffer-Grabiel, Michelle Habell-Pallán, J. Jack Halberstam, Laura Gutiérrez, Louis Mendoza, Marie "Keta" Miranda, Deborah Pacini Hernández, Deborah Paredez, Catherine Ramírez, Juana Maria Rodriguez, Ana Patricia Rodriguez, Sandra Soto, and Alexandra Vazquez. Other colleagues came through in the most amazing ways, and their support is symbolized by the binding that holds this book together. My deep thanks to Roderick Ferguson for offering to read the first drafts of these chapters and really helping me believe I could write a book. Since graduate school, I have not encountered a more generous colleague than Sherrie Tucker, who helped me untangle so many knots. A heartfelt thanks to Raúl Coronado for sharing his literary history expertise and to Nicole Guidotti-Hernández for her insight on the borderlands. The powerful insight of Kirstie Dorr, Sara Clarke Kaplan, Fatima El-Tayeb, and Tara Javidi carried me through the toughest stages in this process. A significant thanks to my dear *amiga* Gaye Teresa Johnson for our monthly book-writing sessions. There are no other scholars I have enjoyed listening to, dancing with, critically engaging with, and learning more from about the power of race, gender, sexuality, and sound than Dolores Inés Casillas, Roshanak Khesti, and Kirstie Dorr. Thank you to my research assistants Cristina Garcia and Rosie Bermudez for doing all the tedious work. I am so appreciative for the transcription labor of Patricia Espinosa Artiles.

During my year at the University of Texas at Austin I was fortunate to engage with extremely supportive colleagues, including Shirley Marshall-Thompson, Eric Pritchard, Elizabeth Englehart, and Ann Cvetcovich. I thank José Limón and the Center for Mexican American Studies and am especially grateful to librarian Margo Gutiérrez of the Benson Latin American Collection for her all-around dynamic librarian skills. In Austin, I gained rich insight through collaborative exchanges with Clay Shorkey of the Texas Music Museum. I offer sincere thanks to music historians Manuel Peña, Chris Strachwitz, and Juan Tejeda for generously sharing their musical knowledge with me.

The shelf space for this book was carved out by fierce feminist theorists who mentored me on this journey: Antonia Castañeda, Cynthia

Orozco, Emma Pérez, Yvonne Yarbro-Bejarano, and Norma Cantú. I am especially grateful to Angie Chabram-Dernersesian for her postdoctoral mentorship and to Sonia Saldívar-Hull for her book mentorship and for reminding me to embrace my Tejana feminist perspectives. My analysis of music is especially indebted to the scholarship of Frances Aparicio, Licia Fiol-Matta, Frances Negrón-Muntaner, and Raquel Rivera.

The LOUD (feminist of color) writing collective gave life to this book. My heartfelt thanks to Maylei Blackwell, Jayna Brown, Erica Edwards, Aisha Finch, Mishuana Goeman, Macarena Gómez-Barris, Yogita Goyal, Grace Hong, Arlene Keizer, Kara Keeling, Jodi Kim, Mignon Moore, and Tiffany Willoughby-Herard. I give an extra-special LOUD shout-out to Grace Hong for giving feedback on the entire book and to Yogita Goyal for our post-LOUD happy hours.

Thank you to Lynn Fujiwara for being my homegirl; she never left my side and saved my sanity and spirit. I am grateful for the love and friendship of Nancy San Martin and Julie Marsh; anything accurately and beautifully translated from Spanish to English is thanks to you. A major thanks to Maylei Blackwell for *consejos,* spiritual guidance, and a kick when I needed it. This book has been blessed by Ricardo Bracho (including his dynamic indexing skills), Denise Contreras, Persephone Gonzales, Vicky Grise, Delia Marez, Gloria Ramírez, Carmen Varela, and Laura Varela. I offer my most special song dedication to Erica Edwards, whose "eyes make the stars look like they're not shining." Thank you for sharing this life with me, for being my amazing friend, writing partner, and soul mate throughout. You bring the "bidi bidi bom bom" to my heart, and I know that "I can live, I can love, I can be better with you . . . for real."

I physically left San Antonio, the "home" I was born and raised in, when I was eighteen, but San Antonio has never left my soul. I will always be a Westside kid at heart who continues to believe the Spurs can make another run at the title and who never ceases to crave flour tortillas. To paraphrase Gloria Anzaldúa, like a turtle I will always carry "home" on my back and the love of multiple families in my heart. Thanks to Deborah Paredez, Frank Guridy, and my goddess daughter Zaya Alegría for creating an intellectual and love-filled home for me. Mari Infante has always fed my soul and my stomach and she is the true definition of friendship. I thank my mother, Enriqueta Ramos Vargas, for giving me a strong tongue. I offer my deepest gratitude for support to my brothers, Robert, Hector, Pedro Jr., to my sister-in-law Jacqueline López Vargas, my niece Allyson, and my nephew Aaron. My father, Pedro Ruíz Vargas, is the best example of feminist masculinity I know. I thank him for exemplifying unconditional love, for being strong enough to raise a masculine daughter in the face of judgment, and for being the best history storyteller I know. Dad, every time I see cotton fields in Texas I will think of you and your experiences growing up *mexicano* in *Tejas.* I will always carry your light in me and it is to you that this book is dedicated.

Notes

Introduction

1. See Deborah R. Vargas, "Rita's Pants: The *charro traje* and Trans-sensuality," *Woman and Performance: A Journal of Feminist Theory* 20:1 (2010): 3–14.

2. Although it is outside the scope of this project, there remain a vast number of Chicana singers to be analyzed, including 1930s singer Adelina Garcia; the cohort of post–World War II women duets such as Carmen y Laura, Las Hermanas Góngora, Las Hermanas Cantú, and others; 1970s singer Laura Canales.

3. I will sometimes use "Chicano/Tejano" to emphasize the intertwined relationship between two distinct yet connected musics. While Tejano music may fall within the umbrella reference of Chicano music, it does not work the other way around.

4. I refer to terms "heteronormative" and "heteronormativity" throughout the book to refer to queer-studies theorizations addressing dominant gender and sexuality ideologies that assume binaries of man/woman, female/male, and of heterosexuality as the norm with regard to social identities, cultural productions, and social constructions of family, citizenship, and home, among others. Moreover, these terms also convey a perceived deviance and pathology associated with gender subjectivities and performances most often labeled "gay," "lesbian," bisexual," and "transgender." See Michael Warner, *Fear of a Queer Planet: Queer Politics and Social Theory* (Minneapolis: University of Minnesota Press, 1993); Cathy J. Cohen, "Punks, Bulldaggers, and Welfare Queens: The Radical Potential of Queer Politics?" in E. Patrick Johnson and Mae G. Henderson, eds., *Black Queer Studies: A Critical Anthology* (Durham, N.C.: Duke University Press, 2005); Robyn Wiegman, "The Desire for Gender," in George E. Haggerty and

Molly McGarry, eds., *A Companion to Lesbian, Gay, Bisexual, Transgender, and Queer Studies* (Malden, Mass.: Blackwell, 2007), 217–36.

5. Examples include Paul F. Berliner, *Thinking Jazz: The Infinite Art of Improvisation* (Chicago: University of Chicago Press, 1994), and the now standard source of jazz history, Ken Burns's documentary *Jazz: A Film by Ken Burns,* dir. Ken Burns, Public Broadcasting System, 2001.

6. Alicia Schmidt Camacho, *Migrant Imaginaries: Latino Cultural Politics in the U.S.–Mexico Borderlands* (New York: New York University Press, 2008), 5–6. Schmidt Camacho draws on the work of Charles Taylor, *Modern Social Imaginaries* (Durham, N.C.: Duke University Press, 2004), and Parameshwar Gaonker, "Toward New Imaginaries: An Introduction," *Public Culture* 14:1 (2002).

7. Manuel Peña, *Música Tejana* (College Station: Texas A&M University Press, 1999), 19. Guadalupe San Miguel Jr. refers to "La onda Chicana" as "the particular type of sound played by the orquestas of the 1960s and 1970s" (Guadalupe San Miguel Jr., *Tejano Proud: Tex-Mex Music in the Twentieth Century* [College Station: Texas A&M University Press, 2002], 77). See also Manuel Peña, *The Mexican American Orquesta: Music, Culture, and the Dialectic of Conflict* (Austin: University of Texas Press, 1999); Rafaela G. Castro, *Chicano Folklore: A Guide to the Folktales, Traditions, Rituals, and Religious Practices of Mexican Americans* (London: Oxford University Press, 2001).

8. See, for example, Américo Paredes, *With His Pistol in His Hand: A Border Ballad and Its Hero* (Austin: University of Texas Press, 1958); Manuel Peña, *The Texas-Mexican Conjunto: History of a Working-Class Music* (Austin: University of Texas Press, 1985); David Reyes and Tom Walden, *Land of a Thousand Dances: Chicano Rock 'n' Roll from Southern California* (Albuquerque: University of New Mexico Press, 1998); Steven Loza, *Barrio Rhythm: Mexican American Music in Los Angeles* (Urbana: University of Illinois Press, 1999); San Miguel, *Tejano Proud.*

9. See Gloria Anzaldúa, *Borderlands/La Frontera: The New Mestiza* (San Francisco: Spinsters/Aunt Lute, 1987); Emma Pérez, *The Decolonial Imaginary: Writing Chicanas into History* (Bloomington: Indiana University Press, 1999); Sonia Saldívar-Hull, *Feminism on the Border: Chicana Gender Politics and Literature* (Berkeley: University of California Press, 2000); Rosa Linda Fregoso, *MeXicana Encounters: The Making of Social Identities on the Borderlands* (Berkeley: University of California Press, 2003).

10. Anthony Macías, *Mexican American Mojo: Popular Music, Dance, and Urban Culture in Los Angeles, 1935–1968* (Durham, N.C.: Duke University Press, 2008). See also *www.americansabor.org* and Michelle Habell-Pallán, *Loca-Motion: The Travels of Chicana and Latina Popular Culture* (New York: New York University Press, 2005).

11. Ajay Heble, *Landing on the Wrong Note: Jazz, Dissonance, and Critical Practice* (London: Routledge, 2000), 4.

12. Ibid., x. See also Daniel Fischlin and Ajay Heble, "Introduction: The Other Side of Nowhere: Jazz, Improvisation, and Communities in Dialogue," in Daniel Fischlin and Ajay Heble, eds., *The Other Side of Nowhere: Jazz, Improvisation, and Communities in Dialogue* (Middletown, Conn.: Wesleyan University Press, 2004), 1.

13. Heble, *Landing on the Wrong Note,* 9.

14. I thank Deborah Paredez for our conversations about her current research on Latina and African American divas from a critical race and feminist perspective and for encouraging me to think critically about the ways divas of color shape and reimagine race, gendered, sexual, national, temporal, and aesthetic categories. See also Daphne A. Brooks, *Bodies in Dissent: Spectacular Performances of Race and Freedom, 1850–1910* (Durham, N.C.: Duke University Press, 2006).

15. See Broyles-González, *Lydia Mendoza's Life in Music: Norteño Tejano Legacies* (New York and London: Oxford University Press, 2001), and Chris Strachwitz and James Nicolopulos, *Lydia Mendoza: A Family Autobiography* (Houston: Arte Público Press, 1993).

16. See Pérez, *The Decolonial Imaginary,* 3–30.

17. Mary Pat Brady, "Border," in Bruce Burgett and Glenn Hendler, eds., *Keywords for American Cultural Studies* (New York: New York University Press, 2007), 31.

18. The use of "j" in the term also is intended to symbolize the Spanish pronunciation of the letter as *jota,* which in turn represents a symbolic gesture to center nonheteronormative genders and sexualities.

19. The book moves back and forth through the terms *mexicano* (generally speaking, a term often claimed by people of Mexican descent; it may also contest discrete identities such as "Mexican" and "Mexican American" that are aligned according to the socially constructed border between the United States and Mexico); "Tejano" and "Texas-Mexican" (terms that designate *mexicanos* who reside in or claim Texas as their birthplaces); "Mexican" (in reference to Mexican nationality and cultural production). My use of these multiple terms emphasizes the social identities, histories, languages, and cultural citizenships negotiated by the singers in my project and validates the multiple and simultaneous use of the terms to describe themselves and their experiences.

20. Licia Fiol-Matta, "Body, Space, Sexuality," New Directions in Queer Latino Studies conference, University of Southern California and University of California, Los Angeles, November 2005.

1. Remember the Alamo, Remember Rosita Fernández

1. I refer to Rosita Fernández by her first name in this chapter because it was her stage name and because it acknowledges the unique iconic singing persona that her music career represented (similar to the spirit of other single first-name artists such as Selena or Cher).

2. Rosita Fernández, interview with the author, August 18, 1999, San Antonio, Texas.

3. Lamar R. Howard, *Texas Crossings: The Lone Star State and the American Far West, 1836–1986* (Austin: University of Texas Press, 1991), xiii; quoted in George Lipsitz, "No Shining City on a Hill: American Studies and the Problem of Place," *American Studies* 40:2 (summer 1991): 54.

4. I acknowledge the shortcomings of this chapter and parts of this book that too often remain within the brown/white binary of Mexican–Anglo relations. See the following books for examples of analysis of Chicanos/*mexicanos* in the United States that go beyond the brown/white binary: Nicole Guidotti-Hernández, *Unspeakable Violence: Remapping U.S. and Mexican National Imaginaries* (Durham, N.C.: Duke University Press, 2011); Luis Álvarez and Daniel Widener, "A History of Black and Brown: Chicano/a–African American Cultural and Political Relations," *Aztlán: A Journal of Chicano Studies* 33:1 (spring 2008): 143–54; Gaye Teresa Johnson, "Constellations of Struggle: Luisa Moreno, Charlotta Bass, and the Legacy for Ethnic Studies," *Aztlán: A Journal of Chicano Studies* 33:1 (spring 2008): 155–72.

5. In fact, it was Lady Bird Johnson, wife of then President Lyndon B. Johnson, who bestowed on Rosita the title "San Antonio's First Lady of Song" after an event at which she saw Rosita perform. The name borrows from the description of legendary singer Etta Fitzgerald as the "First Lady of Song." In fact, Lady Bird Johnson's favorite song was "Tierra del sol." In our conversations, Rosita would often mock Anglo Texans trying to pronounce songs in Spanish: "Ella lo decía 'tee-era-dell-sole, poor fa-vor Rosita" (Rosita Fernández, interview with the author, August 18, 1999, San Antonio, Texas). Rosita recalled the time when Lady Bird Johnson brought a group of nearly fifty ambassadors to San Antonio and Rosita was the main attraction of a show organized by the city along San Antonio's Riverwalk. The quote "Rosita y San Antonio son inseparables" that opens this chapter comes from the back record cover of Fernández's record *San Antonio* (circa mid-1970s) sung with el Mariachi Chapultepec.

6. See Frank Thompson, *The Alamo: A Cultural History* (Dallas: Taylor Trade Publishing, 2001). According to Thompson, any San Antonio cultural production becomes, by default, inseparable from the city's ties to the Alamo

monument and its myths and legacies. In fact, any motion picture produced in San Antonio, no matter the time period or plot, is compelled to include the Alamo, even when it has little to do with the story.

7. Mary Louise Pratt, "Back Yard with Views," in Andrew Ross and Kristen Ross, eds., *Anti-Americanism* (New York: New York University Press, 2004), 35.

8. See Raúl Coronado, *A World Not to Come: A History of Nineteenth-Century Latino Writing, Print Culture, and the Disenchantment of the World* (Cambridge: Harvard University Press, 2012). Coronado goes on to argue that these battles resulted in hatred of all things Indian and Mexican. This meant genocide for Native Americans and conquest and displacement for Texas Mexicans. By the late 1840s, the majority of Mexicans had fled the sexual-racial terror that had taken over San Antonio. When many of the Mexicans returned in the 1850s, they found their property and land taken over by squatters. See also Arnoldo De León, *The Tejano Community, 1836–1900* (Albuquerque: University of New Mexico Press, 1982), 14–15; Timothy Matovina, *Tejano Ethnicity and Religion, San Antonio, 1821–1860* (Austin: University of Texas Press, 2010), 50–52. Matovina draws our attention to the percentages of property ownership that in 1840 is marked by an 85 percent ownership by Mexicans; ten years later, in 1850, that percentage had been reduced to 9 percent.

9. Ibid., 280.

10. Jesús F. de la Teja, *A Community on New Spain's Northern Frontier* (Albuquerque: University of New Mexico Press, 1995).

11. See *The Handbook of Texas Online,* a project of the Texas State Historical Association (http://www.tshaonline.org).

12. Six national flags have flown over Texas since the arrival of Hernán Cortés to the region in 1519: Texas under Spain (1519–1685; 1690–1821); France (1685–90); Mexico (1821–36); Texas as a Republic (1836–45); Texas in the Confederacy (1861–65); Texas in the United States (1845–61; 1865–present).

13. Donald E. Chipman and Harriett Denise Joseph, *Spanish Texas, 1519–1821,* 2d ed. (Austin: University of Texas Press, 2010).

14. Paul Lack, "Occupied Texas: Bexar and Goliad, 1835–1836," in Emilio Zamora, Cynthia Orozco, and Rodolfo Rocha, eds., *Mexican Americans in Texas History* (Austin: Texas State Historical Association, 2000), 35.

15. Andrés Tijerina, *Tejanos and Texas under the Mexican Flag, 1821–1836* (College Station: Texas A&M University Press, 1994).

16. Lack, "Occupied Texas," 49.

17. Ibid. See also Raúl A. Ramos, *Beyond the Alamo: Forging Mexican Ethnicity in San Antonio, 1821–1861* (Chapel Hill: University of North Carolina Press, 2008).

18. Coronado, *A World Not to Come;* Ramos, *Beyond the Alamo,* 137–65.

19. Lack, "Occupied Texas," 5.

20. Ibid., 49. See also Ramos, *Beyond the Alamo;* Matovina, *Tejano Ethnicity and Religion,* 24–28.

21. Timothy M. Matovina, *The Alamo Remembered: Tejano Accounts and Perspectives* (Austin: University of Texas Press, 1995), 5. See also Paul D. Lack, *The Texas Revolutionary Experience: A Political and Social History, 1835–1836,* 1st ed., vol. 10 (College Station: Texas A&M University Press, 1992), 183–207.

22. Matovina, *The Alamo Remembered,* 3.

23. For examples of works that address this issue, see Richard Flores, *Remembering the Alamo: Memory, Modernity, and the Master Symbol* (Austin: University of Texas Press, 2002); Ramos, *Beyond the Alamo.*

24. See Rodolfo Acuña, *Occupied America: The Chicano's Struggle toward Liberation,* 2d ed. (New York: Harper and Row, 1981); David Montejano, *Anglos and Mexicans in the Making of Texas, 1836–1986* (Austin: University of Texas Press, 1987).

25. *Handbook of Texas Online,* http://www.tsha.utexas.edu/handbook/online/articles/SS/qes4.html.

26. One of the eight inscriptions on the exterior base of the San Jacinto Monument reads: "Measured by its results, San Jacinto was one of the decisive battles of the world. The freedom of Texas from Mexico won here led to annexation and to the Mexican War, resulting in the acquisition by the United States of the states of Texas, New Mexico, Arizona, Nevada, California, Utah, and parts of Colorado, Wyoming, Kansas, and Oklahoma. Almost one-third of the present area of the American nation, nearly a million square miles of territory, changed sovereignty."

27. David J. Weber, *Troubles in Texas, 1832: A Tejano Viewpoint from San Antonio with a Translation and Facsimile* (Dallas: Wind River Press for the Degolyer Library of Southern Methodist University Library, 1982), 11.

28. The more precise battle cry is said to have been "Remember the Alamo! Remember Goliad!" in reference to another battle that preceded the Battle of San Jacinto. Yet, "Remember the Alamo!" has gone down in folklore history without the reference to Goliad.

29. I borrow this phrase from David Montejano, *Anglos and Mexicans in the Making of Texas, 1936–1986* (Austin: University of Texas Press, 1987). See also San Miguel Jr., *Tejano Proud,* 41.

30. Maylei Blackwell, *¡Chicana Power! Contested Histories of Feminism in the Chicano Movement* (Austin: University of Texas Press, 2011), 95.

31. Examples of movies include *Martyrs of the Alamo* (1915) directed by D. W. Griffith; *The Alamo* (1960) starring John Wayne; *Thirteen Days to Glory*

(1987); *The Alamo* (2004) starring Billy Bob Thornton and Dennis Quaid. Public television programs include *The History Channel Presents the Alamo* (2003) and *American Experience: Remember the Alamo* (2004). It is interesting to note that the 1960s John Wayne movie *The Alamo* has been re-marketed various times—for example, as a double-feature DVD box set paired with *The Magnificent Seven* and as a "restored original Director's cut" in 1993 and as a "original uncut version" in 1995. For an example of Tejano filmmakers producing cinematic counternarratives of Texas history and of Tejanos within the context of San Antonio, see the work of director Jim Mendiola, including *Pretty Vacant* (1996), *Come and Take It Day* (2002), and *Speeder Kills* (2003).

32. Richard Flores, *Remembering the Alamo: Memory, Modernity, and the Master Symbol* (Austin: University of Texas Press, 2002), 16.

33. The quotations cited appear on huge concrete plates at the entrance to the various exhibits in the museum.

34. Ernest Renan, "What Is Nation?" in Homi K. Bhabha, ed., *Nation and Narration* (New York: Routledge, 1990), 19.

35. Rosa Linda Fregoso, *The Bronze Screen: Chicana and Chicano Film Culture* (Minneapolis: University of Minnesota Press, 1993); Fregoso, *MeXicana Encounters.*

36. Chicana feminist scholarship addressing Tejanas and racialized women includes Leticia M. Garza-Falcón, *A Borderlands Response to the Rhetoric of Dominance* (Austin: University of Texas Press, 1998); Teresa Paloma Acosta and Ruthe Winegarten, *Las Tejanas: 300 Years of History* (Austin: University of Texas Press, 2003); María Cotera, *Native Speakers: Ella Deloria, Zora Neale Hurston, Jovita González, and the Poetics of Culture* (Austin: University of Texas Press, 2008).

37. The word *gente* generally means "people," but in this case "our *gente,*" or sometimes *mi gente,* is equivalent to *mi raza* and conveys a nationalist imaginary of community or a homogeneous people.

38. Shelly Streeby, *American Sensations: Class, Empire, and the Production of Popular Culture* (Berkeley: University of California Press, 2002), 37. Streeby's discussion of the feminized notion of Mexico in relationship to the dominant or masculine notion of the United States is helpful for understanding how the name Rose or Rosita is uniquely gendered feminine by the racialized discourse of Mexico and *mexicanidad.*

39. Examples of popular publications devoted to the myth include Denise McVea, *Making Myth of Emily: Emily West de Zavala and the Yellow Rose of Texas Legend* (San Antonio: Auris Books, 2006), and Anita Richmond Bunkley, *Emily, the Yellow Rose: A Texas Legend* (Cypress, Tex.: Rinard Publishing, 2011).

40. See Trudier Harris, "The Yellow Rose of Texas: A Different Cultural View," *Callaloo* 20:1 (1997): 10.

41. *Yellow* has often been used to refer to someone of light-skinned color and as an equivalent for *mulatta*. For an analysis of the racialized politics of skin color and hair texture, see Noliwe M. Rooks, *Hair Raising: Beauty, Culture and African American Women* (Piscataway, N.J.: Rutgers University Press, 1996); Ingrid Banks, *Hair Matters: Beauty, Power, and Black Women's Consciousness* (New York: New York University Press, 2000).

42. For some examples of black feminist analysis of black women's sexuality, see bell hooks, *Black Looks: Race and Representation* (Boston: South End Press, 1999); Patricia Hill Collins, *Black Sexual Politics: African Americans, Gender, and the New Racism* (New York: Routledge, 2005); Arlene Keizer, "'Are Posteriors Our Posterity?': The Problem of Embodiment in Suzan-Lori Parks's *Venus* and Kara Walker's *Camptown Ladies*," *Social Dynamics* 37:2 (2011): 200–212.

43. Quoted from the tour guide at the Alamo in San Antonio, Texas.

44. Harris, "The Yellow Rose of Texas," 15.

45. Some discographies have the date listed as 1938.

46. Although the song's official name is "New San Antonio Rose," it was circulated as "San Antonio Rose."

47. Frank Jennings, *San Antonio: The Story of an Enchanted City* (San Antonio: San Antonio Express News Press, 1998).

48. Al Strickland, *My Years with Bob Wills*, 2d ed. (Burnet, Tex.: Eakin Press, 1980), 27.

49. Ibid.

50. See Neil Foley, *The White Scourge: Mexicans, Blacks, and Poor Whites in Texas Cotton Culture* (Berkeley: University of California Press, 1997).

51. Charles Townsend, *San Antonio Rose: The Life and Music of Bob Wills* (Urbana: University of Illinois Press, 1986), 28.

52. Rose is the English equivalent of Spanish Rosa. Rosita is a diminutive form of Rosa. In some cases, young girls named Rosa are called "Rosita" in their younger years and/or if they are the youngest in a family. Sometimes "Rosita" carries an extra-special or endearing connotation.

53. Rosarita Foods is a brand owned by the Conagra Food Company. Pedro Guerrero of Arizona founded what he first named "Rosita Foods" in the 1940s. After transitioning from the popularity of his tamales to canned beans, the brand name changed to "Rosarita Foods." One of his sons designed the now iconic Mexican woman for the brand label.

54. Rosita Fernández, interview with the author, August 18, 1999, San Antonio, Texas. At moments during the interview Raúl, Rosita's husband, stopped by to join the conversation.

55. Daniel D. Arreola, *Tejano South Texas: A Mexican American Cultural Province* (Austin: University of Texas Press, 2002), 165.

56. Ibid.

57. Rosita Fernández, interview with the author, August 18, 1999, San Antonio, Texas.

58. Ibid. Rosita Fernández, interview with Ruthie Winegarten, April 29, 1997, San Antonio, Texas.

59. Jackson was commonly referred to as "the Strongman," a popular circus performer of his time. After retiring sometime in the 1930s, he went into the entertainment business, showing Mexican movies in makeshift tents. Jackson's *carpas* were located in Alice, Robstown, and Kingsville. Rosita and Raúl Almaguer chose Jackson to be their first child's godfather. See Peter Haney, "Me hago la . . . ilusión: Genre Play and Status Consciousness in the Mexican American Carpa," In *Proceedings of the First Annual Conference on the Emerging Literature of the Southwest Culture* (El Paso: University of Texas Press, 1996); Peter Haney, "Sol, sombra y media luz: History, Parody, and Identity Formation in the Mexican American Carpa," *Pragmatics* 10:1 (2000): 99–123.

60. After Jackson retired in the 1930s, he went into the entertainment business in the Coastal Bend area, primarily showing Mexican movies in secondhand tents. See Peter Haney, "Carpa y teatro, sol y sombra: Show Business and Public Culture in San Antonio's Mexican Colony, 1900–1940," dissertation, University of Texas, 2004, 83.

61. Aside from Rosita, some of more well-known Tejana singers, including Lydia Mendoza and Las Hermanas Góngora, also performed in *carpas*. See Haney, "Sol, sombra y media luz."

62. Rosita Fernández, interview with the author, August 18, 1999, San Antonio, Texas. See also Sergio de la Mora, *Cinemachismo: Masculinities and Sexuality in Mexican Film* (Austin: University of Texas Press, 2006).

63. See Susan Douglas, *Listening In: Radio and the American Imagination* (Minneapolis: University of Minnesota Press, 1999), 48. She emphasizes that radio did not begin in 1920 and had a twenty-five-year history as a wireless telegraphy, then as a wireless telephony, when the human voice was transmitted. The word *radio* became popularized in the 1920s.

64. Ibid., 6.

65. *La hora Anáhuac* represents the seeds of what at that time could not even be imagined: full-time Spanish language radio in the United States. Although not the first full-time Spanish-language radio station, KEDA is said to be the first dedicated to the promotion of regional Tejano music. Founded by Manuel Dávila in 1966, in 2008 KEDA became the longest-running and last-remaining independent family-owned radio station in San Antonio.

66. Rosita Fernández, interview with the author, August 18, 1999, San Antonio, Texas. Rosita recalled that the Manuel Dávila family were early buyers

of these slots. Raúl Córtez Sr. eventually started KCOR, the first all-Spanish-language radio station in San Antonio.

67. Ibid. Also, personal conversation with music historian and record collector Ramón Hernández, 2009.

68. In later years, Rosita also appeared in print media advertising. She even appeared on a calendar for White Wing Flour Tortillas and on television commercials.

69. Rosita Fernández, interview with the author, July 15, 2000, San Antonio, Texas. Smithsonian Latin Music Oral History Project.

70. Félix F. Gutiérrez and Jorge R. Schement, *Spanish-Language Radio in the Southwestern United States* (Austin: University of Texas, Center for Mexican American Studies, 1979). WOAI claims that its first broadcast in Spanish was in 1928.

71. Rosita met her husband Raúl during one of these classes.

72. Manuel Peña, *The Texas-Mexican Conjunto: History of a Working-Class Music* (Austin: University of Texas Press, 1985), 41.

73. Ibid., 42.

74. Rosita Fernández, interviews with the author, August 24, 1999, and July 15, 2000, San Antonio, Texas.

75. Rosita Fernández, interview with the author, August 24, 1999, San Antonio, Texas. During our interview, Raúl Almaguer recalled: "I'm the only one in my family that did not know music, but I am the only one in my family that wrote songs that were recorded by Rosita."

76. Rosita Fernández, interview with the author, July 15, 2000, San Antonio, Texas. Smithsonian Latin Music Oral History Project.

77. Although all of the music contained in this portfolio was drawn from Mexican composers, it was marketed to non-Spanish-speaking musicians and became the source of many tunes shared between Texas Anglos and Hispanic communities. "A song like 'Sobre las Alas' became a standard in the old-time fiddle playlist under the title 'Over the Waves.'" There seems to be a typographical error or mistranslation here in the title because the word for "waves" is *olas,* not *alas.* The quote appears in an exhibit on Texas music history in the Texas History Museum titled "Mexican sheet music dated 1930 published by Thomas Googan and Brothers Galveston," Second Floor Exhibit, Austin, Texas.

78. Vicki Ruiz counters such limited representations by highlighting women in the public social sphere in *From Out of the Shadows: Mexican Women in Twentieth-Century America* (New York: Oxford University Press, 1998).

79. Thanks to Rosita Fernández for allowing me access to her personal record collection. In 1937, she recorded a two-sided 78 with the Trío San Miguel

and the songs "Elevo al cielo" and "El Ranchero Afamado" on Vocalion (Brunswick Record Corporation). She was paid twenty-five dollars per song with Brunswick.

80. Rosita Fernández, interview with the author, August 24, 1999, San Antonio, Texas.

81. Rosita Fernández, interview with the author, July 15, 2000, San Antonio, Texas. Smithsonian Latin Music Oral History Project.

82. Ibid.

83. Fregoso, *MeXicana Encounters,* 50.

84. José E. Limón, *Dancing with the Devil: Society and Cultural Poetics in Mexican-American South Texas* (Madison: University of Wisconsin Press, 1994), 59.

85. Press release, April 1986, City of San Antonio, Department of Parks and Recreation. See also letter from City of San Antonio dated February 17, 1981, where Mayor Lila Cockrell extends an invitation to Rosita Fernández to sing "San Antonio" for the city's commemoration of the 250th anniversary of the founding of its municipal government.

86. These music postcard records were popular souvenirs of the time.

87. See Richard R. Flores, *Remembering the Alamo: Memory, Modernity, and the Master Symbol* (Austin: University of Texas Press, 2002).

88. Some literature suggests that *Sancho the Homing Steer* was filmed in Hollywood even though it was actually filmed in Arizona. Rosita lived in New York for about a year, and appeared on the *Arthur Godfrey Show* and in various clubs.

89. Rosita Fernández, interview with the author, 2000, San Antonio, Texas. Smithsonian Latin Music Oral History Project.

90. My emphasis.

91. Flores, *Remembering the Alamo,* xv. See also Marita Sturken, *Tangled Memories: The Vietnam War, the AIDS Epidemic, and the Politics of Remembering* (Berkeley: University of California Press, 1997).

92. Gutiérrez distinguishes "lo mexicano" as fixed understandings whereas *mexicandidad* is a malleable concept. *Mexicanidad* marks the deployment of performance strategies to disrupt "lo mexicano" but that do not completely delink the artist from dominant notions of national and cultural belonging. As such, Rosita could be said to be "performing *mexicanidad.*" See Laura G. Gutiérrez, *Performing* Mexicanidad: Vendidas y Cabareteras *on the Transnational Stage* (Austin: University of Texas Press, 2010), 19–21.

93. Two costumes were acquired by the Smithsonian in 2001; the other, acquired later in the year, belonged to Lydia Mendoza. The Mendoza costume was featured in the Smithsonian's traveling exhibit "Corridos" throughout 2002.

94. Rosita Fernández, interview with the author, 1999, San Antonio, Texas. Rosita often switched between English and Spanish during our interviews and personal chats.

95. Later in her career she had some of her costumes made in Mexico by a Monterey designer named Mr. Tenis (ibid.).

96. Kimberley Randall, "The Traveler's Eye: Chinas Poblanas and European-Inspired Costume in Postcolonial Mexico," in Regina A. Root, ed., *The Latin American Fashion Reader* (New York: Berg Publishers, 2005), 72.

97. Ibid., 57.

98. Catherine Ramírez makes similar observations of the manipulation and excessive use of fabric in light of social rules by pachucos and pachucas during World War II (Catherine S. Ramírez, *The Woman in the Zoot Suit: Gender, Nationalism, and the Cultural Politics of Memory* [Durham, N.C.: Duke University Press, 2009]).

99. Randall, "The Traveler's Eye," 56. Randall is quoting Pedro Calderón de la Barca, *La estatua de Prometeo,* a critical edition by Margaret Rich Greer (Princeton, N.J.: Princeton University Press, 1982). For more analysis of the *china poblana* costume and female figure, see Jennifer Gillespie, "Gender, Ethnicity, and Piety: The Case of the China Poblana," in Eva P. Bueno and Terry Caesar, eds., *Imagination beyond Nation: Latin American Popular Culture* (Pittsburgh: University of Pittsburgh Press, 1998), 19–40.

100. "Bexareños" refers to ethnic Mexicans from Béxar (Ramos, *Beyond the Alamo,* 2); "indios civilizados" is italicized by the author. Ramos quotes from Junta Patriótica Notes, Béxar, August 22, 1835, BA.

101. Flores, *Remembering the Alamo,* 61–92.

102. Ramos, *Beyond the Alamo,* 3.

103. Norma Alarcón, "The Theoretical Subjects of *This Bridge Called My Back* and Anglo-American Feminism," in Steven Seidman, ed., *The Postmodern Turn: New Perspectives on Social Theory* (Cambridge: Cambridge University Press, 1994), 140–52.

104. Weber, *Troubles in Texas,* 5–7.

105. Ibid., 5.

106. Rosa Linda Fregoso, "Seguín: The Same Side of the Alamo," in Gary Keller, ed., *Chicano Cinema: Research, Reviews, and Resources* (Binghamton, N.Y.: Bilingual Review/Press, 1985), 148–49.

107. Ibid., 149.

108. Ibid., 148; De León, *The Tejano Community,* 5.

109. In a handwritten letter from then Mayor Henry Cisneros to Rosita, he states: "I am very proud to be able to inform you officially that the City Council

recently voted to name the bridge which spans the San Antonio River in front of the Arneson Theatre 'Rosita's Bridge.' We are looking forward to coordinating with you to set a date for the ceremonies officially designating the bridge and honoring you as you so richly deserve. Best wishes! Henry" (Rosita Fernández Archives, University of Texas Institute of Texan Cultures, San Antonio, Texas).

110. Rosita Fernández, interview with the author, 2000, San Antonio, Texas. Smithsonian Latino Music Oral History Project.

111. See Anzaldúa, *Borderlands/La Frontera*; Pérez, *The Decolonial Imaginary*; Saldívar-Hull, *Feminism on the Border*.

112. Weber, *Troubles in Texas*, 11.

113. Examples of the often-held protests that occur in front of and on top of the Alamo range from activists climbing on top of the building to post anti–Texas Independence signs to art installations.

114. For examples of feminist scholarship that works against this reductive move to normalize women singers and musicians in order to historicize and analyze their cultural production, see Frances Aparicio, *Listening to Salsa: Gender, Latin Popular Music, and Puerto Rican Culture* (Boston: Wesleyan Press, 1998); Angela Y. Davis, *Blues Legacies and Black Feminism: Gertrude "Ma" Rainey, Bessie Smith, and Billie Holliday* (New York: Vintage Books, 1999); bell hooks, *Black Looks: Race and Representation* (Boston: South End Press, 1999); Sherrie Tucker, *Swing Shift: "All-Girl Bands" of the 1940s* (Durham, N.C.: Duke University Press, 2000); Raquel Z. Rivera, *New York Ricans from the Hip Hop Zone* (New York: Palgrave Macmillan, 2003); special issue of *Meridians: Feminism, Race, Transnationalism* devoted to hip-hop, 8:1 (2007).

115. Mexico never recognized the Republic of Texas but considered it a renegade state. Mexican leaders mocked its recognition as exemplified by this quote from 1839 stating that "the supreme government is not aware of the existence of a nation called the republic of Texas, but only a horde of adventurers in rebellion against the laws of the government of the [Mexican] republic" (Randolph Campbell, *Gone to Texas: A History of the Lone Star State* [New York: Oxford University Press, 2004], 173).

116. Chicana feminist scholarship has analyzed the history of Malintzín Tenepal's figure within the construction of Chicano nationalism and, in particular, the way the discourse of her history is executed within Chicano *movimiento* discourse in order to classify Chicanas who did not fit heteronormative constructions of gender as *vendidas* or traitors of the nation or Aztlán. See, for example, Norma Alarcón, "Traddutora, Traditora: A Paradigmatic Figure of Chicana Feminism," in Matthew C. Gutmann, Félix V. Matos Rodríguez, Lynn Stephen, and Patricia Zavella, eds., *Perspectives on Las Américas: A Reader in Culture, History,*

and Representation (Malden, Mass.: Blackwell, 2003), 33–49; Rita Cano Alcalá, "From Chingada to Chingona: La Malinche Redefined or, A Long Line of Hermanas," *Aztlán* 26:2 (2001): 33–61; Anzaldúa, *Borderlands/La Frontera;* Adelaida R. Del Castillo, "Malintzín Tenepal: A Preliminary Look into a New Perspective," *Encuentro Femenil* 1:2 (1974): 58–77.

2. Borders, Bullets, *Besos*

1. The conference was sponsored by the University of California, Santa Barbara, May 8–10, 2008.

2. José Limón states that although "new heroic corridos are infrequent and their impact is increasingly diluted by commercial limitations after 1930, the 'authentic' texts produced in the earlier time continue to remind their listeners of the prior period of open, epic confrontation and thus go on playing an active role as an ideological focal point and expression of resistance" (James Nicolopulos, "The Heroic Corrido: A Premature Obituary?" *Aztlán: A Journal of Chicano Studies* 22:1 [1997]).

3. http://www.corridos.org.

4. Saldívar-Hull, *Feminism on the Border,* 70.

5. David L. Eng with Judith Halberstam and José Esteban Muñoz, "What's Queer about Queer Studies Now?" *Social Text* 23:2–3, 84–85 (fall–winter 2005): 1.

6. An exception to this is the acknowledgment of Silva's early radio and music career in Ramón Saldívar, *The Borderlands of Culture: Américo Paredes and the Transantional Imaginary* (Durham, N.C.: Duke University Press, 2006).

7. Interview with Angélica Silva and Margarita Ríos by Manuel Medrano, March 15, 2003, Brownsville, Texas.

8. Angélica Silva, interview with the author, August 6, 2003, San Antonio, Texas.

9. Mary Ann Villarreal, "Chelo Silva (1922–1988)," in Vicki Ruiz and Virginia Sánchez-Korrol, eds., *Latinas in the United States: An Historical Encyclopedia* (Bloomington: Indiana University Press, 2006), 682.

10. Abel Salas, "The Shunned Homegirl: Chelo Silva a Worldwide Legend," *Brownsville Herald,* May 15–31, 1999, 10.

11. Ibid. Salas states that Crixell's and Carlota Cuellar's songs were two of several songs composed in honor of Silva during her early days of performing.

12. Ibid. Juan Montoya, "Chelo Silva, like Her Story, Shunned in Bordertown," *Harlingen News,* Internet posting, November 18, 2009.

13. Thanks to Angélica Silva for allowing me permission to view the document. Although the paper looks extremely old and yellowed, Angélica Silva was not sure if Cuellar had given her the original document or if she had copied the lyrics years later onto another sheet of paper. In his 1995 *Brownsville Herald* feature, Abel Salas states that "La Cancionera de Emoción was composed jointly by a Mrs. Carlota R. de Cuellar, a Brownsville widow, and by a Mrs. Flavia O. de Gutiérrez" (10). The document Angélica shared with me only gives credit to Carlota Cuellar. Angélica Silva, interview with the author, August 6, 2003, San Antonio, Texas.

14. Leticia Del Toro, liner notes, *Chelo Silva: La Reina Tejana del Bolero,* El Cerrito, Arhoolie Productions, 1995.

15. Rita Vidaurri, interview with the author, May 6–7, 2001, San Antonio, Texas.

16. "Es más importante una voz que se acople a las canciones populares, opina Chelo Silva," *Excelsior,* March 4, 1958, 24A.

17. Saldívar, *The Borderlands of Culture,* 47. Saldívar draws from Leticia Del Toro in the liner notes to *Chelo Silva: La Reina Tejana del Bolero.*

18. Ibid., 48.

19. According to Mary Lee Grant, Silva's marriages are rumored to have ended because of her infidelity (Mary Lee Grant, "Tejana Legends: A Look at Tejan Music Pioneers—Radical in Their Time—and the Path They Paved for Selena and Others," October 27, 2011, http://www.aarp.org/entertainment/music/info-19-2011/tejan-legends.htm).

20. Saldívar, *The Borderlands of Culture,* 49.

21. Angélica Silva, interview with the author, August 6, 2003, San Antonio, Texas.

22. Interview with Angélica Silva and Margarita Ríos by Manuel Medrano, March 15, 2003, Brownsville, Texas. Garnette Pérez is the daughter of Chelo Silva and Leopoldo Pérez Morales. Other children from her marriage with Pérez include Leslie and René.

23. See Pablo Dueñas, *Bolero: Historia gráfica y documental* (Mexico City: Asociación Mexicana de Estudios Fonográficos, 2005), 74.

24. Américo Paredes, *With His Pistol in His Hand: A Border Ballad and Its Hero*; Saldívar, *The Borderlands of Culture,* 398.

25. Saldívar, *The Borderlands of Culture,* 111.

26. José David Saldívar, "Chicano Border Narratives as Cultural Critique," in Héctor Calderón and José David Saldívar, eds., *Criticism in the Borderlands: Studies in Chicano Literature, Culture, and Ideology* (Durham, N.C.: Duke University Press, 1994), 172. Saldívar identifies three other points established by

Paredes in his close reading of corridos: (1) they are a multifaceted discourse; (2) as social texts, they tend to be historical and personal; (3) they make assertions that derive from the collective outlook and experience of the Mexican ballad community on the border. Moreover, Saldívar reminds us of the central discourses of heroism and conflict in the corrido's structure that in turn function as a community/collective voice of resistance to racial subordination or "to reconcile individual experience into a collective identity." He asserts that "Corridos appear to be built of three structural elements: a hero or protagonist, with whom the Chicano or Mexican audience is presumed to identify in some way; a world in which the hero acts and is acted on by antagonistic, often Anglocentric forces, which is presumably a reflection of the audience's conception of the world; and an oral narrative, in which the interaction of the protagonist and the world is described" (José David Saldívar, *Border Matters: Remapping American Cultural Studies* [Berkeley: University of California Press, 1997], 61).

27. Saldívar, *The Borderlands of Culture,* 49.

28. For example, see José E. Limón, *Dancing with the Devil: Society and Cultural Poetics in South Texas* (Madison: University of Wisconsin Press, 1994); María Herrera-Sobek, "Américo Paredes: A Tribute," *Mexican Studies/Estudios Mexicanos* 16:2 (2000); Saldívar, *The Borderlands of Culture;* José R. López Morín, *The Legacy of Américo Paredes* (College Station: Texas A&M University Press, 2006).

29. Sandra K. Soto provides a critical assessment of the power of Paredes in Chicano studies in *Reading Chican@ like a Queer: The De-mastery of Desire* (Austin: University of Texas Press, 2010), 90–92.

30. José David Saldívar, "Chicano Border Narratives as Cultural Critique," in Calderón and Saldívar, *Criticism in the Borderlands,* 178. See also Richard R. Flores, "The Corrido and the Emergence of Texas-Mexican Social Identity," *Journal of American Folklore* 105:416 (spring 1992): 166–82.

31. Richard Bauman, "Introduction," in Richard Bauman, ed., *Folklore and Culture on the Texas–Mexican Border* (Austin: University of Texas Press, 1993), xiv–xv.

32. Soto, *Reading Chican@ like a Queer,* 98.

33. Daniel F. Chamberlain, "El Corrido: Identity, Narrative, and Central Frontiers," in Richard Young, ed., *Music, Popular Culture, Identities* (Amsterdam: Editions Rodopi, 2002), 61.

34. Soto, *Reading Chican@ like a Queer,* 97.

35. Limón, *Dancing with the Devil,* 79.

36. José Limón further states that although "new heroic corridos are infrequent and their impact is increasingly diluted by commercial limitations after 1930, the 'authentic' texts produced in the earlier time continue to remind their

listeners of the prior period of open, epic confrontation and thus go on playing an active role as an ideological focal point and expression of resistance" (Nicolopulos, "The Heroic Corrido," 118).

37. Paredes also made the distinction that border corridos reflected a narrative form of "shifting scenes and by means of action and dialogue," while Mexican corridos held "long, continuous and detailed narrative" (Paredes, *With His Pistol in His Hand,* 187).

38. Américo Paredes coined the term "Greater Mexico" to refer to "all areas inhabited by people of a Mexican culture—not only within the present limits of the Republic of Mexico but in the United States as well—in a cultural rather than a political sense." See Américo Paredes, *A Texas–Mexican Cancionero* (Urbana: University of Illinois Press, 1976), xv.

39. Limón, *Dancing with the Devil,* 26–29.

40. Mark Pedalty, "The Bolero: The Birth, Life, and Decline of Mexican Modernity," *Latin American Music Review* 20:1 (1999): 43.

41. María Herrera-Sobek, *The Mexican Corrido: A Feminist Analysis* (Bloomington: Indiana University Press, 1990), xviii. For a Chicana feminist reworking of Paredes's book title, *With His Pistol in His Hand,* see Catrióna Rueda Esquibel, *With Her Machete in Her Hand: Reading Chicana Lesbians* (Austin: University of Texas Press, 2006).

42. Herrera-Sobek, *The Mexican Corrido,* xiii–xviii.

43. Pedalty, "The Bolero," 32.

44. Ramón Salídvar, *Chicano Narrative: Dialectics of Difference* (Madison: University of Wisconsin Press, 1990). Manuel Peña refers to the differences between a "victim" corrido where the protagonist is subject to injustice and the "heroic" corrido that centers a protagonist as not only resisting injustice but overcoming and defeating the oppressor's actions (Manuel Peña, "Folksong and Social Change: Two Corridos as Interpretive Sources" *Aztlán: A Journal of Chicano Studies* 12:1–2 [1982]: 38).

45. Saldívar, "Chicano Border Narratives as Cultural Critique," 171.

46. Morín, *The Legacy of Américo Paredes,* 71.

47. For example, see Calderón and Saldívar, *Criticism in the Borderlands;* José E. Limón, *Mexican Ballads, Chicano Poems: History and Influence in Mexican American Social Poetry* (Berkeley: University of California Press, 1992); Limón, *Dancing with the Devil;* Renato Rosaldo, *Culture and Truth: The Remaking of Social Analysis* (Boston: Beacon Press, 1993); Saldívar, *Chicano Narrative.*

48. The book focuses on the origins of the corrido form as well as the protagonist Cortez, a border Mexican who flees for his life after killing former Texas Ranger Sheriff W. T. Morris over a heated misunderstanding after Cortez was accused of being a horse thief.

49. Morín, *The Legacy of Américo Paredes,* 76.

50. Limón, *Dancing with the Devil,* 82.

51. See Alma García, *Chicana Feminist Thought: The Basic Historical Writings* (New York: Routledge, 1997); Saldívar-Hull, *Feminism on the Border*; Pérez, *The Decolonial Imaginary*; Maylei Blackwell, *¡Chicana Power!*.

52. Partial lyrics. The English translation appears as in liner notes. See Tish Hinojosa, *Frontejas* (Rounder Records, 1995). Paredes passed away on May 5, 1999. May 5 or "cinco de mayo" is celebrated annually by Mexicans and Chicanos in commemoration of the historic Mexican victory over the French at the Battle of Puebla.

53. Saldívar, "Chicano Border Narratives as Cultural Critique," 179.

54. *The Ballad of Gregorio Cortez,* directed by Robert Young, starred Edward James Olmos as the heroic protagonist.

55. Angie Chabram-Dernersesian, *The Chicana/o Cultural Studies Reader* (New York: Routledge, 2006), 28.

56. Chamberlain, "El Corrido," 55.

57. Manuel Peña, *The Mexican American Orquesta* (Austin: University of Texas Press, 1999), 149, 163.

58. Ibid., 143.

59. Anthony Macias, *Mexican American Mojo: Popular Music, Dance, and Urban Culture in Los Angeles, 1935–1968* (Durham, N.C.: Duke University Press, 2008), 266.

60. Dionne Espinoza, "'Tanto Tiempo Disfrutamos . . .': Revisiting the Gender and Sexual Politics of Chicana/o Youth Culture in East Los Angeles in the 1960s," in Alicia Gaspar de Alba, ed., *Velvet Barrios: Popular Culture and Chicana/o Sexualities* (New York: Palgrave Macmillan, 2003).

61. Ibid., 89; Steven Loza, *Barrio Rhythm: Mexican American Music in Los Angeles* (Urbana: University of Illinois Press, 1993), 103.

62. Espinoza, "'Tanto Tiempo Disfrutamos . . . ,'" 90. Espinoza goes on to say, emphasizing the power of bolero song for Chicanas in the 1960s, that "Sabor a mí" "provided a language of human interaction and construct of love that imaged partnership as a long-term struggle" (98).

63. Dueñas, *Bolero,* 194.

64. Adela Pineda Franco, "The Cuban Bolero and Its Transculturation to Mexico: The Case of Agustín Lara," *Studies in Latin American Popular Culture* 15 (1996): 122.

65. Mark Pedalty, "Themes of Social Justice and Cultural Decadence in the Mexican Bolero: Agustín Lara's Life and Music," unpublished paper presented at Latin American Studies Association, Chicago, September 24–26, 1998, 7.

66. See Pineda Franco, "The Cuban Bolero and Its Transculturation to Mexico," 123–24, and Carlos Monsiváis, *Mexican Postcards,* trans. John Kraniauskas (New York and London: Verso Press, 1997), 173.

67. Pineda Franco, "The Cuban Bolero and Its Transculturation to Mexico," 126.

68. Frances Aparicio, *Listening to Salsa: Gender, Latin Popular Music, and Puerto Rican Culture* (Middletown, Conn.: Wesleyan University Press, 1998), 127.

69. Monsiváis, *Mexican Postcards,* 179.

70. Pedalty, "The Bolero," 40.

71. See Iris M. Zavala, *Bolero: Historia de un Amor* (Mexico City: Celeste, 2000); Rodrigo Bazán Bonfil, *Y si vivo cien años . . . : Antología del bolero en México* (Mexico City: Fondo de Cultural Económica, 2001); Jaime Rico Salazar, *Cien años de boleros* (Bogotá: Centro de Estudios Musicales de Latino América, 1998).

72. Pedalty, "The Bolero," 43.

73. See Vicki L. Ruiz, *From Out of the Shadows: Mexican Women in Twentieth-Century America* (New York: Oxford University Press, 1998), 61–67.

74. Spanish-language recordings appear in catalogs such as *Berliner* and on recording company labels such as Columbia as early as the 1890s. Such "foreign-language-Spanish" recordings functioned as racialized marketing categories very much like the African American jazz "race records" that began as early as the 1920s. See William G. Roy, "'Race Records' and 'Hillbilly Music': Institutional Origins of Racial Categories in the American Commercial Recording Industry," *Poetics* 32 (2004).

75. Pedalty, "The Bolero," 43.

76. Paredes, *With His Pistol in His Hand,* 1.

77. Pedalty, "The Bolero," 35.

78. Ibid., 24. Pedalty quotes Néstor García Canclini, *Transforming Modernity: Popular Culture in Mexico* (Austin: University of Texas Press, 1993), x.

79. Vanessa Knights, "Tears and Screams: Performances of Pleasure and Pain in the Bolero," in Sheila Whiteley and Jennifer Rycenga, eds., *Queering the Popular Pitch* (New York: Routledge, 2006), 86.

80. Although there is no one institution devoted to acquiring Silva's recordings, ephemera, and interviews with family, there are more recent attempts by scholars and music collectors to begin documenting her history. I am grateful for the collaborative experiences with those dedicated to this work, including Clay Shorkey, Texas Music Museum, Austin, Texas; Professor Manuel Medrano, University of Texas, Brownsville; Professor Mary Ann Villarreal, University of Colorado, Boulder; Chris Strachwitz, Strachwitz Frontera Collection of Mexican and Mexican American Music, UCLA Chicano Studies Research Center.

81. Juan Montoya, "Chelo Silva, like Her Story, Shunned in Bordertown," *Harlingen News,* Internet posting, November 18, 2009.

82. Interview with Angélica Silva and Margarita Ríos by Manuel Medrano, March 15, 2003, Brownsville, Texas.

83. Original members who formed the group in 1956 included Francisco Escamilla, José Luis Segura, and Joaquín Ruiz. One of their earliest performances was in Laredo, Texas, in 1957.

84. Rodríguez recalled a huge fight with her father when she initiated her plan to open a bar that would serve beer and have live music for dancing. Her father referred to her as a *cantinera* or woman associated with working-class bar culture and most often assumed to be sexually promiscuous (interview with Sofía Rodríguez by Mary Ann Villarreal, March 28, 2001, Corpus Christi, Texas).

85. Ibid.

86. Mary Lee Grant, "Tejana Legends," http://www.aarp.org/entertainment/music/ionfo-10-2011/tejana-legends.html.

87. Niko Besnier, *Gossip and the Everyday Production of Politics* (Manoa: University of Hawaii Press, 2009), 8.

88. Michel Foucault, *The Archeology of Knowledge and the Discourse on Language,* trans. A. M. Sheridan Smith (New York: Vintage Books, 1982), 96.

89. Michel Foucault, "On the Archeology of the Sciences: Response to the Epistemology Circle," in James D. Faubion, Paul Rabinow, and Robert Hurley, eds., *Aesthetics, Method, and Epistemology, Essential Works of Foucault, 1954–1984,* vol. 2 (New York: New Press, 1999), 309.

90. Lisa Lowe, *Immigrant Acts: On Asian American Cultural Politics* (Durham, N.C.: Duke University Press, 1996), 13–14.

91. Besnier, *Gossip,* 8.

92. Ibid.

93. Field notes, conversations with fans at Tejano Conjunto Festivals, 2000–2009.

94. Roland Barthes, "The Grain of the Voice," in *Image, Music, Text* (New York: Hill and Wang, 1977), 157.

95. Millie Taylor, "Exploring the Grain: The Sound of the Voice in Bruce Nauman's Raw Materials," *Studies in Theatre and Performance* 26:3 (October 2006): 291.

96. At the end of their interview, Medrano and his co-interviewer are seen taking pictures with their video camera of some of these same images of Silva that I have seen, and state, "There are hardly any pictures of her."

97. Personal conversation with Chris Strachwitz and others, 2006.

98. For feminist analysis of Chicana/o gender representations, see Fregoso, *The Bronze Screen.*

99. Monsiváis, *Mexican Postcards,* 173.

100. Salas, "The Shunned Homegirl," 10.

101. Chris Strachwitz, "KCOR Announcer and Presentation," liner notes, *Chelo Silva: La Reina Tejana del Bolero.* Text appears as track number 21.

102. Pérez, *The Decolonial Imaginary,* 6.

103. *Las que viven en ciudad bolero,* VHS, 136 min. (Mexico City: Consejo Nacional Para la Cultura y las Artes, Unidad de Producciones Audiovisuales: Fondo Nacional Para la Cultura y las Artes, Calacas y Palomas, 1993).

104. Alejo Peralta and Díaz Ceballos, *Bolero: Clave del Corazón* (Mexico City: Línea Continua S.A. de C.V., 2004), 161, and *Las que viven en ciudad bolero.*

105. Translation from Spanish by the author.

106. Biographical sketch of Valdelamar by the Sociedad de Autores y Compositores de México (Mexican Society of Authors and Composers), http://www.sacm.org.mx/archivos/biografias.

107. See comments by women composers in *Las que viven en ciudad bolero.*

108. See liner notes to *Chelo Silva: La Reina Tejana del Bolero* (Tejano Roots Series, Arhoolie Productions, 1995).

109. Monsiváis, *Mexican Postcards,* 173.

110. Dan William Dickey, *The Kennedy Corridos: A Study of the Ballads of a Mexican American Hero* (Austin: Center for Mexican American Studies, University of Texas, 1978), 9.

111. Ibid.

112. Ventura Alonzo, interview with the author, San Antonio, June 17, 2000; Beatriz Llamas, interview with the author, May 23–24, 2000, San Antonio, Texas; Rosita Fernández, interview with the author, August 18 and 24, 1999, San Antonio, Texas; Sofía Rodríguez interview by Mary Ann Villarreal, March 28, 2001, Corpus Christi, Texas.

113. Leonardo Quiroz, conversation with the author, July 2000, Corpus Christi, Texas.

114. Monsiváis, *Mexican Postcards,* 176.

115. Richard Leppert, *Sight of Sound: Music, Representation, and the History of the Body* (Berkeley: University of California Press, 1993).

116. Author conversation with Rita Vidaurri, August 2001, San Antonio, Texas. Chris Strachwitz recalls with confidence that this was Silva's last concert performance broadcast live over radio. In fact, he recalls KCOR having done this rare live radio broadcast at the music festival in honor of Silva's recognition that evening (author conversation, El Cerrito, California, June 1999).

117. Leticia Del Toro, liner notes, *Chelo Silva: La Reina Tejana del Bolero,* Arhoolie Productions, 1995.

118. Deborah Paredez, *Selenidad: Selena, Latinos, and the Performance of Memory* (Durham, N.C.: Duke University Press, 2009), 33.

119. Ibid.

120. Olga Nájera-Ramírez, "Unruly Passions: Poetics, Performance, and Gender in the Ranchera Song," in Denise A. Segura and Patricia Zavella, eds., *Women and Migration in the U.S.–Mexico Borderlands* (Durham, N.C.: Duke University Press, 2007), 456–76. Nájera-Ramírez argues that studies "have failed to acknowledge women's participation as performers, composers, and consumers of the ranchera," especially as a musical site where women make feminist interventions (456–57). I believe this is also the case with the lack of sustained attention to boleros, and especially Chicana performances of boleros within the field of Chicano studies.

121. Interview with Angélica Silva and Margarita Ríos by Manuel Medrano, March 15, 2003, Brownsville, Texas.

122. Pedalty, "The Bolero," 38.

123. Chelo Silva was accompanied in her performance by Flaco Jiménez y su Conjunto. Silva tells the audience that her boleros will be "al estilo Tejano" (Tex-Mex conjunto style).

124. See liner notes to *Chelo Silva: La Reina Tejana del Bolero* (1995).

125. Arhoolie Records Web site: http://www.arhoolie.com/titles/423.shtml.

126. Tony de la Rosa recorded the song on 45 rpm for Bego, BG-729. Conjunto Ideal recorded it on 45 rpm for Discos Ideal, 1316-A (Strachwitz Frontera Collection of Mexican and Mexican American Recordings, UCLA Chicano Studies Research Center; no years are provided on labels).

127. One of the 45 rpm recordings is listed as Falcon FEP-15-AA-2. Both sides contain "Pregúntame a mí." The second recording also for the Falcon label, listed as A554, includes a side B recording, "Como un perro" (Strachwitz Frontera Collection of Mexican and Mexican American Recordings, UCLA Chicano Studies Research Center; no years are provided on labels).

128. E-mail to the author from Chris Strachwitz, August 6, 2007.

129. Author-inserted ellipsis to mark the transition between *el* and *la*.

130. Aparicio, *Listening to Salsa*, 183.

131. Self-produced CD compilation of music and poetry shared with me by author (Rosa Canales Pérez, *Para Mi Pueblo*, 2002). Pérez came to know of Silva from hearing her parents talk about Silva's music in the 1950s. When Pérez moved to Brownsville in the mid-1980s, she was surprised to hear very little about her in Brownsville and initially was not aware that Silva was married to Paredes.

132. Francisco Fregoso, interview with the author, June 1, 2004, Corpus Christi, Texas.

133. "La actuación de Paquita la del Barrio," *Houston Chronicle*, www.chron.com ("La butaca" blog, October 31, 2008).

134. Interview with Angélica Silva and Margarita Ríos by Manuel Medrano, March 15, 2003, Brownsville, Texas.

135. "Paquita la del Barrio defiende su música," *El Siglo de Torreón*, Espectáculos, September 23, 2004, http://www.elsiglodetorreon.com.mx.

136. Ibid.

137. Interview with Angélica Silva and Margarita Ríos by Manuel Medrano, March 15, 2003, Brownsville, Texas.

138. www.laFarandilla.com, May 13, 2009.

139. Ann Cvetkovich, "In the Archives of Lesbian Feelings: Documentary and Popular Culture," *Camera Obscura 49: Feminism, Culture, and Media Studies* 17:1 (2002): 116.

140. Ibid.

141. Ibid., 117.

142. Catherine S. Ramírez, *The Woman in the Zoot Suit: Gender, Nationalism, and the Cultural Politics of Memory* (Durham, N.C.: Duke University Press, 2009), 56. Interestingly, in March 2010 Paquita made homophobic remarks when she said during an interview, responding to the passage of Mexico City legislation granting marriage and adoption rights to gay couples, that she would much rather see children dead than adopted by gay foster parents. This created a public backlash against her from her Latino queer fans ("Mexican Singer Paquita La del Barrio on Gay Adoption: 'It's Better That the Child Die,'" *Los Angeles Times*, March 17, 2010).

143. Author's emphasis. "Don Américo" was often used in reference to Paredes when professors (especially those who were students of Paredes) referred to him. Although there is no direct equivalent of *Don* in English, the closest term would be "sir." It is a mark of respect and deference.

144. This phrase is taken from the title of Carla Trujillo's *Chicana Lesbians: The Girls Our Mothers Warned Us About* (Berkeley: Third Woman Press, 1991).

145. My "Chicana butch tribute" draws from the analysis of power, queer sexuality, and desire that is possible in queer receptions of songs as argued by Yvonne Yarbro-Bejarano, "Crossing the Border with Chabela Vargas: A Chicana Femme's Tribute," in Daniel Balderston and Donna J. Guy, eds., *Sex and Sexuality in Latin America* (New York: New York University Press, 1997), 33–43.

146. Ibid., 38.

147. Gloria Anzaldúa, "Introduction," in Gloria Anzaldúa, ed., *Making Face, Making Soul/Haciendo Caras: Creative and Critical Perspectives by Feminists of Color* (San Francisco: Aunt Lute Books, 1990), xv.

148. Saldívar, *Chicano Narrative*, 41.

3. Tex-Mex Conjunto Accordion Masculinity

1. The term *Tejas* is not merely the Spanish-language translation of Texas but a self-conscious reference encompassing geographic landscape, contested histories of Mexican presence, and cultural imaginary of Tejanas/os. When *Tejas* is referenced, it channels counterdiscourses of Tejano history as well as the contradictions therein.

2. Scholarship has long grappled with the hegemony of ocularcentrism. See Josh Kun, *Audiotopias: Music, Race, and America* (Berkeley: University of California Press, 2005); David Michael Levin, *Modernity and the Hegemony of Vision* (Berkeley: University of California Press, 1983); Ronald M. Radano and Philip V. Bohlman, eds., *Music and the Racial Imagination* (Chicago: University of Chicago Press, 2000); and Martin Jay, *Downcast Eyes: The Denigration of Vision in Twentieth-Century French Thought* (Berkeley: University of California Press, 1993).

3. Martha Mockus, *Sounding Out: Pauline Oliveros and Lesbian Musicality* (New York: Routledge, 2008), 89.

4. E. Annie Proulx, *Accordion Crimes* (New York: Simon & Schuster, 1996).

5. Some examples include Kun, *Audiotopias;* María Elena Cepeda, *Musical ImagiNation: U.S.–Colombian Identity and the Latin Music Boom* (New York: New York University Press, 2010); John Connell and Chris Gibson, *Sound Tracks: Popular Music, Identity, and Place* (New York: Routledge, 2002).

6. Manuel Peña, *The Texas-Mexican Conjunto: History of a Working-Class People* (Austin: University of Texas Press, 1985); Manuel Peña, *Música Tejana: The Cultural Economy of an Artistic Transformation* (College Station: Texas A&M University Press, 1999); Juan Tejeda and Avelardo Valdez, eds., *¡Puro Conjunto! An Album in Words and Pictures* (Austin: Center for Mexican American Studies, University of Texas Press, 2001).

7. The button accordion has held prominence within the Tex-Mex conjunto music scene, although the piano accordion is a well-documented part of this history during the earlier decades of the twentieth century.

8. See Arnoldo De León, *They Called Them Greasers: Anglo Attitudes toward Mexicans in Texas, 1821–1900* (Austin: University of Texas Press, 1983); David Montejano, *Anglos and Mexicans in the Making of Texas* (Austin: University of Texas Press, 1987); Pérez, *The Decolonial Imaginary.*

9. Américo Paredes, *George Washington Gomez: A Mexicotexan Novel* (Houston: Arte Público Press, 1990), 242.

10. "Among accordionists, the first recording honor, at least with large American companies belongs to Bruno in 1928" (Clay Shorkey in Tejeda and Valdez, *¡Puro Conjunto!*, 308).

11. Arnaldo Valdez and Jeffrey A. Halley, "Gender in the Culture of Mexican American Conjunto Music," *Gender and Society* 10:2 (1996): 158. This kind of analysis does not challenge the discourse of sound beyond the conventional gender dichotomies of instrument/singer, masculinity/femininity, public/private.

12. Margaret Sarkissian, "Gender and Music," in Helen Meyer, ed., *Ethnomusicology: An Introduction* (London: Macmillan, 1992), 15.

13. Manuel Peña, "Conjunto Music: The First Fifty Years," in Tejeda and Valdez, *¡Puro Conjunto!*, 67.

14. Eng, Halberstam, and Muñoz, "Introduction: What's Queer about Queer Studies Now?": 1–17.

15. Ventura Alonzo, interview with the author, June 2000, San Antonio, Texas.

16. Valdez and Halley, "Gender in the Culture of Mexican American Conjunto Music," 148–67.

17. Ibid., 154.

18. Rosa Linda Alonzo-Saenz, "Houston Big Band Leaders," family biography, April 1982. In a 1930 survey of "Selected Occupations of the Mexican Population in Houston," no females were listed as "musicians and music teachers."

19. Peña, *The Mexican American Orquesta*, 153.

20. Carol Rust, "Ventura Alonzo Honored in Mural/Queen of the Accordion," *Houston Chronicle*, August 14, 1996, 1. Alonzo came onto the Houston *mexicano* music scene from the Magnolia barrio in Houston, one of the city's oldest *mexicano* ethnic enclaves. Arguably, Magnolia is where Houston *mexicano* culture emerged. By the late 1920s, Magnolia had developed its own business district, including grocery stores, restaurants, bakeries, barbershops, and Spanish "talkie" theaters. See Arnoldo De León, *Ethnicity in the Sunbelt: A History of Mexican Americans in Houston* (Houston: Mexican American Studies Program Monograph Series, University of Texas, 1989). Formerly an all-white area, Magnolia Park become the site of the greatest increase in *mexicano* arrivals from South Texas and Mexico, including Alonzo, in the 1920s and 1930s. In 1996, a mural of Alonzo was dedicated in her honor in Magnolia Park. Ironically, the artist states in the *Houston Chronicle* that people would stop him often to ask who Alonzo was, even though "she was a pioneer in this community" (ibid.).

21. San Miguel states that Alonzo, like Rosita Fernández, was mostly a local phenomenon who had a limited impact on Tejano music. See San Miguel, *Tejano Proud*, 45.

22. Peña, *The Mexican American Orquesta*, 153.

23. Rust, "Ventura Alonzo Honored in Mural/Queen of the Accordion," 1.

24. Peña, *The Texas-Mexican Conjunto*, 40; Clay Shorkey, Texas Museum director, interview with the author, June 2000, Austin, Texas.

25. Frank and Mrs. Alonzo, interview with Manuel Peña, April 25, 1993. According to ledgers shared with me by Ventura Alonzo, the contract was between Alonzo y Sus Rancheros and Falcon Record Company. They were paid one dollar by Falcon, which then held rights to these songs.

26. I believe "AC Records" is misspelled and should be ACA Recording Studios in Houston (Alonzo-Saenz, "Houston Big Band Leaders"). Other songs Alonzo recalled include "Mi Tejanita," "Mi Juanita," "Del Río Polka," and "Socorro" on Alameda Records. She also recalled recording "Gracias Soñadoras" and "Conchita Del Mar" for Broadway Records, but could not recall the years for either set of recordings (Ventura Alonzo, interview with the author, May 2000).

27. Ventura Alonzo, interview with the author, May 2000.

28. Peña, *The Mexican American Orquesta,* 156–57.

29. She was the fifth child of eight, including, in order of age, Luis, María Magdalena, Beatríz, Amado, José, Uvaldo, and Pilar.

30. Both of Alonzo's parents were musically inclined. Her father was a music instructor who played clarinet and her mother often sang in the church choir. Her father taught his children music, and eventually her sister and brother taught piano as well (Ventura Alonzo, interview with the author, May 2000).

31. Rosa Linda Alonzo-Saenz, family biography.

32. Ventura Alonzo, interview with the author, May 2000.

33. Throughout the 1920s and 1930s, Mexican American women in Houston worked in cotton fields, textile factories, laundries, restaurants, and, of course, at home. At home, they cooked, cleaned, laundered clothes by hand, ironed, cared for children of their own and of other women, and sometimes for their sisters' children or their *comadres'* (women-centered alternative models of kinship) children. In short, women worked outside and inside the home, which dispels the myth that women did not work if they stayed at home.

34. Ventura Alonzo was one of the earliest accordionists to record: she recorded "Magnolia" in 1947. Some of her recordings for Alameda, her first record label, include "Mi Tejanita," "Mi Juanita," "Del Río Polka," and "Socorro." For Broadway, she recorded "Gracias Soñadoras" and "Conchita Del Mar." Her songwriting was not vast, but included "Si yo te quiero," "Magnolia Polka," "Navigation Waltz," and "Chaparita." In May 1950, Alonzo and her husband Frank signed a recording contract with Falcon Record Company, owned by Arnaldo Ramírez of Mission, Texas. They were hired as an orquesta to record four record sides during one session for eighty dollars.

35. Ventura Alonzo, interview with the author, May 2000, San Antonio, Texas.

36. Ventura Alonzo, interview with the author, June 2000, San Antonio, Texas.

37. Rust, "Ventura Alonzo Honored in Mural."

38. Frank Alonzo was a welder who arrived to Houston from San Antonio to weld metal at a junkyard. Interestingly, Alonzo claims that she married Frank Alonzo in order to get rid of her first husband, who used to harass and stalk her.

39. See Emma Pérez, "Oral Narratives as Chicano (His)story Text," Working Paper No. 32, Southwest Institute for Research on Women (Tucson: University of Arizona, 1994).

40. Ibid., 14.

41. Ventura Alonzo, interview with the author, June 2000.

42. Rust claims that "when Frank discovered his wife's piano ability, the self-taught guitar player immediately thought 'band'" ("Ventura Alonzo Honored in Mural"). In her oral history, Alonzo states that this is incorrect and that she taught Frank to play musical instruments (Ventura Alonzo, interview with the author, May 2000, San Antonio).

43. Ventura Alonzo, interview with the author, May 2000, San Antonio, Texas.

44. Ibid.

45. Ibid.

46. Ibid.

47. From her second marriage to Francisco she had her only daughter Mary, with whom she lived until her death, Frank Alonzo Jr., and Alonzo Alonzo.

48. Ventura Alonzo, interview with the author, May 2000, San Antonio.

49. Angela Y. Davis, *Blues Legacies and Black Feminism* (New York: Pantheon Books, 1998), 71.

50. Ventura Alonzo, interview with the author, June 2000, San Antonio, Texas.

51. Ibid.

52. Before La Terraza opened, Houston's nightlife included such popular dance/music spots as Stafford, Rosenberg, Acapulco, and Tropical, some more popular than others among Houston's *mexicano* public.

53. Ventura Alonzo, interview with the author, June 2000, San Antonio, Texas.

54. Ibid.

55. In 2001, more than five decades after she began playing, Alonzo was inducted into the Tejano Music Hall of Fame in Alice, Texas, where her story is now situated alongside those of many of her contemporaries.

56. Mockus, *Sounding Out*, 90.

57. Ibid.

58. Carlos Guerra's reference in his essay about the Lawrence Welk comedy bits about "buxom female accordionists" points to the ways the accordion

fastened to the female breast area as "funny" and "odd" and therefore an "unnatural" fit (Carlos Guerra, "Accordion Menace . . . Just Say Mo'!" in Tejeda and Valdez, *¡Puro Conjunto!,* 115–20).

59. Eva Ybarra, interview with the author, July 2009.

60. Ibid. Ybarra also mentioned that her chromatic button accordion tends to be heavier than her smaller diatonic accordion, so this also has contributed to this area of her arm becoming harder.

61. Accordionist Valerio Longoria is credited with being the first accordionist to shift from a seated to a standing position while playing.

62. Juan Tejeda, "Eva Ybarra," in Tejeda and Valdez, *¡Puro Conjunto!,* 299.

63. Avelardo Valdez and Jeffrey A. Halley, "Why So Few Women Conjunto Artists?" in Tejeda and Valdez, *¡Puro Conjunto!,* 231.

64. Other women accordionists include Lupita Rodela from East Texas, who played mostly smaller Texas towns during the 1980s and 1990s. Rodela continues to play and at one point fronted El Conjunto de Lupita Rodela, which included her brother and husband as manager. Accordionist Chavela Ortiz, born in Fresno and raised in San Jose, began playing accordion as a child with her family band, Las Incomparables Hermanas Ortiz, which included her mother, grandfather, and sister. In the 1970s, she played for the band Brown Express and, in the 1980s, formed her own band, Chavela y Su Grupo Express, before her untimely death in 1992. Ortiz was married to Jorge Hernández of Los Tigres del Norte. What is unique about Ybarra's gender presentation is that, unlike most women accordionists, her femininity is not shaped by having biological family around her. Thus she is not represented as mother, wife, or sister, nor has she been married or had a boyfriend or husband as manager. Also, unlike her contemporaries, such as Victoria Galván, Cecilia Saenz, or Houston-based Mickey (of the conjunto Mickey y Sus Carnales), Ybarra wears gender-neutral clothing, such as jeans and boots. She rarely wears sultry tops and wears little makeup.

65. Valdez and Halley, "Why So Few Women Conjunto Artists?" 231.

66. Ibid.

67. Tejeda and Valdez, *¡Puro Conjunto!,* 272.

68. Ibid., 271.

69. For a wonderful analysis of masculinity, homosociality, and meat, see "Carne, Carnales, and the Carnivalesque," in José E. Limón, *Dancing with the Devil,* 123–40.

70. The song's title connotes both the diminutive form of Texas Mexican women and Texas Mexican girls. "Mi Tejanita" is sung by Los Pingüinos del Norte in *Chulas Fronteras* (1975).

71. In 2005, Galán released *I Love My Freedom, I Love My Texas; On the Road with Mingo Saldívar y Los Cuatro Espadas* featuring accordionist Mingo

Saldívar (the dancing cowboy), which, as described by Galán on his Web site, "captures the passionate spirit of one of conjunto's most admired and popular accordion masters who is considered a National Treasure."

72. George Revill, "Music and the Politics of Sound: Nationalism, Citizenship, and Auditory Space," *Environment and Planning D* 18:5 (2000): 610.

73. Examples of Chicana feminist scholarship that has challenged cultural-nationalist discourses include Marta Cotera, *Diosa y Hembra: History and Heritage of Chicanas in the U.S.* (Austin: Information Systems Development, 1976); Alma García, *Chicana Feminist Thought: The Basic Historical Writings* (New York: Routledge, 1997); Pérez, *The Decolonial Imaginary;* Blackwell, *¡Chicana Power!.* Cathy Ragland's work on Norteño music provides a productive critique of Chicano/Tejano music scholarship by asserting that it has fallen short of addressing Tejano conjunto music within a transnational framework. Yet, similar to Chicano music scholarship, Ragland's attention to migration and transnationalism in Norteño music focuses on race, class, and nation. See Cathy Ragland, *Música Norteña: Mexican Migrants Creating a Nation between Nations* (Philadelphia: Temple University Press, 2009), 12–13.

74. Tejeda and Valdez, *¡Puro Conjunto!,* 100.

75. The terms *cholo* and *chola* are loosely translated as "gang-identified" male or female. See Joan W. Moore, *Going Down to the Barrio: Homeboys and Homegirls in Change* (Philadelphia: Temple University Press, 1991), and Diego Vigil, *Barrio Gangs: Street Life and Identity in Southern California* (Austin: University of Texas Press, 1988). Several studies provide gender and feminist analysis of *cholas,* homegirls, and pachucas in the twentieth century. See Norma Mendoza-Denton, *Homegirls: Language and Cultural Practice among Latina Youth Gangs* (Malden, Mass.: Blackwell, 2008), for examples of *chola* style, including makeup, hair, eyebrow shapes, and rules of speech. See also Marie Keta Miranda's Oakland-based study of girls in gangs, *Homegirls in the Public Sphere* (Austin: University of Texas Press, 2003), and Ramírez, *The Woman in the Zoot Suit.*

76. Caren Kaplan, Norma Alarcón, and Minoo Moallem, eds., *Between Woman and Nation: Nationalisms, Transnational Feminism, and the State* (Durham, N.C.: Duke University Press, 1999).

77. Valdez and Halley, "Why So Few Women Conjunto Artists?" 235.

78. Leppert, *The Sight of Sound,* xxi.

79. For examples of feminist music scholarship that works against this, see Sherrie Tucker, *Swing Shift: "All-Girl" Bands of the 1940s* (Durham, N.C.: Duke University Press, 2000).

80. Mockus, *Sounding Out,* 90.

81. Eva Ybarra, interview with the author, June 2002, July 2009.

82. Sheila Whiteley, Andy Bennett, and Stan Hawkins, eds., *Music, Space and Place: Popular Music and Cultural Identity* (Burlington, Va.: Ashgate Publishing Company, 2004), 2.

83. According to Kun, audiotopias are movements and moments represented as "contact zones" of sonic and social spaces "where disparate identity-formations, cultures, *and* geographies historically kept and mapped separately are allowed to interact with each other as well as enter into relationships whose consequences for cultural identification are never predetermined" (Kun, *Audiotopias,* 23).

84. See Steve Waksman, *Instruments of Desire: The Electric Guitar and the Shaping of Musical Experience* (Cambridge: Harvard University Press, 1999); Tucker, *Swing Shift.*

85. Sara Cohen, "Men Making a Scene: Rock Music and the Productions of Gender," in Sheila Whiteley, ed., *Sexing the Groove: Popular Music and Gender* (New York: Routledge, 1997), 28. Cohen's assertions about music and meanings in relation to rock are useful in the case of the accordion as well: within particular social and cultural groups, music signifies collective ideas, images, and meanings, some of which concern gender. Particular instruments, sounds, structures, and styles may, for example, connote male or female stereotypes: for instance, in Euro-American cultures, rock music has commonly symbolized masculinity.

86. Roshanak Kheshti, "Touching Hearing: The Aural Imaginary in the World Music Industry," unpublished manuscript.

87. Fregoso, *MeXicana Encounters,* 74.

88. Eva Ybarra, interview with the author, 2002, San Antonio.

89. Ibid.

90. According to Valdez and Halley ("Why So Few Women Conjunto Artists?"), Ybarra is said to have been encouraged by her father and brothers to play, although neither ever taught her. Her mother and grandmother seemed adamant that they did not want her to play the accordion, especially in public.

91. Eva Ybarra, interview with the author, 2002, San Antonio, Texas.

92. Ibid.

93. Ibid. Italics represents stress of term by Ybarra. Subsequent references in the text are from this interview.

94. Eva Ybarra, interview with the author, July 2009.

95. Eva Ybarra, interview with the author, July 2002; fieldwork notes, Tejano Conjunto Festivals, 2001–7.

96. Eva Ybarra, interview with the author, July 2009.

97. Eva Ybarra, interview with the author, June 2002. All subsequent quotes are from this interview.

4. Sonido de Las Américas

1. Author's field notes, Havana, Cuba, September 2007.

2. Ibid.

3. Flora Pimenta Gutiérrez was born in 1938 in "un campo de La Habana," what she described as the more rural area adjacent to the urban center of the city. She recalled her love of music began in her mid-teens after she won a scholarship to attend school. Her study of music included a rigorous education in classical music. Gutiérrez's love of music, and her formal and informal knowledge acquisition of music, offer a dynamic archive of Cuban music: "Particularmente, siempre me gustaba la música mexicana. Porque donde yo vivía en mi pueblo me quedaba con mi abuela. Había un radio en casa de mi abuela, aunque éramos pobres había un radio desde pequeña y me acostumbré a oír música mexicana que me encantaba como Lola Beltrán, Toña La Negra me encantaba. Ellas llegaban aquí y cantaban en radio, en la RHC Cadena Azul" (I especially enjoyed Mexican music. In the area of town where I lived I used to stay over at my grandmother's. There was a radio in my grandmother's home; even though we were poor, there was always a radio, from the time I was a child and I got used to listening to Mexican music that I loved, such as Lola Beltrán, Toña La Negra, I loved them. They [the singers] would also come and sing on the radio, on RHC Cadena Azul).

4. "Without omitting the spatial and places, of course, he makes himself more sensitive to times than to spaces. He will come to 'listen' to a house, a street, a town, as an audience listens to a symphony" (Henri Lefebvre, *Rhythmanalysis: Space, Time, and Everyday Life,* trans. Stuart Elden and Gerald Moore [London: Continuum, 2004], 22).

5. Pierre Nora distinguishes between memory as "in permanent evolution, open to the dialectic of remembering and forgetting" and history, which "is the reconstruction . . . of what is no longer" (Pierre Nora, "Between Memory and History: Les Lieux de Mémoire," *Representations* 26 [spring 1989]: 8). See also Diana Taylor, *The Archive and the Repertoire: Performing Cultural Memory in the Americas* (Durham, N.C.: Duke University Press, 2003).

6. Norma Alarcón, "Chicana Feminism: In the Tracks of 'the' Native Woman," in Norma Alarcón, Caren Kaplan, and Minoo Moallem, eds., *Between Woman and Nation: Nationalisms, Transnational Feminisms, and the State* (Durham, N.C.: Duke University Press, 1999), 67.

7. Michael Lassing, "Different Methods, Different Places: Feminist Geography and New Directions in US Western History," *Journal of Historical Geography* 29:2 (2003): 238.

8. Neil Smith, "Contours of a Spatialized Politics: Homeless Vehicles and the Production of Geographical Scale," *Social Text* 33 (1992): 67–68.

9. Gayatri Gopinath, "Queer Regions: Locating Lesbians in Sancharram," in George E. Haggerty and Molly McGary, eds., *A Companion to Lesbian, Gay, Bisexual, Transgender, and Queer Studies* (Malden, Mass.: Blackwell, 2007), 343.

10. Gerhard Kubik, "Analogies and Differences in African-American Musical Cultures across the Hemisphere: Interpretive Models and Research Strategies," *Black Music Journal* 1/2 (1998): 206.

11. Sallie Marston, "The Social Construction of Scale," *Progress in Human Geography* 24:2 (2000): 221. See also Erik Swyngedouw, "Neither Global nor Local: 'Glocalization' and the Politics of Scale," in Kevin R. Cox, ed., *Spaces of Globalization: Reasserting the Power of the Local* (New York and London: Guilford Press, 1997), 169.

12. Smith, "Contours of a Spatialized Politics," 66.

13. A key example of such feminist scholarship in Chicana music is the analysis of Chicana punk artists by Michelle Habell-Pallán, "'Soy punkera, ¿y qué?': Sexuality, Translocality, and Punk in Los Angeles and Beyond," in Deborah Pacini Hernandez, Héctor Fernández L'Hoeste, and Erick Zolov, eds., *Rockin' Las Américas: The Global Politics of Rock in Latin/o America* (Pittsburgh: University of Pittsburgh Press, 2004), 160–78.

14. José David Saldívar, *Border Matters: Remapping American Cultural Studies* (Berkeley: University of California Press, 1997); Sonia Saldívar-Hull, *Feminism on the Border: Chicana Gender Politics and Literature* (Berkeley: University of California Press, 2000).

15. Licia Fiol-Matta, "Body, Space, Sexuality," New Directions in Queer Latino Studies conference, University of Southern California and University of California Los Angeles, November 2005.

16. David Montejano, *Anglos and Mexicans in the Making of Texas, 1836–1986* (Austin: University of Texas Press, 1987), 114.

17. Ibid.

18. Eva's sister Tina Moore could not recall the specific theater, but considering the time period and based on my interviews with artists from the same generation, it was most likely the Texas Theatre or the Teatro Nacional.

19. Tina Moore, interview with the author, March 25–26, 2006, San Antonio, Texas.

20. Gary Hartman, *The History of Texas Music* (College Station: Texas A&M University Press, 2008), 5.

21. Manuel Peña, *The Texas Mexican Conjunto: A History of a Working-Class Music* (Austin: University of Texas Press, 1985), 45n20, citing Manuel Gamio, *Mexican Immigration to the United States* (Chicago: University of Chicago Press, 1971). See also Gary Hickinbotham, "A History of the Texas Recording Industry," *Journal of Texas Music History* 4:1 (spring 2001): 19.

22. Hickinbotham, "A History of the Texas Recording Industry," 21.

23. Montejano, *Anglos and Mexicans in the Making of Texas, 1836–1986*, 159–61.

24. Hickinbotham, "A History of the Texas Recording Industry," 21.

25. Colin J. Bray and Jack Litchfield, "Label Types of Bluebird Records," http://78rpmrecord.com/blblabl.htm.

26. Hickenbotham, "A History of the Texas Recording Industry," 21.

27. See *Ethnic Music on Records*, vol. 6 (Artist Index, Title Index) for a complete list of Garza's recordings in the United States up to 1942.

28. Borrowed from title of the book by Alarcón, Kaplan, and Moallem, *Between Woman and Nation*.

29. Gisela Cramer and Ursula Prutsch, "Nelson A. Rockefeller's Office of Inter-American Affairs (1940–1946) and Record Group 229," *Hispanic American Historical Review* 86:4 (2006): 785–806.

30. Ibid., 786. See also Catherine L. Benamou, *Orson Welles's Pan-American Odyssey* (Berkeley: University of California Press, 2007), 10–11.

31. Leonardo Ferreira, *Centuries of Silence: The Story of Latin American Journalism* (Westport, Conn.: Praeger Publishers, 2006), 188.

32. *The Columbia Program Book* (New York: Columbia Broadcasting System, November 1, 1944), 4.

33. Columbia Broadcasting System, *Annual Report* (fiscal year ending December 28, 1940), March 31, 1941, 7.

34. Ibid., 6.

35. The distribution of information to Latin America by the Rockefeller office—of which radio was merely one along with motion pictures, newsreels, and magazines—was designed with four objectives in mind. The first objective was to convince Latin Americans that the "Good Neighbor" policy was a "sincere and permanent reversal of our nineteenth-century policies of dollar diplomacy and manifest destiny." The second objective sought to not interfere with the independent sovereignty of Latin American nations. The third was to defend Latin American countries from German economic imperialism. The final objective was to convince Latin Americans of the "sincere attempt to bring about a lasting friendship between peoples of this hemisphere" (Donald Meyer, "Toscanini and the Good Neighbor Policy: The NBC Symphony Orchestra's 1940 South American Tour," *American Music* [fall 2000]: 233–37). See also "Offers a Subsidy on Latins' News: This Government Would Help Short-Wave Stations Sending Unbiased Matter," *New York Times*, October 7, 1941, 13.

36. Ferreira, *Centuries of Silence*, 179–80. See also Columbia Broadcasting System, *Annual Report* (fiscal year ending December 29, 1945), March 22, 1946, 7. CBS created the most extensive network of short-wave and long-wave stations

to date, La Cadena de las Américas (Network of the Americas), which began transmission in 1941. See also Meyer, "Toscanini and the Good Neighbor Policy," 240.

37. Meyer, "Toscanini and the Good Neighbor Policy," 240. The U.S. government helped the situation by expediting Federal Communications Commission (FCC) approval for upgrading twelve commercial short-wave stations to fifty thousand watts and by providing the content of a news service. The eventual goal was to have these short-wave networks become major commercial ventures after the war ended, but the required backing by advertising never materialized. In early 1942, the Network of the Americas featured a ninety-minute dedicatory broadcast over seventy-six stations reaching both domestic and Latin American audiences.

38. *Time,* June 1, 1942, 62.

39. Columbia Broadcasting System, *Annual Report,.* March 22, 1946, 7; *The Columbia Program Book* (New York: Columbia Broadcasting System, April 1, 1942), 4.

40. Ibid., 64.

41. See Tucker, *Swingshift: "All-Girl" Bands of the 1940s.*

42. Tina Moore, interview with the author, March 25–26, 2006, San Antonio, Texas. Moore lost a box of Garza's memorabilia, including this newspaper clipping. I have not been able to locate it because she does not remember the newspaper or the exact date, but recalls that it was toward the beginning of the war.

43. For analysis of Latino racial hierarchies of language, skin color, hair texture in film and televions, see Arlene Dávila, *Latinos Inc.: The Marketing and Making of a People* (Berkeley: University of California Press, 2001); Charles Ramírez-Berg, *Latino Images in Film: Stereotypes, Subversion, Resistance* (Austin: University of Texas Press, 2002); Priscilla Peña Ovalle, *Dance and the Hollywood Latina* (New Brunswick, N.J.: Rutgers University Press, 2011).

44. Tina Moore, interview with the author, May 2001, San Antonio, Texas.

45. *New York Times,* January 23, 1944, X9.

46. Jay Hickerson, *The 2nd Revised Ultimate History of Network Radio Programming and Guide to All Circulating Shows* (Hamden, Conn.: Presto Print II, 2001).

47. "CBS Plans Chain in Latin America: Paley Says US Programs Will Be Rebroadcast an Hour Daily in 18 Countries," *New York Times,* December 24, 1940, 21.

48. See Doreen Massey, *Space, Place, and Gender* (Minneapolis: University of Minnesota Press, 1994), 170.

49. Tina Moore, interview with the author, May 2001, San Antonio, Texas.

50. Holly Knox, *Sally Rand: From Film to Fans* (Bend, Ore.: Maverick Publications, 1988), 6. The stage name "Sally Rand" was given to her by legendary movie director Cecil B. DeMille when he hired her as a player in one of his stock companies. Rand's dream was to become a Hollywood actor, and although she did appear in numerous silent films, her lisp is said to have blocked her successful acquisition of talking picture roles. Rand's biggest movie part was as third lead along with George Raft and Carole Lombard in the 1934 movie *Bolero*.

51. Brad Redford, "Sally Rand—The Woman Who Brought Nudity to Dallas," http://www.oocities.org/~jimlowe/sally/redford.html.

52. The feature reads: "He aquí seis diversos aspectos de la famosa artista de teatro, Sally Rand, que provocativamente sorprende al público con sus bailables, en los que sólo usa abanicos o globos par 'evitar miradas indiscretas'" (Here we have six different aspects of the famous performance artist Sally Rand, who provocatively surprises the public with her dances, using only fans or balloons in order to "avoid indiscrete looks") ("La Bella Artista Sally Rand Cambia Sus Globos y Abanicos," *La Prensa [Diario Popular Independiente]*, 1937).

53. Tina Moore, interview with the author, May 2001, San Antonio, Texas.

54. There is much debate as to the true composer of the song; among those mentioned is Moisés Simons. The recording was by Don Azpiazú and his Havana Casino Orchestra in 1930 for Victor Records.

55. Alicia Arrizón, "Latina Subjectivity, Sexuality and Sensuality," *Women and Performance: A Journal of Feminist Theory* 18:3 (2008): 193.

56. Alarcón, "Chicana Feminism," 67.

57. Pablo Dueñas, *Bolero: Historia gráfica y documental*, 3d ed. (Mexico City: Asociación Mexicana de Estudios Fonográficos, 2005), 201. See Jaime Rico Salazar, *Cien Años de Boleros: Su historia, sus compositores, sus intérpretes y 500 boleros inolvidables* (Bogotá: Centro de Estudios Musicales de Latinoamerica, 1988), 56–119.

58. Originally, Felipe "El Charro" Gil and brother Alfredo were part of "Los Corporales," but when Felipe decided to leave the group in order to become Eva's manager, Alfredo, Chucho Navarro, and Hernando Avilés would form the Trío Los Panchos.

59. Tina Moore, interview with the author, March 25–26, 2006, San Antonio, Texas. Twenty years after her initial recording for Columbia Records in Mexico, the company would ask her to return to record a commemorative album of some of her most popular songs recorded for the label.

60. "Recordando a Curiel y Pardavé" (Discos Columbia, n.d.). Songs include "Vereda Tropical," "Caminos de Ayer," "Me Acuerdo de tí," "Noche de

Luna," "Sin Lágrimas," "Déjame," "Aburrido me Voy," "La Panchita," "Caminito de la Sierra," "No Hagas Llorar a esa Mujer," "Negra Consentida," "Varita de Nardo."

61. Gilles Deleuze and Félix Guattari, *A Thousand Plateaus: Capitalism and Schizophrenia,* trans. Brian Massumi (Minneapolis: University of Minnesota Press, 1987), 23.

62. Tina Moore shared the fact that Garza recorded and performed in Colombia, Argentina, and Brazil (Tina Moore, interview with the author, March 25–26, 2006, San Antonio, Texas).

63. See Massey, *Space, Place, and Gender;* Katherine McKittrick, *Demonic Grounds: Black Women and the Cartographies of Struggle* (Minneapolis: University of Minnesota Press, 2006); Katherine McKittrick and Linda Peake, "What Difference Does Difference Make to Geography?" in Noel Castree, ed., *Questioning Geography: Fundamental Debates* (New York: Wiley-Blackwell, 2005).

64. Adela Pineda Franco, "The Cuban Bolero and Its Transculturation to Mexico: The Case of Agustín Lara," *Studies in Latin American Popular Culture* 15 (1996): 119–31.

65. Tina Moore, interview with the author, May 2001, San Antonio, Texas. Moore shared the fact that while Garza agreed that claiming she was a Mexican was a good way to obtain work, Gil persisted in telling those in the record business that Garza was *mexicana* in ways that suggested he was ashamed of the fact that Garza was born and raised in the United States.

66. I often had to make an extra effort to convince *mexicanos* and *cubanos* that Garza was actually *norteamericana.*

67. Helio Orovio, interview with the author, September 2007, Havana.

68. Manuel Villar, interview with the author, September 2007, Havana.

69. Helio Orovio, interview with the author, September 2007, Havana. "During the war years, RHC-Cadena Azul and CMQ together accounted for as much as 80% of the audience in Havana's 30-plus station market" (Michael B. Salwen, "The Origins of CMQ" pre-Castro Cuba's leading radio network," *Historical Journal of Film, Radio, and Television* 13:3 [1993]: 317).

70. Ibid.

71. For a list of Garza and other artists who performed in Cuba during the 1950s, see Cristóbal Díaz Ayala, *Música Cubana del Areyto al Rap Cubano,* 4th ed. (San Juan, P.R.: Fundación Musical, 2003), 258.

72. Ramón Fajardo Estrada, *Rita Montaner: Testimonio de una época* (Havana: Fondo Editorial Casa de las Américas, 1997), 274.

73. Smith, "Contours of a Spatialized Politics."

74. Frances Aparicio, *Listening to Salsa,* 101–2; Aparicio's translation of original Spanish version.

75. Newspaper article, Havana; from the private collection of Helio Orovio. No date or name of publication are given; my translation.

76. See Aparicio, *Listening to Salsa*, 155; Helio Orovio, *Cuban Music from A to Z* (Durham, N.C.: Duke University Press, 2004), 101–2.

77. Aparicio, *Listening to Salsa*, 177.

78. Fernández was born in Santiago de Cuba in 1901 and began to gain popularity for his compositions by the age of fifteen. He gave up a career in baseball to join the Castillo Quartet and spent ten years with the band, touring around the country. After returning to Santiago to form the Guaracheros de Oriente, he eventually took that group to tour Venezuela in 1950. He stayed for ten years, until the Cuban Revolution enticed him to return to Cuba. Saquito spent most of his later years playing in Havana. Helio Orovio, interview with the author, September 2007, Havana. See also Helio Orovio, *El Bolero Latino* (Havana: Editorial Letras Cubanas, 1995).

79. José Reyes Fortín, interview with Ana Casanova, September 2007, Havana.

80. Josh Kun, "Bagels, Bongos, and Yiddishe Mambos, or The Other History of Jews in America," *Shofar: An Interdisciplinary Journal of Jewish Studies* 23:4 (summer 2005): 57.

81. Thanks to Raúl Fernández for his help with clarifying details about Unión Radio and Teatro Rívoli.

82. Back cover of *Eva Garza Interpreta a Agustín Lara*, n.d., MUSART Records DM1252; my translation.

83. See Taylor, *The Archive and the Repertoire*.

84. Tina Moore, interview with the author, March 25–26, 2006, San Antonio, Texas.

85. Garza's roles in these movies included singing and dancing, as a common narrative strategy in *cabaretera* films was to include musical interludes within the main narrative structure. These scenes were not given to or wasted on anonymous musical artists; rather, the bonus for viewers was the opportunity to see performances by popular bolero singers of the time, including the Trío Los Panchos, Toña La Negra, Luis Alcaráz, Pedro Vargas, and the legendary Agustín Lara. Lucho Bermúdez, notable Colombian musician and composer of boleros, recalled accompanying artists in Medellín, among them Pedro Vargas, Eva Garza, Miguelito Valdés, Avelina García, and Toña La Negra.

86. Mark Pedalty, "The Bolero: The Birth, Life, and Decline of Mexican Modernity," *Latin American Music Review* 20:1 (1999): 36–38, 41. For feminist queer analysis of the *cabaretera*, see Sergio de la Mora, *Cinemachismo: Masculinities and Sexuality in Mexican Film* (Austin: University of Texas Press, 2006); Laura Gutiérrez, *Performing Mexicanidad: Vendidas y Cabareteras on the Transnational Stage* (Austin: University of Texas Press, 2010).

87. De la Mora, *Cinemachismo.*

88. Ana M. López, "Tears and Desire: Women and Melodrama in 'Old' Mexican Cinema," in Diane Carson, Linda Dittmar, and Janice R. Welsch, eds., *Multiple Voices in Feminist Film Criticism* (Minneapolis: University of Minnesota Press, 1994), 255.

89. When San Antonio's Teatro Alameda opened on March 9, 1949, it was the largest movie palace dedicated to Spanish-language movies, often featuring movies of the golden age of Mexican cinema.

90. Aparicio, *Listening to Salsa;* José Quiroga, *Tropics of Desire: Interventions from Queer Latino America* (New York: New York University Press, 2000), 145–68; Vanessa Knights, "Tears and Screams: Performances of Pleasure and Pain in the Bolero," in Sheila Whiteley and Jennifer Rycenga, eds., *Queering the Popular Pitch* (New York: Routledge, 2006), 83–100.

91. See interviews with Mexican composers and singers of boleros, including María Grever, Emma Elena Valdelamar, and Amparo Montes, in *Las que viven en ciudad bolero.*

92. Knights, "Tears and Screams," 85.

93. Felipe Gil Jr., interview with the author, July 2004, Mexico City.

94. Quoted in Aparicio, *Listenining to Salsa,* 127.

95. Mary Pat Brady, *Extinct Lands, Temporal Geographies: Chicana Literature and the Urgency of Space* (Durham, N.C.: Duke University Press, 2002), 8.

96. Ibid.

97. Garza also appeared on Colombia radio station Radio Pipatón and made numerous appearances on the television station La Nueva Grande de Bogotá R.C.R. along with famed Trío Fantasía (composed of Tony, Carmenza, and Elizabeth).

5. Giving Us That Brown Soul

1. Matt S. Meier and Margo Gutiérrez, "Brown Power," in Matt S. Meier and Margo Gutiérrez, eds., *Encyclopedia of the Mexican American Civil Rights Movement* (Westport, Conn.: Greenwood Press, 2000), 30. See also Rodolfo Acuña, *Occupied America: A History of Chicanos,* 2d ed. (New York: Harper & Row, 1981); Carlos Muñoz, *Youth, Identity, Power: The Chicano Movement* (London: Verso, 1991).

2. Carlos Arce, "A Reconsideration of Chicano Culture and Identity," *Daedalus* 110:2 (spring 1981): 179.

3. Little Joe's given name is José María de León Hernández.

4. Little Joe y La Familia, *Para La Gente,* 1972, LP.

5. Manuel Peña, *Música Tejana* (College Station: Texas A&M University Press, 1999), 152.

6. Musicologists and music biographers often state that Hernández's rock-and-roll influence was a by-product of the Americanization of his generation of Mexican Americans. For example, Manuel Peña observes: "like many tejano youngsters, Little Joe and his fellow band members were grounding at least part of their identities in American musical culture" (ibid., 153). I maintain that the complex and interconnected influences of rock, blues, and jazz are blurred by the assimilationist catchall "American musical culture" and can more precisely be termed a set of African-derived musical influences.

7. Portia K. Maultsby, "Soul," in Mellonee V. Burnim and Portia K. Maultsby, eds., *African American Music: An Introduction* (New York: Routledge, 2006), 272.

8. Ibid., 271.

9. Little Joe's decision to change the name of his band from The Latinaires to La Familia in the early 1970s is reflective of what Manuel Peña refers to as Little Joe's "drift toward the ideology of Chicanismo" (Peña, *Música Tejana,* 164).

10. "La onda Chicana" or sometimes "la onda Tejana" is not the same term as my use of *la onda*. "La onda Chicana" is defined in Chicano musicology as the "pinnacle of *orquesta* tradition" prominent in the 1960s–70s. See ibid., 150–83; San Miguel, *Tejano Proud,* 46, 77.

11. José Esteban Muñoz, "Feeling Brown, Feeling Down: Latina Affect, the Performativity of Race, and the Depressive Position," *Signs: Journal of Women in Culture and Society* 31:3 (2006): 679.

12. Ralph E. Rodríguez, *Brown Gumshoes: Detective Fiction and the Search for Chicana/o Identity* (Austin: University of Texas Press, 2005).

13. Curtis Marez, "The Politics of Working-Class Chicano Style," *Social Text 48* 14:3 (fall 1996): 109.

14. For various definitions and debates about what Tejano music means, see Peña, *Música Tejana,* 184–218; San Miguel, *Tejano Proud,* 3–19; Walter Aaron Clark, *From Tejano to Tango* (New York: Routledge, 2002), 97–125.

15. Angelo Figueroa, "Editor's Statement by Angelo Figueroa," *People en Español, Time* 3:2 (March 2000): 15.

16. Gloria Anzaldúa, "Introduction," in *Making Face, Making Soul/Haciendo Caras,* xv.

17. Some examples include Anthony Macías, *Mexican Mojo: Popular Music, Dance, and Urban Culture in Los Angeles, 1935–1968* (Durham, N.C.: Duke University Press, 2008); George Lipsitz, *Footsteps in the Dark: The Hidden Histories of Popular Music* (Minneapolis: University of Minnesota Press, 2007); Josh Kun, *Audiotopia: Music, Race, and America* (Berkeley: University of California Press, 2005); Steven Loza, *Barrio Rhythm: Mexican American Music in Los Angeles*

(Urbana: University of Illinois Press, 1993). See also Raquel Z. Rivera, "Between Blackness and Latinidad," in *New York Ricans from the Hip Hop Zone* (New York: Palgrave Press, 2003).

18. Frances Aparicio, "Jennifer as Selena: Rethinking Latinidad in Media and Culture," *Latino Studies* 1:1 (March 2003): 90–105; Deborah Paredez, *Selenidad, Selena, Latinos, and the Performance of Memory* (Durham, N.C.: Duke University Press, 2009).

19. See, for example, *Selena: The Movie,* directed by Gregory Nava; San Miguel, *Tejano Proud;* Clark, *From Tango to Tejano.*

20. Roderick Ferguson, *Aberrations in Black: Toward a Queer of Color Critique* (Minneapolis: University of Minnesota Press, 2004), 4.

21. Suzette Quintanilla, interview with the author, 2000, Corpus Christi, Texas.

22. Rosa Ybarra, "Selena's Death Reshaped Family's Life," *Corpus Christi Monitor,* March 31, 2005.

23. The Tejano Music Awards do not offer an overall "Entertainer of the Year" category; instead, they split top vocalist and entertainer honors by sex—for example, "Female Vocalist of the Year" and "Female Entertainer of the Year."

24. At the Tejano Music Awards, 1993, San Antonio.

25. Deborah Pacini Hernandez, *Oye Como Va! Hybridity and Identity in Latino Popular Music* (Philadelphia: Temple University Press, 2010).

26. Héctor Fernández L'Hoeste, "All Cumbias, the Cumbia: The Latin Americanization of a Tropical Genre," in Sandhya Shukla and Heidi Tinsman, eds., *Imagining Our Americas: Toward a Transnational Frame* (Durham, N.C.: Duke University Press 2007), 338.

27. Ibid., 340.

28. Ibid., 339.

29. Once a regional South Texas program, the show eventually aired over television networks in northern Mexico in the mid-1980s and eventually in television markets around Latin America.

30. *The Johnny Canales Show,* aired live from Matamoros, Tamaulipas, 1987.

31. See Brady, *Extinct Lands, Temporal Geographies.*

32. Author's video copy of the *Johnny Canales Show* television special that aired on Univision, includes a compilation of Selena appearances on his television show that aired shortly after her passing.

33. "Let the Music Play" was originally recorded by Shannon in 1983 for Emergency Records. After being a hit in U.S. and British dance clubs for several months, the single was eventually picked up by Mirage Records, and in 1984 it reached the Top 10 on U.S. charts and the Top 20 on British charts. In

2006, the Mexican pop group RDB recorded the song as a cover for release through iTunes. Alexandra Vázquez notes that "freestyle represented a cohesive response by Latin sonic practitioners to the material conditions of the mid-1980s to early 1990s" (Alexandra T. Vazquez, "Instrumental Migrations: The Transnational Movements of Cuban Music," PhD thesis, New York University, 2006, 9).

34. See, for example, bell hooks, *Black Looks: Race and Representation* (Boston: South End Press, 1992); Ramírez, *The Woman in the Zoot Suit*; Deborah Paredez, *Selenidad: Selena, Latinos, and the Performance of Memory* (Durham, N.C.: Duke University Press, 2009).

35. "Missing My Baby," included on Selena's CD *Dreaming of You*, was produced by Brooklyn-based Full Force, who worked closely with Cult Jam. See the 1985 album *Lisa Lisa & Cult Jam with Full Force*, which included the classic freestyle hit "I Wonder If I Take You Home."

36. Cristina Verán, "Let the Music Play (Again)," *Village Voice*, April 18, 2006. For more discussion on the lyrical characteristics of freestyle as "overwhelmingly about love, required or not," see Alexandra T. Vázquez, "Can You Feel the Beat? Freestyle's System of Living, Loving, and Recording," *Social Text* 102 (spring 2010): 111.

37. Estefan also repopularized the 1970s disco hit "Turn the Beat Around" with her release single in 1994 and performed the song on the 1998 *VHI Divas* concert.

38. See Marlon Riggs, *Tongues Untied*, for a discussion of snapology.

39. See Deborah R. Vargas, "Bidi Bidi Bom Bom: Selena and Tejano Music in the Making of Tejas," in Michelle Habell-Pallán and Mary Romero, eds., *Latino Popular Culture* (New York: New York University Press, 2002), 114.

40. For an excellent performance studies analysis of Selena's Astrodome performance, see Paredez, *Selenidad*, 31–55.

41. See Joshua Gamson, *The Fabulous Sylvester: The Legend, the Music, the Seventies in San Francisco* (New York: Picador, 2005).

42. EMI Latin would go on to sign other Tejano artists, including Roberto Pulido, Laura Canales, Mazz, David Lee Garza, and Emilio Navaira.

43. Joe Nick Patoski, *Selena: Como la flor* (Boston: Little, Brown, 1996), 128.

44. See liner notes to the posthumously released CD *Dreaming of You* (1995) for more on how the English-language CD was being produced (at the time of her death) to capture "Selena's sound" and voice, said to be "multidimensional and within the scope of R & B style." The CD includes a song reproduced and recorded with 1980s hip-hop band Full Force. Based out of Brooklyn, Full Force wrote and performed hit singles with artists such as Lisa Lisa and Cult

Jam—including their smash hit "I Wonder If I Take You Home"—James Brown, and Patti LaBelle. Full Force coproduced "Missing My Baby," a song previously recorded on an older album, with brother A.B.

45. Frances Aparicio, "Jennifer as Selena," 102.

46. For further discussion of "Techno Cumbia," see Patoski, *Selena: Como la flor.*

47. "Selena Remembered Five Years Later," special issue, *Estylo Magazine* 4:2 (2000): 54.

48. Ibid.; Suzette Quintanilla, interview with the author, 2000, Corpus Christi, Texas.

49. Suzette Quintanilla, interview with the author, 2000, Corpus Christi, Texas.

50. Ibid.

51. Ibid.

52. In fact, during a visit to Q Productions in Corpus Christi a few years after her death, I inquired about a room directly next to the recording studio that was obviously in disarray. A staff member informed me that the room was being renovated in order to expand the recording studio because it was formerly the room in which Selena used to design and sew her costumes.

53. Tomás Ybarro-Frausto, "Rasquachismo: A Chicano Sensibility," in Richard Griswold del Castillo, Teresa McKenna, and Yvonne Yarbro-Bejarano, eds., *Chicano Art: Resistance and Affirmation, 1965–1985* (Los Angeles: University of California Wright Art Gallery, 1991), 155.

54. See Dick Hebdige, *Subculture: The Meaning of Style* (London and New York: Routledge, 1991); Angela McRobbie, *Zoot Suits and Second Hand Dresses: An Anthology of Fashion and Music* (Boston: Unwin Hyman Press, 1988); Angela McRobbie, *Postmodernism and Popular Culture* (New York: Routledge, 1994); bell hooks, *Black Looks: Race and Representation* (Boston: South End Press, 1992).

55. Larry Rohter, "A Legend Grows, and So Does an Industry," *New York Times,* January 12, 1997, 38H. See also Angharad N. Valdivia, "Xuxa! Can Latin Americans Be Blonde or Can the United States Tolerate a Latin American?" in *A Latina in the Land of Hollywood and Other Essays on Media Culture* (Tucson: University of Arizona Press, 2000).

56. Suzette Quintanilla, interview with the author, 2000, Corpus Christi, Texas.

57. bell hooks, *Outlaw Culture: Resisting Representations* (New York: Routledge, 1994), 180.

58. Suzette Quintanilla, interview with the author, 2000, Corpus Christi, Texas.

59. Pacini Hernandez, *Oye Como Va!,* 120–21.

60. Suzette Quintanilla, interview with the author, 2000, Corpus Christi, Texas.

61. Carmina Danini, "In Mexico Singer's Fans Mourn Loss," *San Antonio Express-News,* April 1, 1995, 12A.

62. Suzette Quintanilla, interview with the author, 2000, Corpus Christi, Texas.

63. Frances Aparicio, "The Blackness of Sugar: Celia Cruz and the Performance of (Trans)nationalism," *Cultural Studies* 13: 2 (April 1999): 223–36.

64. Angie Chabram-Dernersesian, "En-countering the Other Discourse of Chicano-Mexicano Difference," in "Special Issue: Chicana/o Latina/o Cultural Studies: Transnational and Transdisciplinary Movements," *Cultural Studies* 13:2 (1999): 283.

65. See, for example, Peña, *The Texas-Mexican Conjunto;* San Miguel, *Tejano Proud.*

66. Simon Jones, "'Crossover' and the Politics of Race," in Will Straw, Stacey Johnson, Rebecca Sullivan, and Paul Friedlander, eds., *Popular Music: Style and Identity* (Montreal: Centre for Research on Canadian Cultural Industries and Institutions, 1995), 167.

67. See Reebee Garofalo, "Crossing Over: 1939–1992," in Jannette L. Dates and William Barlow, eds., *Split Image: African Americans and the Mass Media* (Washington, D.C.: Howard University Press, 1993), 57–127.

68. George Lipsitz, *Dangerous Crossroads: Popular Music, Postmodernism, and the Poetics of Place* (London and New York: Verso, 1994), 61.

69. See Simon Frith, "Ain't No Mountain High Enough: The Politics of Crossover," in Simon Frith, ed., *Facing the Music* (New York: Pantheon Books, 1988), 51–87; John Szwed, *Crossovers: Essays on Race, Music, and American Culture* (Philadelphia: University of Pennsylvania Press, 2005); María Elena Cepeda, *Musical ImagiNation: U.S.–Colombian Identity and the Latin Music Boom* (New York: New York University Press, 2010).

70. David Brackett, "The Politics and Musical Practice of 'Crossover,'" in Straw, Johnson, Sullivan, and Friedlander, *Popular Music,* 23.

71. Lipsitz, *Dangerous Crossroads,* 120.

72. For black/queer histories in disco, see Alice Echols, *Hot Stuff: Disco and the Remaking of American Culture* (New York: W. W. Norton, 2010).

73. Suzette Quintanilla, interview with the author, 2000, Corpus Christi, Texas.

74. I thank Laura Gutiérrez for pushing me to think further about the "browning" of the Latina/o diaspora that takes place via figures like Selena.

75. Interview with "María" by the author, August 12, 2005, El VIP, Mexico City.

76. Angie Chabram-Dernersesian, "Introduction: Chicana/o Latina/o Cultural Studies Transnational and Transdisciplinary Movements," *Cultural Studies* 13:2 (April 1999): 173–94.

77. See Frances Negrón-Muntaner, "Selena's Butt," *Aztlán: A Journal of Chicano Studies* 22:2 (1997): 181–94; Deborah Paredez, "Remembering Selena, Re-membering Latinidad," *Theatre Journal* 54:1 (2002): 63–83; Frances Aparicio, "Jennifer as Selena," 90–105.

78. Alexandra T. Vázquez, *Listening in Detail: Performances of Cuban Music* (Durham, N.C.: Duke University Press, forthcoming). For further analysis of freestyle by Vazquez, see "Can You Feel the Beat?" 107–24.

79. Cathy J. Cohen, "Punks, Bulldaggers, and Welfare Queens: The Radical Potential of Queer Politics?" in E. Patrick Johnson and Mae G. Henderson, eds., *Black Queer Studies: A Critical Anthology* (Durham, N.C.: Duke University Press, 2005), 25.

80. Ibid. See also Eng, Halberstam, and Muñoz, "Introduction," special issue, "What's Queer about Queer Studies Now?," 1–17.

81. Cohen, "Punks, Bulldaggers, and Welfare Queens," 23.

82. See Gamson, *The Fabulous Sylvester;* Tim Lawrence, "I Want to See All My Friends at Once: Arthur Russell and the Queering of Gay Disco," *Journal of Popular Music Studies* 18:2 (2006): 144–66; and Echols, *Hot Stuff.*

83. John-Manuel Andriote, *Hot Stuff: A Brief History of Disco* (New York: Harper Entertainment, 2001), 20.

84. Kobena Mercer, *Welcome to the Jungle: New Positions in Black Cultural Studies* (New York: Routledge, 1994), 140.

85. For example, see José Esteban Muñoz, "Feeling Brown: Ethnicity and Affect in Ricardo Bracho's 'The Sweetest Hangover' (and Other STDs)," *Theatre Journal* 52:1 (March 2000): 67–79.

86. Vázquez, "Instrumental Migrations," 6.

87. Ibid., 10. Houston's musical milieu, especially in radio, surrounded Selena during her formative years in Lake Jackson, Texas, a community/suburb/town about fifty-five miles from Houston.

88. For fuller discussion of Latina singers of freestyle, see Vázquez, "Can You Feel the Beat?"

89. Paredez, *Selenidad,* 43.

90. The terms *jota* (feminine) and *joto* (masculine) or *jota/o* are most similar to, but not a direct translation of, *queer.* Yet, like *queer, jota/o* has been reclaimed by Latinas/os (most often of Mexican descent) as a positive self-identity for those who claim nonnormative gender and sexuality and by organizations addressing issues of social injustice for gay, lesbian, transgender, bisexual, and other nonnormative genders and sexualities.

Epilogue

1. Jenn Alva and Phanie Díaz, online interview with the author, September 17, 2010.

2. Stuart Hall, "New Ethnicities," in David Morely and Kuan-Hsing Chen, eds., *Stuart Hall: Critical Dialogues in Cultural Studies* (New York: Routledge, 1996), 442–51.

3. Ahmed Mori, "Girl in a Coma: San Antonio Punk," zinkmagazine.com (spring 2010).

4. http://www.girlinacoma.com.

5. Ibid.

6. Jenn Alva and Phanie Díaz, online interview with the author, September 17, 2010.

7. http://www.girlinacoma.com.

8. Anonymous, "Girl in a Coma Wakes Up Local Punk Scene," *San Antonio Express-News* (*http://www.mysanantonio.com*, May 26, 2009).

9. Bill Freeman, http://www.allmusic.com/album/trio-bc-r1568808/review.

10. See Eric Zolov, *Refried Elvis: The Rise of the Mexican Counterculture* (Berkeley: University of California Press, 1999).

11. Julia Palacios and Tere Estrada, "'A contra corriente': A History of Women Rockers in Mexico," in Deborah Pacini Hernandez, Héctor Fernández L'Hoeste, and Erick Zolov, eds., *Rockin' Las Américas: The Global Politics of Rock in Latin/o America* (Pittsburgh: University of Pittsburgh Press, 2004), 146.

12. Ibid.

13. Alicia Arrizón, *Latina Performance: Traversing the Stage* (Bloomington: Indiana University Press, 1999), provides a key feminist analysis of Chata Noloesca.

14. Regina Martínez, interview with the author, December 2010.

15. *Gloria Ríos: La Leyenda del Rock & Roll*, prod. Regina Martínez, dir. Arturo Lara (DVD, 2006). This video of Ríos's life is self-produced by Ríos's daughter Regina Martínez and thus has no institutional publishing or marketing sponsor.

16. 50 Aniversario del Rock en México exhibition, Instituto Cultural Mexicano, San Antonio, Texas, November 9, 2007.

17. *Gloria Ríos: La Leyenda del Rock & Roll.*

18. Ibid.

19. For a discussion of Mexican middle-class youth and the elision of blackness in the arrival of American rock and roll in Mexico, see Zolov, *Refried Elvis*, 17–61.

20. Ibid., 20.

21. As for the social, economic, and political context for the entry of rock and roll in Mexico, Eric Zolov and other Mexican music scholars assert that, generally speaking, Mexicans viewed rock and roll as an imperialist import from the United States, introducing a space in which to question the social order, particularly by Mexican youth. While youth found rock and roll a means for challenging adult authority, adults engaged with the music as a means to access modern global culture. Broadly speaking, rock and roll became a discursive site for negotiating fears and anxieties about Mexico's rapid modernization. Zolov's history of rock in Mexico marks a trajectory from its entry in the mid-1950s into what he refers to as Mexico's *desmadre* or collapse of social order, to its reappropriation as "high culture" by the middle classes in the early 1960s, to the influence of countercultural values during the 1968 student rebellions (ibid., 17–92).

22. The twist dance movement is especially interesting because Chubby Checker didn't release his single "The Twist" (a cover of Hank Ballard's 1959 single), or in turn invent the now-legendary dance, until 1960.

23. Regina Martínez, interview with the author, March 20, 2011, San Antonio, Texas.

24. This segment of Ríos's performance also raises questions about the racialized construction of rock and roll in its entry into Mexico. A general thesis has been that the rise of rock-and-roll singers like Elvis and Bill Halley whitewashed African American presence out of the music in the United States and, in turn, made more palatable the racialized representation of the music as less black or, according to racist discourse, less sexualized. Yet, a sustained analysis of Ríos and other women rock-and-roll performers of the time based on this thesis has not been done. In other words, such racialized discourse about rock and roll's palatability in Mexico was never not gendered or sexualized. See Eric Zolov, "La Onda Chicana: Mexico's Forgotten Rock Counterculture," in Hernandez, L'Hoeste, and Zolov, *Rockin' Las Américas,* 22–42.

25. 50 Aniversario del Rock en México.

26. Zolov, *Refried Elvis,* 35–36.

27. Jim Mendiola, conversation with the author, May 15, 2011.

28. The *cantinera* figure, yet to be fully analyzed in Chicano studies, can be traced back to the spaces of fandango dance and music in the nineteenth-century Southwest. Arnoldo De León notes that the fandango was identified with lewd passions and lascivious señoritas described as sensuous.

29. "Clumsy Sky," lyrics by Nina Díaz, *Both Before I'm Gone,* Blackheart Records, 2007.

30. Phanie Díaz, online interview with the author, November 17, 2010.

31. For Chicana feminist analysis of gender and sexuality of Chicana *punkeras,* see Michelle Habell-Pallán, "'Soy punkera, ¿y qué?': Sexuality, Translocality,

and Punk in Los Angeles and Beyond," in Hernandez, L'Hoeste, and Zolov, *Rockin' Las Américas,* 160–78.

32. Phanie Díaz, online interview with the author, November 17, 2010.

33. Carla Meyer, "Girl in a Coma Bringing Head Full of Influences to Harlow," *Sacramento Bee,* http://sacbee.com, November 29, 2011.

34. Jim Mendiola, conversation with the author, May 15, 2011.

35. For a feminist-queer analysis, see Catrióna Rueda Esquibel, "Velvet Malinche: Fantasies of 'the' Aztec Princess in the Chicana/o Sexual Imagination," in Alicia Gaspar de Alba, ed., *Velvet Barrios: Popular Culture and Chicana/o Sexualities* (New York: Palgrave Macmillan, 2003), 295–310.

Permissions

Portions of chapter 1 were published as "Rosita Fernández: La Rosa de San Antonio," special issue *(Gender on the Borderlands), Frontiers: A Journal of Women's Studies* 24, no. 2/3 (2003): 168–84.

Portions of chapter 2 were published as "Borderland Bolerista: The Licentious Lyricism of Chelo Silva," *Feminist Studies* 34, no. 1–2 (spring/summer 2008): 173–97.

Portions of chapter 5 were published as "Selena: Sounding a Transnational Latina/o Queer Imaginary," *ELN (English Language Notes)* 45, no. 2 (fall/winter 2007): 65–76; as "Cruzando Frontejas: Remapping Selena's Tejano Music Crossover," in *Chicana Traditions: Continuity and Change,* ed. Norma Cantú and Olga Nájera-Ramírez, 224–36 (Urbana: University of Illinois Press, 2002); and as "Bidi Bidi Bom Bom: Selena and Tejano Music in the 'Making of Tejas,'" in *Latino/a Popular Culture,* ed. Michelle Habell-Pállan and Mary Romero, 117–26 (New York: New York University Press, 2002).

Lyrics from "San Antonio," by Walter Jurmann, copyright 1967 Hal Leonard Corporation.

Lyrics from "Con su pluma en su mano," by Tish Hinojosa, from the album *Frontejas,* copyright 1995 Alfred Publishing.

Lyrics from "Que Murmuren," by Rafael Cárdenas and Rubén Fuentes, copyright 1957 Columbia Records.

Lyrics from "La Huella de Mis Besos," written by Severo Mirón and sung by Chelo Silva, copyright Discos Columbia.

Lyrics from "Cheque en Blanco," written by Emma Elena Valdelamar, copyright Editora Musical Musart, S.A. de C.V.

Lyrics from "Pregúntame a mí," written by Luis M. Dueñas and sung live by Chelo Silva, copyright Hal Leonard Corporation.

Lyrics from "Sabor de Engaño," by Mario Alvarez, copyright 1948 Columbia Records.

Lyrics from "Las Nubes," arranged by Joe Callardo and sung by Little Joe Hernandez, copyright Arhoolie Records.

Lyrics from "Las Nubes," arranged by José Calván and sung by Carmen y Laura, copyright Discos Ideal.

Lyrics from "Techno Cumbia," written by A. B. Quintanilla and Pete Austudillo, copyright 1995 Capital–EMI Latin Records.

Lyrics from "Clumsy Sky," written by Nina Díaz and performed by Girl in a Coma, copyright 2007 Jett Pack Music (BMI).

Index

DEBORAH R. VARGAS is associate professor of Chicano/Latino studies at the University of California, Irvine, where she teaches critical race feminisms, cultural studies, and queer studies.